Web Development with

Second Edition

An in-depth practical guide for .NET developers to build interactive UIs with C#

Jimmy Engström

BIRMINGHAM—MUMBAI

Web Development with Blazor
Second Edition

Copyright © 2023 Packt Publishing

All rights reserved. No part of this book may be reproduced, stored in a retrieval system, or transmitted in any form or by any means, without the prior written permission of the publisher, except in the case of brief quotations embedded in critical articles or reviews.

Every effort has been made in the preparation of this book to ensure the accuracy of the information presented. However, the information contained in this book is sold without warranty, either express or implied. Neither the author, nor Packt Publishing or its dealers and distributors, will be held liable for any damages caused or alleged to have been caused directly or indirectly by this book.

Packt Publishing has endeavored to provide trademark information about all of the companies and products mentioned in this book by the appropriate use of capitals. However, Packt Publishing cannot guarantee the accuracy of this information.

Senior Publishing Product Manager: Suman Sen
Acquisition Editor – Peer Reviews: Saby Dsilva
Project Editor: Parvathy Nair
Content Development Editor: Shazeen Iqbal
Copy Editor: Safis Editing
Technical Editor: Aniket Shetty
Proofreader: Safis Editing
Indexer: Tejal Daruwale Soni
Presentation Designer: Rajesh Shirsath
Developer Relations Marketing Executive: Priyadarshini Sharma

First published: June 2021
Second edition: March 2023

Production reference: 1090323

Published by Packt Publishing Ltd.
Livery Place
35 Livery Street
Birmingham
B3 2PB, UK.

ISBN 978-1-80324-149-4

www.packt.com

Foreword

In 2017, I met Jimmy at an event in Stockholm, where I quickly noticed his passion for technology, user experience, and pop culture. We spent the better part of an hour debating Marvel versus DC Comics characters and storylines, and I knew this was a person who studied for both his craft and hobbies. His presentations regarding Blazor, HoloLens, and delivering better applications for our users are always cutting edge and lead the audience to best practices for each technology.

The author has been a Microsoft MVP and community leader for almost a decade. The Swedish developer community has grown under his leadership and benefitted from his insights to build better applications and services. The Blazm components library that he wrote and made available is a prime example of helping other developers in his local community and across the world.

This book has been written for the practical Blazor developer. Clear definitions of why you need to consider each feature of the framework are followed by examples and clear solutions that will make you immediately successful. You'll learn by following along with the very relatable example project of a blog engine. From user interface topics through API design and security considerations, the blog engine you will build with Blazor and ASP.NET Core in this book will run in production and can easily serve your blog. I appreciate that Jimmy introduces and covers bringing your Blazor application to .NET MAUI and building a native application for Windows, MacOS, iOS, and Android as part of the 18th chapter. Jimmy does a great job showing the portability and power of Blazor combined with MAUI and the native application capabilities of that framework. The final chapter of this book is an awesome reference for new and seasoned developers, with answers to the typical problems that will surface during the lifetime of your application, and it should be kept as a desktop reference for years to come.

Jeff Fritz

Principal Program Manager at Microsoft, Executive Producer of the .NET Conf event series, and Leader in Live Video Technical Community Engagement

Contributors

About the author

Jimmy Engström has been developing since he was seven and got his first computer. He loves to be on the cutting edge of technology and try new things. When he got wind of Blazor, he immediately realized the potential and adopted it when it was still in beta. He has been running Blazor in production since it was launched by Microsoft. His passion for the .NET industry and community has taken him around the world, speaking about development. Microsoft has recognized this passion by awarding him the Microsoft Most Valuable Professional award over 9 years in a row.

I dedicate this book to my mom and dad, who got me my first computer, which got me started with programming.

To my brother, who took the time to teach me how to code, and to my sister, who helped me with my English homework growing up.

I would also like to dedicate the book to my wife, Jessica, who has helped me along the way by both reviewing the book and picking up my slack. Love you!

This book would never have been possible without you all! A huge thanks to the reviewers, who have done a tremendous job reviewing the book.

– Jimmy Engström

Since my parents are not fluent in English, here is the same text but in Swedish:

Jag dedikerar den här boken till min mamma och pappa som köpte min första dator, som fick mig att börja programmera. Till min bror som tog sig tiden att lära mig koda och till min syster som hjälpte mig med engelskaläxan när jag växte upp.

Jag vill också dedikera boken till min fru som har hjälpt mig att se över boken och stöttat mig på alla tänkbara sätt. Älskar dig!

Detta hade inte varit möjligt utan er alla.

Ett stort tack till de som sett över boken, ni har gjort ett fantastiskt jobb.

– Jimmy Engström

About the reviewers

Jürgen Gutsch is a .NET addicted web developer. He has worked with .NET and ASP.NET since the early versions in 2002. Before that, he wrote server-side web application using classic ASP. He is also an active person in the .NET developer community. Jürgen writes for the dotnetPro Magazine, one of the most popular German speaking developer magazines. He also publishes articles in English on his blog on "ASP.NET Hacker" and contributes to several open-source projects. Jürgen has been a Microsoft MVP since 2015.

For quite some years, Jürgen does technical reviews for books like this for Packt, and he also wrote a book called *Customizing ASP.NET Core* for ASP.NET Core 5 and ASP.NET Core 6.

He works as a developer, consultant, and trainer for the digital agency YOO Inc. located in Basel (Switzerland). YOO Inc. serves national as well as international clients and specializes in creating custom digital solution for distinct business needs.

Jessica Engström has been a Microsoft MVP for over 9 years. Her passion for the community can be seen in her activities like teaching, organizing, and speaking at conferences all over the world, running a podcast (Coding After Work), and streams (MarriedGeeks & CodingAfterWork).

Recently, she ventured into cybersecurity as a community manager at Detectify, working with ethical hackers.

She spends too much money on Lego in her spare time and loves to drive her EV.

David Vanderheyden is a husband, a father of two sons and a daughter, and is fluent and communicative with a big interest in innovative technologies. From his early childhood years, he was very curious about computers, how they are built, and how they work.

Because of this curiousity, he taught himself the basics of web development and learned about operating systems, infrastructure, and programming. As a true auto-didact, he extended his knowledge of diverse programming languages, technical stacks, and architectures and patterns. On the sides he blogged in his spare time about things learned. After years of building websites and doing Desktop Publishing (DTP) work for non-profits, friends, and family, he changed his career to software development and he worked as a technical consultant on a wide range of projects, from migrating applications to creating new applications on the full stack. He spends his days as a freelance consultant focused on the .NET stack, helping businesses with their software needs and helping fellow developers with migrations to Blazor.

First and foremost, I would like to thank my wife and children for all the love and support in my endeavors. You guys frequently share me with my work, but you will always be my number one priority. A big thanks to Wouter and Packt for this opportunity, and thank you Jimmy and the people at Packt for this cooperation; it's been a true delight.

Join our community on Discord

Join our community's Discord space for discussions with the author and other readers:

https://packt.link/WebDevBlazor2e

Table of Contents

Preface   xxi

Chapter 1: Hello Blazor   1

Technical requirements 2
Why Blazor? 2
Preceding Blazor 3
Introducing WebAssembly 4
Introducing .NET 7 6
Introducing Blazor 7

    Blazor Server • 8

    Blazor WebAssembly • 10

    Blazor WebAssembly versus Blazor Server • 14

    Blazor Hybrid / .NET MAUI • 14

Summary 15
Further reading 15

Chapter 2: Creating Your First Blazor App   17

Technical requirements 17
Setting up your development environment 17

    Windows • 18

    macOS • 19

    Linux (or macOS or Windows) • 20

Creating our first Blazor application 20

    Exploring the templates • 20

        Blazor Server App • 21

        Blazor WebAssembly App • 21

        Blazor Server App Empty • 21

        Blazor WebAssembly App Empty • 21

    Creating a Blazor Server application • 22

    Creating a WebAssembly application • 27

Using the command line 33

    Creating projects using the command line • 34

Figuring out the project structure 35

    Program.cs • 35

        WebAssembly Program.cs • 35

        Blazor Server Program.cs • 36

    Index/_Host • 38

        _Host (Blazor Server) • 38

        Index (WebAssembly) • 41

    App • 42

    MainLayout • 43

    Bootstrap • 44

    CSS • 45

Summary 46

Chapter 3: Managing State — Part 1   47

Technical requirements 47

Creating a data project 48

    Creating a new project • 48

    Creating data classes • 49

    Creating an interface • 50

    Implementing the interface • 51

Adding the API to Blazor 60
Summary 61

Chapter 4: Understanding Basic Blazor Components — 63

Technical requirements 64
Exploring components 64
    Counter • 64
    FetchData • 66
Learning Razor syntax 70
    Razor code blocks • 71
    Implicit Razor expressions • 72
    Explicit Razor expressions • 72
    Expression encoding • 72
    Directives • 73
      Adding an attribute • 73
      Adding an interface • 73
      Inheriting • 74
      Generics • 74
      Changing the layout • 74
      Setting a namespace • 75
      Setting a route • 75
      Adding a using statement • 75
Understanding dependency injection 75
  Singleton • 76
  Scoped • 77
  Transient • 77
  Injecting the service • 77
Figuring out where to put the code 78
  In the Razor file • 78
  In a partial class • 79

Inheriting a class • 80

Only code • 80

Lifecycle events 82

OnInitialized and OnInitializedAsync • 82

OnParametersSet and OnParametersSetAsync • 82

OnAfterRender and OnAfterRenderAsync • 82

ShouldRender • 82

Parameters 83

Cascading parameters • 83

Writing our first component 84

Creating a components library • 85

Using our components library • 86

Creating our own component • 87

Summary 89

Chapter 5: Creating Advanced Blazor Components   91

Technical requirements 91

Exploring binding 92

One-way binding • 92

Two-way binding • 94

Actions and EventCallback 95

Using RenderFragment 96

ChildContent • 97

Default value • 97

Building an alert component • 97

Exploring the new built-in components 100

Setting the focus of the UI • 100

Influencing the HTML head • 101

Component virtualization • 104

Error boundaries • 107

Summary 108

Chapter 6: Building Forms with Validation 109

Technical requirements 109

Exploring form elements 109

EditForm • 110

InputBase<> • 111

InputCheckbox • 112

InputDate<TValue> • 112

InputNumber<TValue> • 112

InputSelect<TValue> • 112

InputText • 112

InputTextArea • 112

InputRadio • 112

InputRadioGroup • 113

InputFile • 113

Adding validation 113

ValidationMessage • 114

ValidationSummary • 115

Custom validation class attributes 115

Looking at bindings 119

Binding to HTML elements • 119

Binding to components • 120

Building an admin interface 121

Listing and editing categories • 123

Listing and editing tags • 126

Listing and editing blog posts • 130

Summary 141

Chapter 7: Creating an API 143

Technical requirements 143

Creating the service **143**

Adding data access • 144

Learning about Minimal APIs • 145

Adding the API controllers • 146

Adding APIs for handling blog posts • 146

Adding APIs for handling categories • 149

Adding APIs for handling tags • 150

Creating the client **151**

Summary **157**

Chapter 8: Authentication and Authorization — 159

Technical requirements **160**

Setting up authentication **160**

Configuring Blazor Server • 161

Securing Blazor Server **164**

Securing Blazor WebAssembly **167**

Adjusting Auth0 • 172

Securing the API **173**

Configure Auth0 • 173

Configure the API • 173

Adding roles **175**

Configuring Auth0 by adding roles • 175

Adding roles to Blazor Server • 176

Adding roles to Blazor WebAssembly • 177

Summary **179**

Chapter 9: Sharing Code and Resources — 181

Technical requirements **182**

Adding static files **182**

Choosing between frameworks • 183

Adding a new style • 183

Table of Contents xv

    Adding CSS to BlazorServer • 184

    Adding CSS to BlazorWebAssembly.Client • 184

    Making the admin interface more usable • 184

    Making the menu more useful • 185

    Making the blog look like a blog • 186

CSS isolation **187**

Summary **190**

Chapter 10: JavaScript Interop   191

Technical requirements **191**

Why do we need JavaScript? **192**

.NET to JavaScript **192**

    Global JavaScript (the old way) • 193

    JavaScript Isolation • 193

JavaScript to .NET **195**

    Static .NET method call • 195

    Instance method call • 196

Implementing an existing JavaScript library **199**

JavaScript interop in WebAssembly **202**

    .NET to JavaScript • 203

    JavaScript to .NET • 204

Summary **206**

Chapter 11: Managing State — Part 2   207

Technical requirements **208**

Storing data on the server side **208**

Storing data in the URL **209**

    Route constraints • 209

    Using a query string • 210

    Scenarios that are not that common • 210

Implementing browser storage **211**

Creating an interface • 212

Implementing Blazor Server • 212

Implementing WebAssembly • 214

Implementing the shared code • 215

Using an in-memory state container service **218**

Implementing real-time updates on Blazor Server • 219

Implementing real-time updates on Blazor WebAssembly • 222

Summary **226**

Chapter 12: Debugging the Code 227

Technical requirements **227**

Making things break **228**

Debugging Blazor Server **228**

Debugging Blazor WebAssembly **230**

Debugging Blazor WebAssembly in the web browser **231**

Hot Reload **233**

Summary **234**

Chapter 13: Testing 235

Technical requirements **236**

What is bUnit? **236**

Setting up a test project **236**

Mocking the API **239**

Writing tests **243**

Authentication • 245

Testing JavaScript • 247

Summary **248**

Chapter 14: Deploy to Production 251

Technical requirements **251**

Continuous delivery options 251
Hosting options 252
  Hosting Blazor Server • 252
  Hosting Blazor WebAssembly • 253
  Hosting on IIS • 253
Summary 253

Chapter 15: Moving from, or Combining, an Existing Site   255

Technical requirements 256
Introducing Web Components 256
Exploring Custom Elements 257
Exploring the Blazor Component 257
Adding Blazor to an Angular site 258
Adding Blazor to a React site 260
Adding Blazor to MVC/Razor Pages 261
Adding Web components to a Blazor site 263
Migrating from Web Forms 265
Summary 266

Chapter 16: Going Deeper into WebAssembly   267

Technical requirements 268
.NET WebAssembly build tools 268
AOT compilation 268
WebAssembly Single Instruction, Multiple Data (SIMD) 269
Trimming 270
Lazy loading 270
PWA 273
Native dependencies 273
Common problems 275
  Progress indicators • 275
  Prerendering on the server • 276

Preloading and persisting the state • 277

Summary 279

Chapter 17: Examining Source Generators — 281

Technical requirements 281

What a source generator is 282

How to get started with source generators 284

Community projects 286

InterfaceGenerator • 286

Blazorators • 286

C# source generators • 286

Roslyn SDK samples • 287

Microsoft Learn • 287

Summary 287

Chapter 18: Visiting .NET MAUI — 289

Technical requirements 289

What is .NET MAUI? 290

Creating a new project 291

.NET MAUI App • 291

.NET MAUI Class Library • 291

.NET MAUI Blazor App • 291

Looking at the template 292

Developing for Android 297

Running in an emulator • 297

Running on a physical device • 299

Developing for iOS 299

Hot restart • 300

Simulator • 301

Developing for macOS 304

Developing for Windows 305

Developing for Tizen 305

Summary 305

Chapter 19: Where to Go from Here — 307

Technical requirements 307

Learnings from running Blazor in production 307

Solving memory problems • 308

Solving concurrency problems • 309

Solving errors • 309

Old browsers • 309

The next steps 310

The community • 310

The components • 311

Summary 312

Other Books You May Enjoy — 317

Index — 323

Preface

Until now, creating interactive web pages meant using JavaScript. But with Blazor, a framework for creating .NET web applications, developers can easily build interactive and rich web applications using C#. This book will guide you through the most commonly encountered scenarios when starting your journey with Blazor.

Firstly, you'll discover how to leverage the power of Blazor and learn what you can do with Blazor Server, Blazor WebAssembly, and Blazor Hybrid. The book will help you overcome some of the common obstacles that developers face by showing you how all of the elements work together practically. As you advance, you'll learn how to create Blazor Server and Blazor WebAssembly projects, how Razor syntax works, and how to validate forms and create your own components. The book then introduces you to the key concepts involved in web development with Blazor, which you can put into practice immediately.

By the end of this Blazor book, you'll have gained the confidence to create and deploy production-ready Blazor applications.

Who this book is for

The book is for web developers and software developers who want to explore Blazor to learn how to build dynamic web UIs. This book assumes familiarity with C# programming and web development concepts.

What this book covers

Chapter 1, Hello Blazor, will teach you the difference between Blazor server and Blazor WebAssembly. You will get an overview of how the technology works and a brief history of where Blazor comes from. Knowing the structure and differences between the hosting models is essential for understanding the technology.

Chapter 2, *Creating Your First Blazor App*, helps you understand how to install and set up your development environment. You will create your first Blazor app (both Blazor Server and Blazor WebAssembly) and learn about the structure of the project template.

Chapter 3, *Managing State – Part 1*, teaches you how to create a repository to store your data (blog posts, categories, and tags).

Chapter 4, *Understanding Basic Blazor Components*, digs deeper into components, life cycle events, adding parameters, and sharing parameters between components. You will also create reusable components in this chapter.

Chapter 5, *Creating Advanced Blazor Components*, digs even deeper into components, adding functionality such as child components, cascading parameters, and values, and covering how to use actions and callbacks.

Chapter 6, *Building Forms with Validation*, looks at forms, how to validate forms, and how to build your own validation mechanism. This chapter will cover the most common use cases when handling forms, such as file upload, text, numbers, and triggering code when checking a checkbox.

Chapter 7, *Creating an API*, looks at creating an API using Minimal API. When using Blazor WebAssembly, we need an API to get data.

Chapter 8, *Authentication and Authorization*, looks at adding authentication and authorization to Blazor and making sure navigation, such as redirecting to a login page, works as expected.

Chapter 9, *Sharing Code and Resources*, teaches you how sharing code between Blazor WebAssembly and Blazor Server projects can be shared by adding all of the things you need into a shared library. In this chapter, you will build a shared library that can be packaged as a NuGet package and shared with others.

Chapter 10, *JavaScript Interop*, explores how you can leverage JavaScript libraries when using Blazor and make calls from C# to JavaScript. You will also look at how JavaScript can call C# functions in our Blazor app.

Chapter 11, *Managing State – Part 2*, looks into the different ways of managing state (persisting data), such as using LocalStorage or just keeping data in memory using dependency injection. You will also implement real-time updates to your blog post using SignalR.

Chapter 12, *Debugging the Code*, teaches you how to debug your applications and add extended logging to figure out what's wrong with your application. You will not only look at traditional debugging but also at debugging C# code directly from within the web browser.

Chapter 13, *Testing*, looks at automated testing so that you can make sure your components work as they should (and continue to do so). There is no built-in method to test Blazor applications, but there is an excellent community project called bUnit.

Chapter 14, *Deploy to Production*, will take you through the different things you need to think about when running Blazor in production.

Chapter 15, *Moving from, or Combining an Existing Site*, will show you how to integrate Blazor into an existing site and combine JavaScript frameworks like Angular or React with Blazor.

Chapter 16, *Going Deeper into WebAssembly*, covers the specific things for Blazor WebAssembly.

Chapter 17, *Examining Source Generators*, covers how Blazor relies heavily on source generators. In this chapter, you will learn how they work and relate to Blazor.

Chapter 18, *Visiting .NET MAUI*, looks at the third hosting model, Blazor Hybrid. Using .NET MAUI, you can build iOS, Android, macOS, Tizen, and Windows applications by leveraging what you have learned in this book.

Chapter 19, *Where to Go from Here*, is a short chapter with a call to action, some resources you can use, and a finale.

To get the most out of this book

I recommend reading the first few chapters to ensure you are up to speed with the basic concepts of Blazor in general. The project we are creating is adapted for real-world use but some parts are left out, such as proper error handing. You should, however, get a good grasp of the building blocks of Blazor.

The book focuses on using Visual Studio 2022; that said, feel free to use whatever version you are comfortable with that supports Blazor.

Software covered in this book	OS requirements
Visual Studio 2022, .NET7	Windows 10 or later, macOS, Linux

If you are using the digital version of this book, we advise you to type the code yourself or access the code via the GitHub repository (link available in the next section). Doing so will help you avoid any potential errors related to the copying and pasting of code.

I would love for you to share your progress while reading this book or in Blazor development in general. Tweet me at @EngstromJimmy.

I hope you have as much fun reading this book as I had writing it.

Download the example code files

The code bundle for the book is hosted on GitHub at https://github.com/PacktPublishing/Web-Development-with-Blazor-Second-Edition. We also have other code bundles from our rich catalog of books and videos available at https://github.com/PacktPublishing/. Check them out!

Download the color images

We also provide a PDF file that has color images of the screenshots/diagrams used in this book. You can download it here: https://packt.link/g0hSv.

Conventions used

There are a number of text conventions used throughout this book.

CodeInText: Indicates code words in text, database table names, folder names, filenames, file extensions, pathnames, dummy URLs, user input, and Twitter handles. For example; "The counter component is implemented similarly for both Blazor WebAssembly and Blazor Server."

A block of code is set as follows:

```
public void ConfigureServices(IServiceCollection services)
{
    services.AddRazorPages();
    services.AddServerSideBlazor();
    services.AddSingleton<WeatherForecastService>();
}
```

Any command-line input or output is written as follows:

```
dotnet new blazorserver -o BlazorServerSideApp
cd Data
```

Bold: Indicates a new term, an important word, or words that you see on the screen, for example, in menus or dialog boxes, also appear in the text like this. For example: "Select **Blazor Server App** from the search results and press **Next**."

Preface

 Warnings or important notes appear like this.

 Tips and tricks appear like this.

Get in touch

Feedback from our readers is always welcome.

General feedback: Email `feedback@packtpub.com`, and mention the book's title in the subject of your message. If you have questions about any aspect of this book, please email us at `questions@packtpub.com`.

Errata: Although we have taken every care to ensure the accuracy of our content, mistakes do happen. If you have found a mistake in this book, we would be grateful if you would report this to us. Please visit, `http://www.packtpub.com/submit-errata`, selecting your book, clicking on the Errata Submission Form link, and entering the details.

Piracy: If you come across any illegal copies of our works in any form on the Internet, we would be grateful if you would provide us with the location address or website name. Please contact us at `copyright@packtpub.com` with a link to the material.

If you are interested in becoming an author: If there is a topic that you have expertise in and you are interested in either writing or contributing to a book, please visit `http://authors.packtpub.com`.

Share your thoughts

Once you've read *Web Development with Blazor, Second Edition*, we'd love to hear your thoughts! Scan the QR code below to go straight to the Amazon review page for this book and share your feedback.

https://packt.link/r/1803241497

Your review is important to us and the tech community and will help us make sure we're delivering excellent quality content.

Download a free PDF copy of this book

Thanks for purchasing this book!

Do you like to read on the go but are unable to carry your print books everywhere? Is your eBook purchase not compatible with the device of your choice?

Don't worry, now with every Packt book you get a DRM-free PDF version of that book at no cost.

Read anywhere, any place, on any device. Search, copy, and paste code from your favorite technical books directly into your application.

The perks don't stop there, you can get exclusive access to discounts, newsletters, and great free content in your inbox daily

Follow these simple steps to get the benefits:

1. Scan the QR code or visit the link below

https://packt.link/free-ebook/9781803241494

2. Submit your proof of purchase
3. That's it! We'll send your free PDF and other benefits to your email directly

1
Hello Blazor

Thank you for picking up your copy of *Web Development with Blazor*. This book intends to get you started as quickly and pain-free as possible, chapter by chapter, without you having to read this book from cover to cover before getting your Blazor on.

This book will start by guiding you through the most common scenarios you'll come across when you start your journey with Blazor and will also dive into a few more advanced scenarios. This book aims to show you what Blazor is – both Blazor Server, Blazor WebAssembly, and Blazor Hybrid – how it all works practically and to help you avoid traps.

This is the book's second edition; much has happened since the first edition. .NET 6 and .NET 7 got released, and in this revision, I have updated the content to reflect the changes and the new functionality we got. Not only that, I have simplified the demos in the book, giving even more focus on Blazor and removing things that aren't directly Blazor (like Entity Framework).

A common belief is that Blazor is WebAssembly, but WebAssembly is just one way of running Blazor. Many books, workshops, and blog posts on Blazor focus heavily on WebAssembly. This book will cover Blazor WebAssembly, Blazor Server, and Blazor Hybrid. There are a few differences between Blazor Server and Blazor WebAssembly; I will point them out as we go along.

This first chapter will explore where Blazor came from, what technologies made Blazor possible, and the different ways of running Blazor. We will also touch on which type is best for you.

In this chapter, we will cover the following topics:

- Why Blazor?
- Preceding Blazor

- Introducing WebAssembly
- Introducing .NET 7
- Introducing Blazor

Technical requirements

It is recommended that you have some knowledge of .NET before you start, as this book is aimed at .NET developers who want to utilize their skills to make interactive web applications. However, it's more than possible that you will pick up a few .NET tricks along the way if you are new to the world of .NET.

Why Blazor?

Not that long ago, I got asked by a random person on Facebook if I was working with Blazor.

I said: Yes, yes I do.

He then continued with a long remark telling me that Blazor would never beat Angular, React, or Vue.

I see these kinds of remarks quite often, and it's essential to understand that beating other SPA frameworks has never been the goal. This is not Highlander, and there can be more than one.

Learning web development has previously been pretty tough. Not only do we need to know ASP.NET for the server, but we also need to learn a SPA framework like React, Angular, or VUE.

But it doesn't end there. We also need to learn NPM, Bower, and Parcel, as well as JavaScript or TypeScript.

We need to understand transpiling and build that into our development pipeline. This is, of course, just the tip of the iceberg; depending on technology, we need to explore other rabbit holes.

Blazor is an excellent choice for .NET developers to write interactive web applications without needing to learn (or keep up with) all the things we just mentioned. We can leverage our existing C# knowledge and the packages we are used to and share code between server and client.

I usually say: "Blazor removes all the things I hate about web development." To be honest, I guess the saying should be, "Blazor can remove all the things I hate about web development." With Blazor, it is still possible to do JavaScript interop and use JavaScript frameworks or other SPA frameworks from within Blazor, but we don't have to.

Blazor has opened a door where I can feel productive, creating a great user experience for my users using my existing C# knowledge.

Preceding Blazor

You probably didn't get this book to read about **JavaScript**, but it helps to remember that we are coming from a pre-Blazor time. I recall that time – the dark times. Many of the concepts used in Blazor are not that far from those used in many JavaScript frameworks, so I will start with a brief overview of our challenges.

As developers, we have many different platforms we can develop for, including desktop, mobile, games, the cloud (or server-side), AI, and even IoT. All these platforms have a lot of different languages to choose from, but there is, of course, one more platform: the apps that run inside the browser.

I have been a web developer for a long time, and I've seen code move from the server to run within the browser. It has changed the way we develop our apps. Frameworks such as Angular, React, Aurelia, and Vue have changed the web from reloading the whole page to updating small parts on the fly. This *new* on-the-fly update method has enabled pages to load quicker, as the perceived load time has been lowered (not necessarily the whole page load).

But for many developers, this is an entirely new skill set; that is, switching between a server (most likely C#, if you are reading this book) to a frontend developed in JavaScript. Data objects are written in C# in the backend and then serialized into JSON, sent via an API, and then deserialized into another object written in JavaScript in the frontend.

JavaScript used to work differently in different browsers, which jQuery tried to solve by having a common API that was translated into something the web browser could understand. Now, the differences between different web browsers are much smaller, which has rendered jQuery obsolete in many cases.

JavaScript differs slightly from other languages since it is not object-oriented or typed, for example. In 2010, Anders Hejlsberg (known for being C#, Delphi, and Turbo Pascal's original language designer) started working on **TypeScript**. This object-oriented language can be compiled/transpiled into JavaScript.

You can use Typescript with Angular, React, Aurelia, and Vue, but in the end, it is JavaScript that will run the actual code. Simply put, to create interactive web applications today using JavaScript/TypeScript, you need to switch between languages and choose and keep up with different frameworks.

In this book, we will look at this in another way. Even though we will talk about JavaScript, our primary focus will be developing interactive web applications mainly using C#.

Now, we know a bit about the history of JavaScript. JavaScript is no longer the only language that can run within a browser, thanks to WebAssembly, which we will cover in the next section.

Introducing WebAssembly

In this section, we will look at how **WebAssembly** works. One way of running Blazor is by using WebAssembly, but for now, let's focus on what WebAssembly is.

WebAssembly is a binary instruction format that is compiled and, therefore, smaller. It is designed for native speeds, which means that when it comes to speed, it is closer to C++ than it is to JavaScript. When loading JavaScript, the JavaScript files (or inline) are downloaded, parsed, optimized, and JIT-compiled; most of those steps are not needed for WebAssembly.

WebAssembly has a very strict security model that protects users from buggy or malicious code. It runs within a sandbox and cannot escape that sandbox without going through the appropriate APIs. Suppose you want to communicate outside WebAssembly, for example, by changing the **Document Object Model (DOM)** or downloading a file from the web. In that case, you will need to do that with JavaScript interop (more on that later, and don't worry – Blazor will solve this for us).

Let's look at some code to get a bit more familiar with WebAssembly.

In this section, we will create an app that sums two numbers and returns the result, written in C (to be honest, this is about the level of C I'm comfortable with).

We can compile C into WebAssembly in a few easy steps:

1. Navigate to `https://wasdk.github.io/WasmFiddle/`.
2. Add the following code:

    ```c
    int main() {
      return 1+2;
    }
    ```

3. Press **Build** and then **Run**.

You will see the number 3 being displayed in the output window toward the bottom of the page, as shown in the following screenshot:

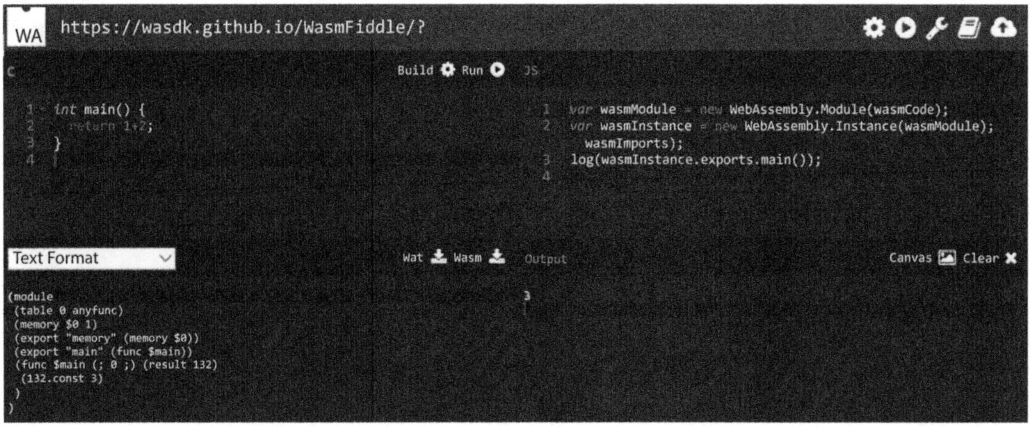

Chapter 1

![WasmFiddle screenshot]

Figure 1.1: WasmFiddle

WebAssembly is a stack machine language, which means that it uses a stack to perform its operations.

Consider this code:

```
1+2
```

Most compilers (including the one we just used) will optimize the code and return 3.

But let's assume that all the instructions should be executed. This is the way WebAssembly would do things:

1. It will start by pushing 1 onto the stack (instruction: i32.const 1), followed by pushing 2 onto the stack (instruction: i32.const 2). At this point, the stack contains 1 and 2.
2. Then, we must execute the add-instruction (i32.add), which will pop (get) the two top values (1 and 2) from the stack, add them up, and push the new value onto the stack (3).

This demo shows that we can build WebAssembly from C code. Now, we have C code that's been compiled into WebAssembly running in our browser.

OTHER LANGUAGES

Generally, it is only low-level languages that can be compiled into WebAssembly (such as C or Rust). However, there are a plethora of languages that can run on top of WebAssembly. Here is a great collection of some of these languages: https://github.com/appcypher/awesome-wasm-langs.

WebAssembly is super performant (near-native speeds) – so performant that game engines have already adapted this technology for that very reason. Unity, as well as Unreal Engine, can be compiled into WebAssembly.

Here are a couple of examples of games running on top of WebAssembly:

- **Angry Bots (Unity)**: https://beta.unity3d.com/jonas/AngryBots/
- **Doom**: https://wasm.continuation-labs.com/d3demo/

This is a great list of different WebAssembly projects: https://github.com/mbasso/awesome-wasm.

This section touched the surface of how WebAssembly works; in most cases, you won't need to know much more. We will dive into how Blazor uses this technology later in this chapter.

To write Blazor apps, we must leverage the power of .NET 7, which we'll look at next.

Introducing .NET 7

The .NET team has been working hard on tightening everything up for us developers for years. They have been making everything simpler, smaller, cross-platform, and open source – not to mention easier to utilize your existing knowledge of .NET development.

.NET core was a step toward a more unified .NET. It allowed Microsoft to reenvision the whole .NET platform and build it in a completely new way.

There are three different types of .NET runtimes:

- .NET Framework (full .NET)
- .NET Core
- Mono/Xamarin

Different runtimes had different capabilities and performances. This also meant that creating a .NET core app (for example) had different tooling and frameworks that needed to be installed.

.NET 5 is the start of our journey toward one single .NET. With this unified toolchain, the experience to create, run, and so on will be the same across all the different project types. .NET 5 is still modular in a similar way that we are used to, so we do not have to worry that merging all the different .NET versions is going to result in a bloated .NET.

Thanks to the .NET platform, you will be able to reach all the platforms we talked about at the beginning of this chapter (web, desktop, mobile, games, the cloud (or server-side), AI, and even IoT) using only C# and with the same tooling.

Blazor has been around for a while now. In .NET Core 3, the first version of Blazor Server was released, and at Microsoft Build in 2020, Microsoft released Blazor WebAssembly.

In .NET 5, we got a lot of new components for Blazor, pre-rendering, and CSS Isolation to name a few things. Don't worry; we will go through all these things throughout the book.

In .NET 6, we got even more functionality like Hot Reload, co-located JavaScript, new components, and much more, all of which we will explore throughout the book.

In November 2022, Microsoft released .NET 7, which has even more enhancements for Blazor developers.

Looking at the enhancements and number of features, I can only conclude that Microsoft believes in Blazor, and so do I.

Now that you know about some of the surrounding technologies, in the next section, it's time to introduce the main character of this book: Blazor.

Introducing Blazor

Blazor is an open-source web UI SPA framework. That's a lot of buzzwords in the same sentence, but simply put, it means that you can create interactive SPA web applications using HTML, CSS, and C# with full support for bindings, events, forms and validation, dependency injection, debugging, and much more. We will take a look at these in this book.

In 2017, Steve Sanderson (well-known for creating the Knockout JavaScript framework and who works for the ASP.NET team at Microsoft) was about to do a session called *Web Apps can't really do *that*, can they?* at the developer conference NDC Oslo.

But Steve wanted to show a cool demo, so he thought, *would it be possible to run C# in WebAssembly?* He found an old inactive project on GitHub called *Dot Net Anywhere*, which was written in C and used tools (similar to what we just did) to compile the C code into WebAssembly.

He got a simple console app running inside the browser. This would have been a fantastic demo for most people, but Steve wanted to take it further. He thought, *is it possible to create a simple web framework on top of this?*, and went on to see if he could get the tooling working as well.

When it was time for his session, he had a working sample to create a new project, create a to-do-list with great tooling support, and run the project inside the browser.

Damian Edwards (the .NET team) and David Fowler (the .NET team) were also at the NDC conferences. Steve showed them what he was about to demo, and they described the event as their heads exploded and their jaws dropped.

And that's how the prototype of Blazor came into existence.

The name Blazor comes from a combination of Browser and Razor (which is the technology used to combine code and HTML). Adding an *L* made the name sound better, but other than that, it has no real meaning or acronym.

There are a couple of different flavors of Blazor, including Blazor Server, Blazor WebAssembly, Blazor Hybrid (using .NET MAUI).

There are some pros and cons of the different versions, all of which I will cover in the upcoming sections and chapters.

Blazor Server

Blazor Server uses SignalR to communicate between the client and the server, as shown in the following diagram:

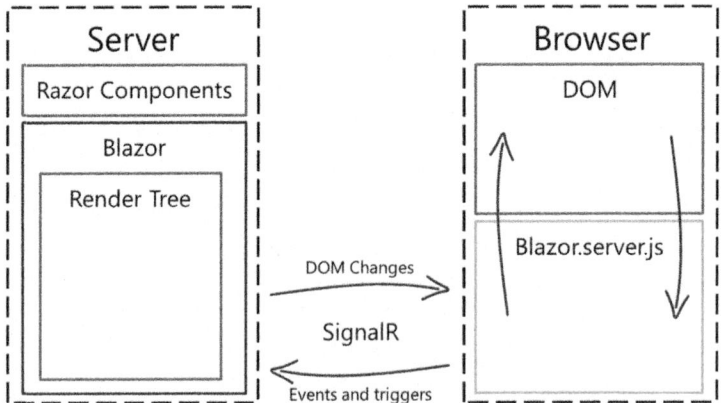

Figure 1.2: Overview of Blazor Server

SignalR is an open-source, real-time communication library that will create a connection between the client and the server. SignalR can use many different means of transporting data and automatically select the best transport protocol based on your server and client capabilities. SignalR will always try to use WebSockets, which is a transport protocol built into HTML5. If WebSockets is not enabled, it will gracefully fall back to another protocol.

Blazor is built with reusable UI elements called **components** (more on components in *Chapter 4, Understanding Basic Blazor Components*). Each component contains C# code, and markup and can even include another component. You can use Razor syntax to mix markup and C# code or do everything in C# if you wish. The components can be updated by user interaction (pressing a button) or triggers (such as a timer).

The components are rendered into a render tree, a binary representation of the DOM containing object states and any properties or values. The render tree will keep track of any changes compared to the previous render tree, and then send only the things that changed over SignalR using a binary format to update the DOM.

JavaScript will receive the changes on the client-side and update the page accordingly. If we compare this to traditional ASP.NET, we only render the component itself, not the entire page, and we only send over the actual changes to the DOM, not the whole page.

There are, of course, some disadvantages to Blazor Server:

- You need to always be connected to the server since the rendering is done on the server. If you have a bad internet connection, the site might not work. The big difference compared to a non-Blazor Server site is that a non-Blazor Server site can deliver a page and then disconnect until it requests another page. With Blazor, that connection (SignalR) must always be connected (minor disconnections are ok).
- There is no offline/PWA mode since it needs to be connected.
- Every click or page update must do a round trip to the server, which might result in higher latency. It is important to remember that Blazor Server will only send the changed data. I have not experienced any slow response times.
- Since we have to have a connection to the server, the load on that server increases and makes scaling difficult. To solve this problem, you can use the Azure SignalR hub to handle the constant connections and let your server concentrate on delivering content.
- Each connection stores the information in the server's memory, increasing memory use and making load balancing more difficult.
- To be able to run it, you have to host it on an ASP.NET Core-enabled server.

However, there are advantages to Blazor Server as well:

- It contains just enough code to establish that the connection is downloaded to the client, so the site has a small footprint, which makes the site startup really fast
- Since everything is rendered on the server, Blazor server is more SEO friendly.

- Since we are running on the server, the app can fully utilize the server's capabilities.
- The site will work on older web browsers that don't support WebAssembly.
- The code runs on the server and stays on the server; there is no way to decompile the code.
- Since the code is executed on your server (or in the cloud), you can make direct calls to services and databases within your organization.

At my workplace, we already had a large site, so we decided to use Blazor Server for our projects. We had a customer portal and an internal CRM tool, and our approach was to take one component at a time and convert it into a Blazor component.

We quickly realized that, in most cases, it was faster to remake the component in Blazor rather than continue to use ASP.NET MVC and add functionality. The **User Experience (UX)** for the end-user became even better as we converted.

The pages loaded faster. We could reload parts of the page as we needed instead of the whole page, and so on.

We found that Blazor introduced a new problem: the pages became *too* fast. Our users didn't understand if data had been saved because *nothing happened*; things *did* happen, but too fast for the users to notice. Suddenly, we had to think more about UX and how to inform the user that something had changed. This is, of course, a very positive side effect from Blazor.

Blazor Server is not the only way to run Blazor – you can also run it on the client (in the web browser) using WebAssembly.

Blazor WebAssembly

There is another option: instead of running Blazor on a server, you can run it inside your web browser using WebAssembly.

Microsoft has taken the mono runtime (which is written in C) and compiled that into WebAssembly.

The WebAssembly version of Blazor works very similarly to the server version, as shown in the following diagram. We have moved everything off the server, and it is now running within our web browser:

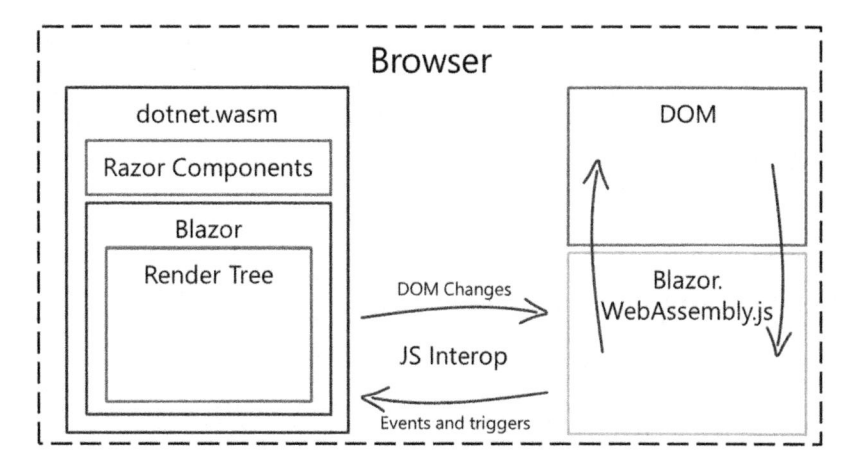

Figure 1.3: Overview of Blazor WebAssembly

A render tree is still created, and instead of running the Razor pages on the server, they are now running inside our web browser. Instead of SignalR, since WebAssembly doesn't have direct DOM access, Blazor updates the DOM with direct JavaScript interop.

The mono runtime that's compiled into WebAssembly is called **dotnet.wasm**. The page contains a small piece of JavaScript that will make sure to load dotnet.wasm. Then, it will download blazor.boot.json, a JSON file containing all the files the application needs to run, as well as the application's entry point.

If we look at the default sample site that is created when we start a new Blazor project in Visual Studio, the Blazor.boot.json file contains 63 dependencies that need to be downloaded. All the dependencies get downloaded and the app boots up.

As we mentioned previously, dotnet.wasm is the mono runtime that's compiled into WebAssembly. It runs .NET DLLs – the ones you have written and the ones from .NET Framework (which is needed to run your app) – inside your browser.

When I first heard of this, I got a bit of a bad taste. It's running the whole .NET runtime inside my browser?! But then, after a while, I realized how amazing that is. You can run any .NET Standard DLLs in your web browser.

In the next chapter, we will look at exactly what happens and in what order code gets executed when a WebAssembly app boots up.

The big concern is the download size of the site. The simple **file new** sample app is about 1.3 MB, which is quite large if you put a lot of effort into the download size. What you should remember, though, is that this is more like a **Single-Page Application (SPA)** – it is the whole site that has been downloaded to the client. I compared the size to some well-known sites on the internet; I then only included the JavaScript files for these sites but also included all the DLLs and JavaScript files for Blazor.

The following is a diagram of my findings:

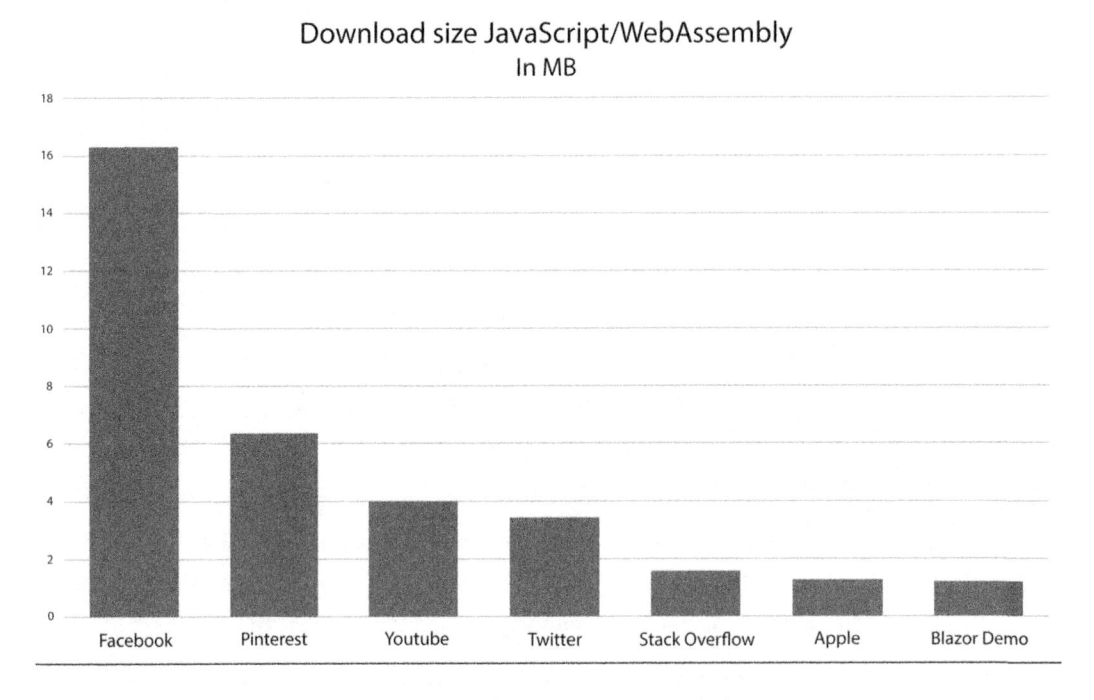

Figure 1.4: JavaScript download size for popular sites

Even though the other sites are larger than the sample Blazor site, you should remember that the Blazor DLLs are compiled and should take up less space than a JavaScript file. WebAssembly is also faster than JavaScript.

There are some disadvantages to Blazor WebAssembly:

- Even if we compare it to other large sites, the footprint of a Blazor WebAssembly is large and there are a large number of files to download.
- To access any on-site resources, you will need to create a Web API to access them. You cannot access the database directly.

- The code is running in the browser, meaning it can be decompiled. This is something all app developers are used to, but it is perhaps not as common for web developers.

There are, of course, some advantages of Blazor WebAssembly as well:

- Since the code runs in the browser, creating a **Progressive Web App** (**PWA**) is easy.
- Does not require a connection to the server. It will work offline.
- Since we're not running anything on the server, we can use any backend server or file share (no need for a .NET-compatible server in the backend).
- No round trips mean that you can update the screen faster (that is why there are game engines that use WebAssembly).

I wanted to put that last advantage to the test! When I was seven years old, I got my first computer, a Sinclair ZX Spectrum. I remember that I sat down and wrote the following:

```
10 PRINT "Jimmy"
20 GOTO 10
```

That was *my* code; I made the computer write my name on the screen over and over!

That was when I decided that I wanted to become a developer to make computers do stuff.

After becoming a developer, I wanted to revisit my childhood and decided I wanted to build a ZX Spectrum emulator. In many ways, the emulator has become my test project instead of a simple *Hello World* when I encounter new technology. I've had it running on a Gadgeteer, Xbox One, and even a HoloLens (to name a few).

But is it possible to run my emulator in Blazor?

It took me only a couple of hours to get the emulator working with Blazor WebAssembly by leveraging my already built .NET Standard DLL; I only had to write the code specific to this implementation, such as the keyboard and graphics. This is one of the reasons Blazor (both Server and WebAssembly) is so powerful: it can run libraries that have already been made. Not only can you leverage your knowledge of C#, but you can also take advantage of the large ecosystem and .NET community.

You can find the emulator here: http://zxbox.com. This is one of my favorite projects to work on, as I keep finding ways to optimize and improve the emulator.

Building this type of web application used to only be possible with JavaScript. Now, we know we can use Blazor WebAssembly and Blazor Server, but which one of these new options is the best?

Blazor WebAssembly versus Blazor Server

Which one should we choose? The answer is, as always, it depends. You have seen the advantages and disadvantages of both.

If you have a current site that you want to port over to Blazor, I recommend going for the server side; once you have ported it, you can make a new decision as to whether you want to go for WebAssembly as well. This way, it is easy to port parts of the site, and the debugging experience is better with Blazor Server.

Suppose your site runs on a mobile browser or another unreliable internet connection. In that case, you might consider going for an offline-capable (PWA) scenario with Blazor WebAssembly since Blazor Server needs a constant connection.

The startup time for WebAssembly is a bit slow, but there are ways to combine the two hosting models to have the best of two worlds. We will cover this in Chapter *16, Going Deeper into WebAssembly*.

There is no silver bullet when it comes to this question, but read up on the advantages and disadvantages and see how those affect your project and use cases.

We can run Blazor server-side and on the client, but what about desktop and mobile apps?

Blazor Hybrid / .NET MAUI

.NET MAUI is a cross-platform application framework. The name comes from .NET Multi-platform App UI and is the next version of Xamarin. We can use traditional XAML code to create our cross-platform application just as with Xamarin however, .NET MAUI also targets desktop operating systems that will make it possible to run our Blazor app on Windows and even macOS.

Using Blazor Hybrid, we also get access to native APIs (not only Web APIs), which makes it possible for us to take our application to another level.

We will take a look at .NET MAUI in *Chapter 18, Visiting .NET MAUI*.

As you can see, there are a lot of things you can do with Blazor, and this is just the beginning.

Summary

In this chapter, you were provided with an overview of the different technologies you can use with Blazor, such as server-side (Blazor Server), client-side (WebAssembly), desktop, and mobile. This overview should have helped you decide what technology to choose for your next project.

We then discussed how Blazor was created and its underlying technologies, such as SignalR and WebAssembly. You also learned about the render tree and how the DOM gets updated to give you an understanding of how Blazor works under the hood.

In the upcoming chapters, I will walk you through various scenarios to equip you with the knowledge to handle everything from upgrading an old/existing site, and creating a new server-side site, to creating a new WebAssembly site.

We'll get our hands dirty in the next chapter by configuring our development environment and creating and examining our first Blazor App.

Further reading

As a .NET developer, you might be interested in the Uno Platform (https://platform.uno/), which makes it possible to create a UI in XAML and deploy it to many different platforms, including WebAssembly.

If you want to see how the ZX Spectrum emulator is built, you can download the source code here: https://github.com/EngstromJimmy/ZXSpectrum.

Join our community on Discord

Join our community's Discord space for discussions with the author and other readers:

https://packt.link/WebDevBlazor2e

2
Creating Your First Blazor App

In this chapter, we will set up our development environment so that we can start developing Blazor apps. We will create our first Blazor app and go through the project structure, highlighting the differences between Blazor Server and Blazor WebAssembly projects.

By the end of this chapter, you will have a working development environment and have created both a Blazor Server app and a Blazor WebAssembly app.

In this chapter, we will cover the following:

- Setting up your development environment
- Creating our first Blazor application
- Using the command line
- Figuring out the project structure

Technical requirements

We will create a new project (a blog engine) and will continue working on that project throughout the book.

You can find the source code for this chapter's result at https://github.com/PacktPublishing/Web-Development-with-Blazor-Second-Edition/tree/main/Chapter02.

Setting up your development environment

In this book, the focus will be on Windows development, and any screenshots are going to be from Visual Studio (unless stated otherwise). But since .NET 7 is cross-platform, we will go through how to set up your development environment on Windows, macOS, and Linux.

The go-to link for all the platforms can be found at https://visualstudio.microsoft.com/.

We can download Visual Studio, Visual Studio Code, or Visual Studio for Mac from the web page.

Windows

On Windows, we have many different options for developing Blazor applications. Visual Studio 2022 is the most powerful tool we can use.

There are three different editions, which are as follows:

- Community 2022
- Professional 2022
- Enterprise 2022

In short, the Community Edition is free, while the others cost money. The Community Edition does have some limitations, and we can compare the different editions here: https://visualstudio.microsoft.com/vs/compare/.

For this book, we can use any of these versions. Take the following steps:

1. Download Visual Studio 2022 from https://visualstudio.microsoft.com/vs/. Choose the version that is right for you.
2. Install Visual Studio and during the installation, make sure to select **ASP.NET and web development**, as shown in *Figure 2.1*:

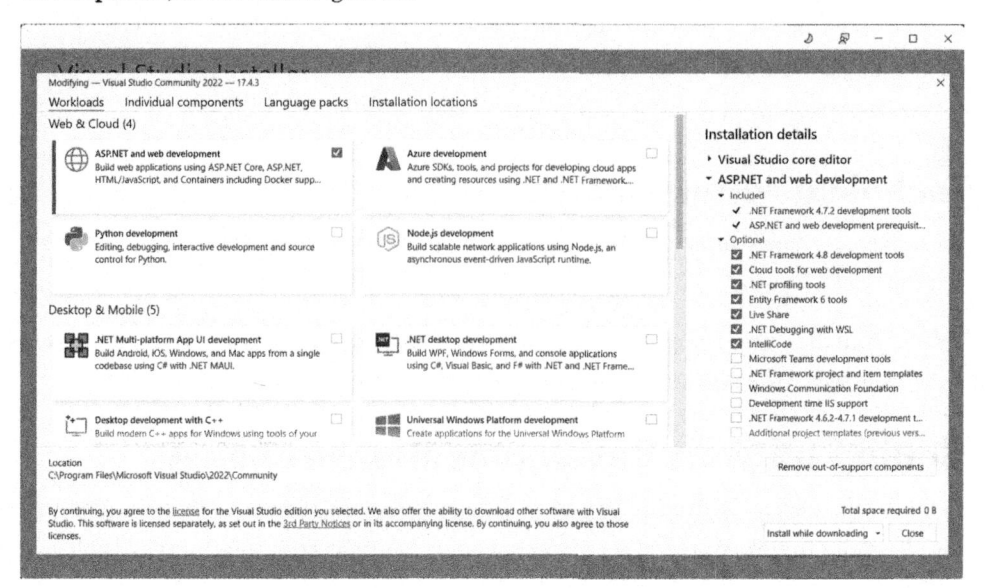

Figure 2.1: Visual Studio 2022 installation on Windows

3. To the right is a list of all the components that will be installed. Check **.NET WebAssembly Build Tools**.

We can also use Visual Studio Code to develop Blazor on Windows, but we won't discuss the installation process for Windows.

macOS

On macOS, we also have some options. Visual Studio for Mac is the most powerful IDE we can use.

Download Visual Studio for Mac from `https://visualstudio.microsoft.com/vs/mac/` as follows:

1. Click on the **Download Visual Studio for Mac** button.
2. Open the file that we downloaded.

Make sure to select **.NET**, as shown in *Figure 2.2*:

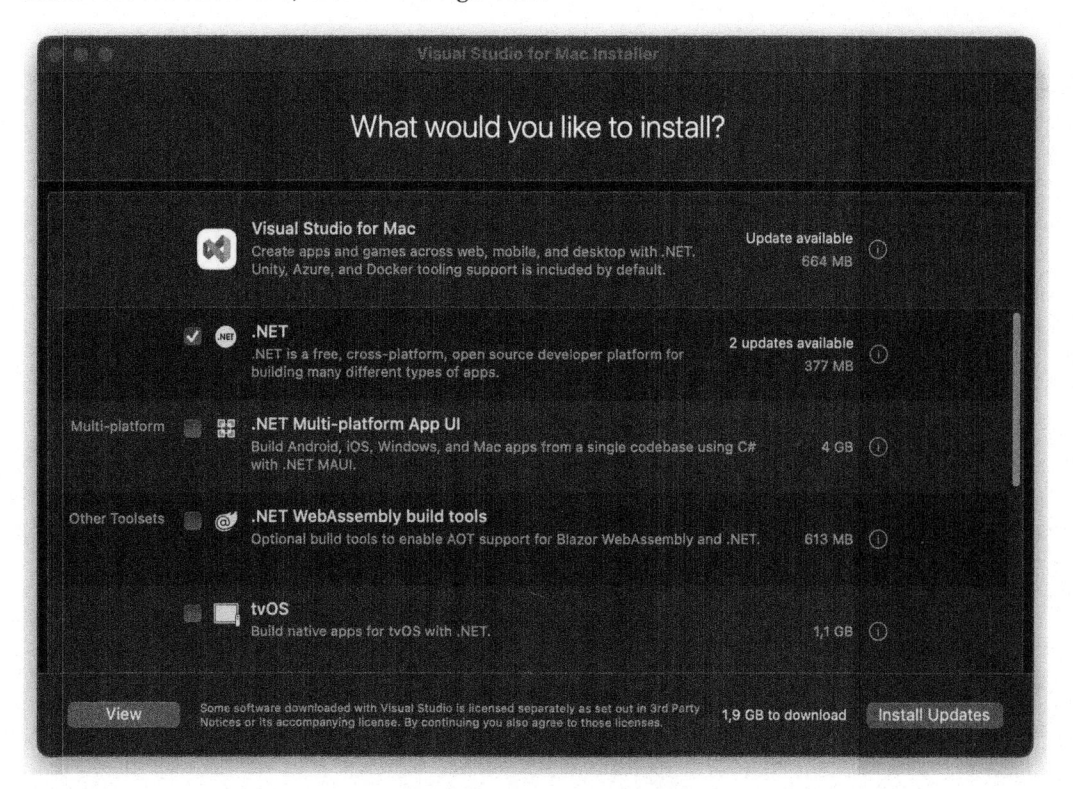

Figure 2.2: Visual Studio for Mac installation screen

Since Visual Studio Code is a cross-platform software, we can use it here as well.

Linux (or macOS or Windows)

Visual Studio Code is cross-platform, which means we can use it on Linux, macOS, or Windows.

The different versions are available at `https://code.visualstudio.com/Download`.

Once installed, we also need to add two extensions:

1. Open Visual Studio Code and press *Ctrl + Shift + X*.
2. Search for `C# for Visual Studio Code (powered by OmniSharp)` and click **Install**.
3. Search for `JavaScript Debugger (Nightly)` and click **Install**.

To create a project, we can use the .NET CLI, which we will return to throughout this book, but we won't do a deep dive into the .NET CLI.

Now that everything is set up, let's create our first app.

Creating our first Blazor application

Throughout the book, we will create a blog engine. There won't be a lot of business logic that you'll have to learn; the app is simple to understand but will touch base on many of the technologies and areas you will be faced with when building a Blazor app.

The project will allow visitors to read blog posts and search for them. It will also have an admin site where you can write a blog post, which will be password-protected.

We will make the same app for both Blazor Server and Blazor WebAssembly, and I will show you the steps you need to do differently for each platform.

> **IMPORTANT NOTE**
>
> This guide will use Visual Studio 2022 from now on, but other platforms have similar ways of creating projects.

Exploring the templates

In .NET 7, we got more templates. We will explore them further in *Chapter 4, Understanding Basic Blazor Components*. This chapter will give you a quick overview. In .NET 7 we have 4 Blazor templates, two Blazor Server, and two Blazor WebAssembly. We also have one Blazor Hybrid (.NET MAUI), but we will get back to it in *Chapter 18, Visiting .NET MAUI*.

Blazor Server App

The **Blazor Server App** template gives us (as the name implies) a Blazor Server app. It contains a couple of components to see what a Blazor app looks like and some basic setup and menu structure. It also contains code for adding Bootstrap, Isolated CSS, and things like that (See *Chapter 9, Sharing Code and Resources*).

This is the template we will use in the book to understand better how things go together.

Blazor WebAssembly App

The **Blazor WebAssembly App** template gives us (as the name implies) a Blazor WebAssembly app. Just like the Blazor Server App template, it contains a couple of components to see what a Blazor app looks like and some basic setup and menu structure. It also contains code for adding Bootstrap, Isolated CSS, and things like that (See *Chapter 9, Sharing Code and Resources*).

This is the template we will use in the book to understand better how things go together.

Blazor Server App Empty

The **Blazor Server App Empty** template is a basic template that contains what is essential to run a Blazor Server App.

It doesn't contain Isolated CSS and things like that. When starting an actual project, this is probably the template to use. But it does require us to implement things we might need that the non-empty templates will give us.

Blazor WebAssembly App Empty

The **Blazor WebAssembly App Empty** template is a basic template that contains what is essential to run a Blazor WebAssembly App.

It doesn't contain Isolated CSS and things like that. When starting an actual project, this is probably the template to use. But it does require us to implement things we might need that the non-empty templates will give us.

Creating a Blazor Server application

To start, we will create a Blazor Server application and play around with it:

1. Start Visual Studio 2022, and you will see the following screen:

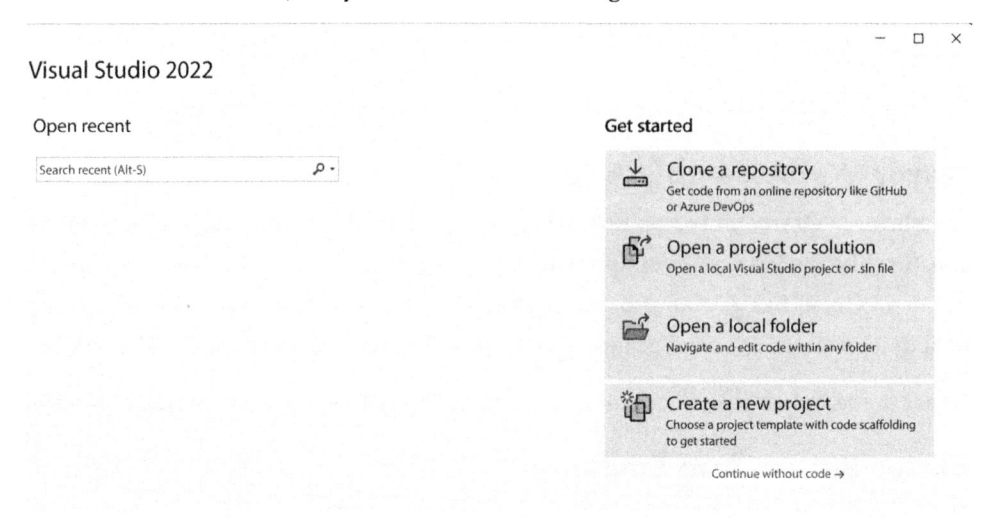

Figure 2.3: Visual Studio startup screen

2. Press **Create a new project**, and in the search bar, type `blazor`.

3. Select **Blazor Server App** from the search results and press **Next**:

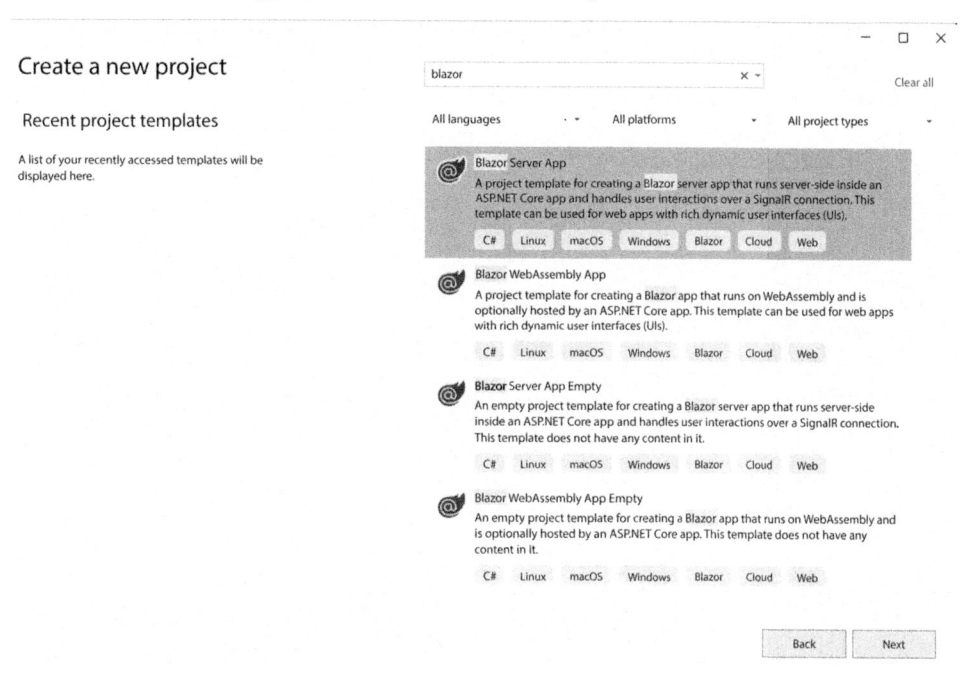

Figure 2.4: The Visual Studio Create a new project screen

4. Now name the project (this is the hardest part of any project, but fear not, I have done that already!). Name the application `BlazorServer`, change the solution name to `MyBlog`, and press **Next**:

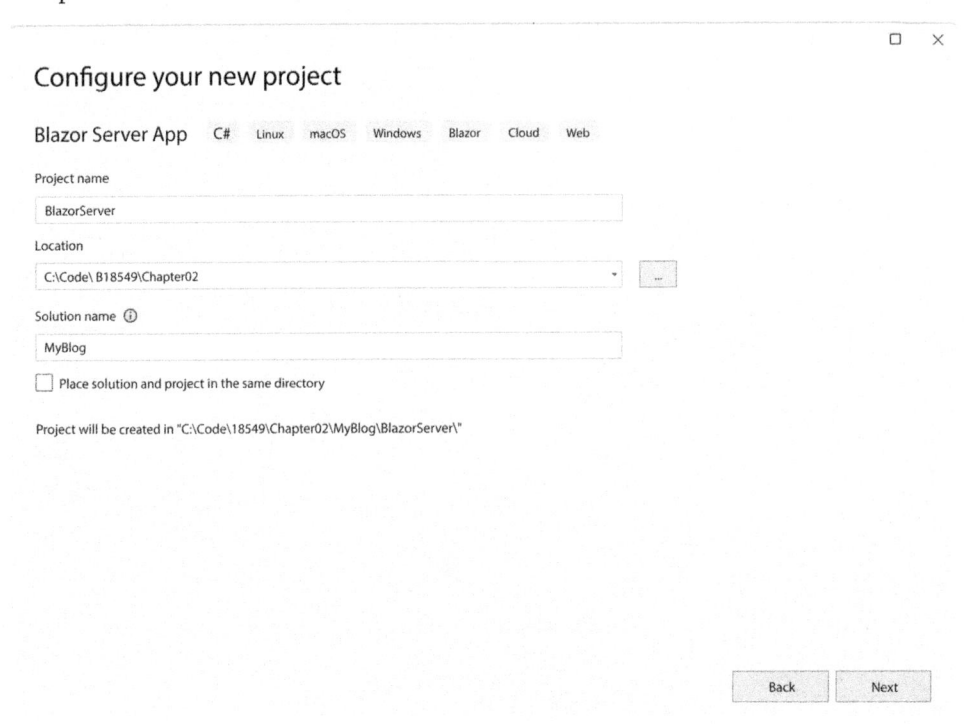

Figure 2.5: The Visual Studio Configure your new project screen

5. Next, choose what kind of Blazor app we should create. Select **.NET 7.0 (Standard Term Support)** from the dropdown menu and press **Create**:

Chapter 2   25

Additional information

Blazor Server App   C#   Linux   macOS   Windows   Blazor   Cloud   Web

Framework ⓘ

.NET 7.0 (Standard Term Support)   ▼

Authentication type ⓘ

None   ▼

☑ Configure for HTTPS ⓘ
☐ Enable Docker ⓘ

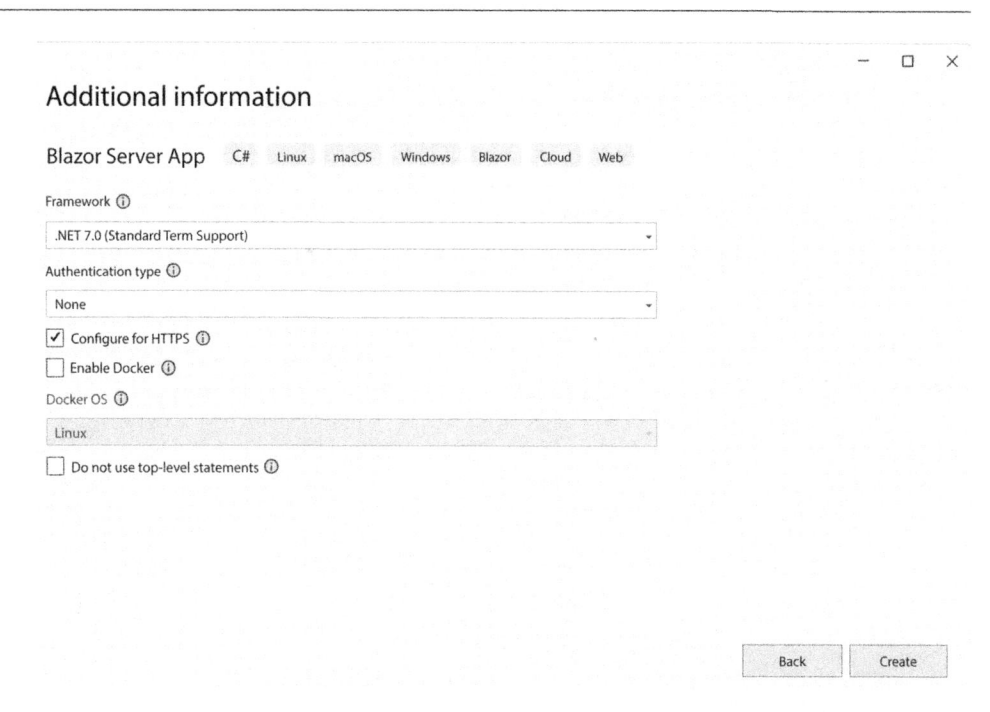

Docker OS ⓘ

Linux   ▼

☐ Do not use top-level statements ⓘ

[Back]   [Create]

Figure 2.6: Visual Studio screen for creating a new Blazor app

6. Now run the app by pressing *Ctrl + F5* (we can also find it under **Debug | Start without debugging**).

Congratulations! You have just created your first Blazor Server application. The site should look something like in *Figure 2.7*:

BlazorServer   About

🏠 Home

➕ Counter

≡ Fetch data

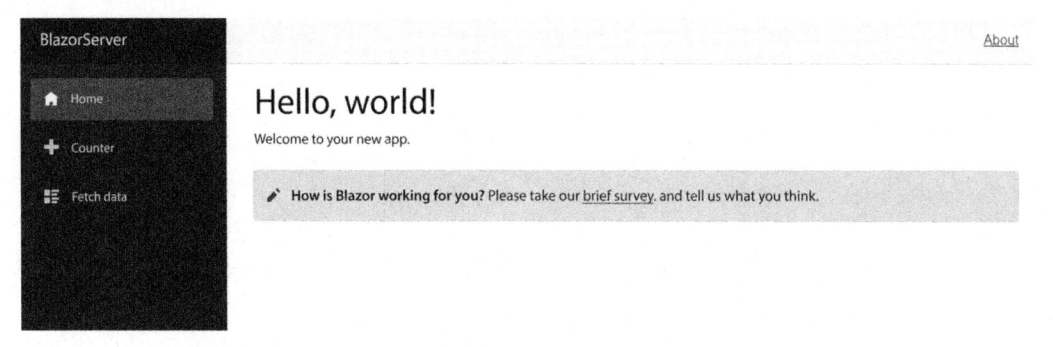

Hello, world!

Welcome to your new app.

✏ **How is Blazor working for you?** Please take our brief survey, and tell us what you think.

Figure 2.7: A new Blazor Server server-side application

Explore the site a bit, navigate to **Counter** and **Fetch data** to get a feeling for the load times, and see what the sample application does.

The sample application has some sample data ready for us to test.

This is a Blazor Server project, which means that for every trigger (for example, a button press), a command will be sent via SignalR over to the server. The server will rerender the component, send the changes back to the client, and update the UI.

Press *F12* in your browser (to access the developer tools), switch to the **Network** tab and then reload the page (*F5*). You'll see all the files that get downloaded to the browser.

In *Figure 2.8*, you can see some of the files that get downloaded:

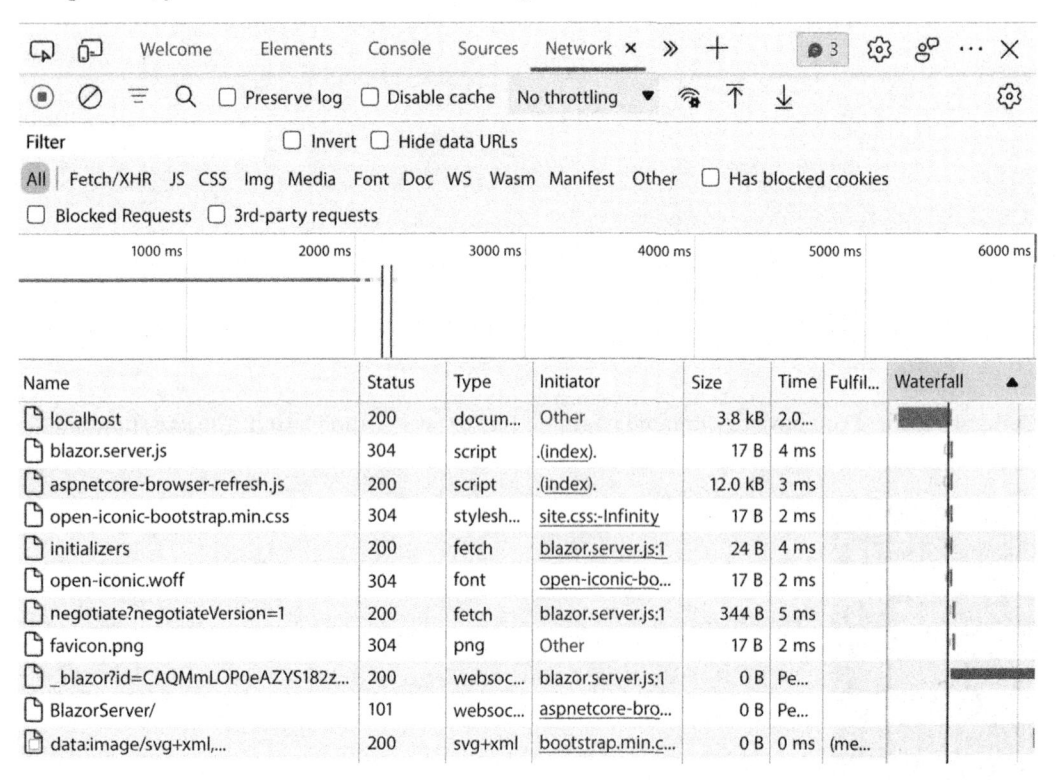

Name	Status	Type	Initiator	Size	Time	Fulfil...	Waterfall
localhost	200	docum...	Other	3.8 kB	2.0...		
blazor.server.js	304	script	(index).	17 B	4 ms		
aspnetcore-browser-refresh.js	200	script	(index).	12.0 kB	3 ms		
open-iconic-bootstrap.min.css	304	stylesh...	site.css:-Infinity	17 B	2 ms		
initializers	200	fetch	blazor.server.js:1	24 B	4 ms		
open-iconic.woff	304	font	open-iconic-bo...	17 B	2 ms		
negotiate?negotiateVersion=1	200	fetch	blazor.server.js:1	344 B	5 ms		
favicon.png	304	png	Other	17 B	2 ms		
_blazor?id=CAQMmLOP0eAZYS182z...	200	websoc...	blazor.server.js:1	0 B	Pe...		
BlazorServer/	101	websoc...	aspnetcore-bro...	0 B	Pe...		
data:image/svg+xml,...	200	svg+xml	bootstrap.min.c...	0 B	0 ms	(me...	

Figure 2.8: The Network tab in Microsoft Edge

The browser downloads the page, some CSS, and then `blazor.server.js`, which is responsible for setting up the SignalR connection back to the server. It then calls the `negotiate` endpoint (to set up the connections).

The call to `_blazor?id=` (followed by a bunch of letters) is a **WebSocket** call, which is the open connection that the client and the server communicate through.

If you navigate to the **Counter** page and press the **Click me** button, you will notice that the page won't be reloaded. The trigger (click event) is sent over SignalR to the server, and the page is rerendered on the server and gets compared to the render tree, and only the actual change is pushed back over the WebSocket.

For a button click, three calls are being made:

- The page triggers the event (for example, a button click).
- The server responds with the changes.
- The page then acknowledges that the **Document Object Model (DOM)** has been updated.

In total, 600 bytes (this example is from the Counter page) are sent back and forth for a button click.

We have created a solution and a Blazor Server project and tried them out. Next up, we will add a Blazor WebAssembly app to that solution.

Creating a WebAssembly application

Now it is time to take a look at a WebAssembly app. We will create a new Blazor WebAssembly app and add it to the same solution as the Blazor Server app we just created:

1. Right-click on the **MyBlog** solution and select **Add | New Project**.

2. Search for blazor, select **Blazor WebAssembly App** in the search results, and press **Next**:

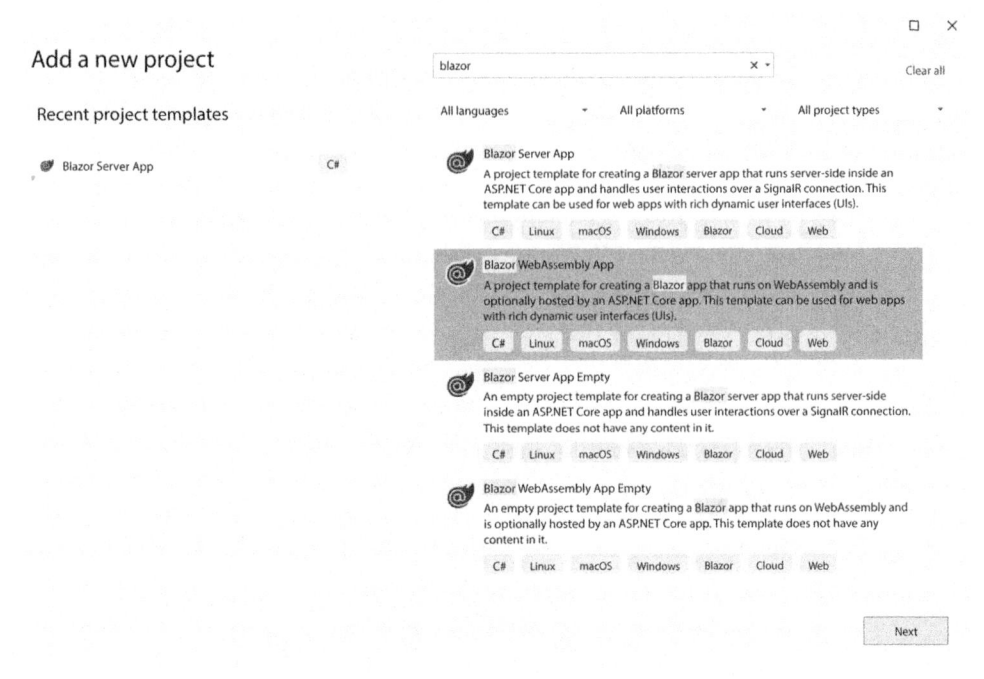

Figure 2.9: The Visual Studio Add a new project screen

3. Name the app `BlazorWebAssembly`. Leave the location as is (Visual Studio will put it in the correct folder by default) and press **Create**:

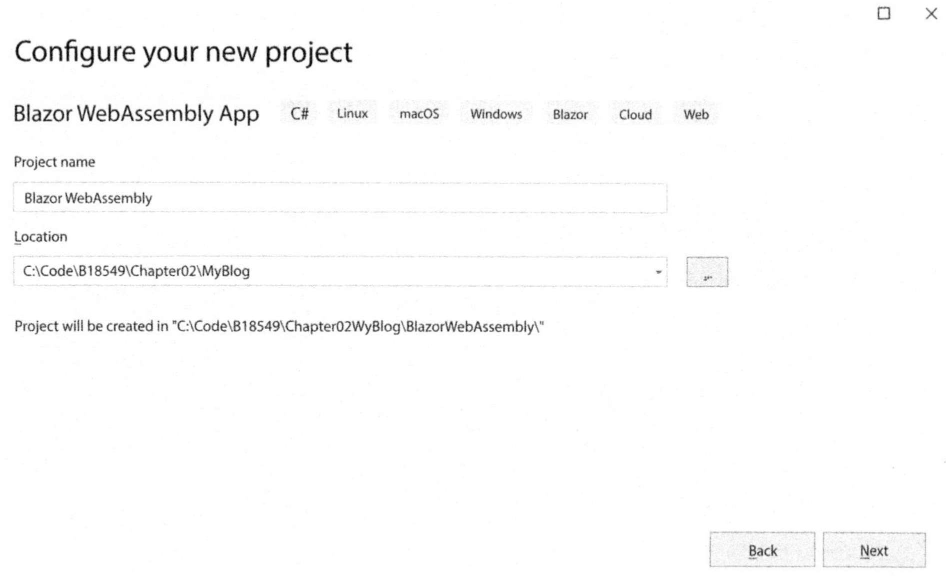

Chapter 2 29

Configure your new project

Blazor WebAssembly App   C#   Linux   macOS   Windows   Blazor   Cloud   Web

Project name

Blazor WebAssembly

Location

C:\Code\B18549\Chapter02\MyBlog

Project will be created in "C:\Code\B18549\Chapter02WyBlog\BlazorWebAssembly\"

Back   Next

Figure 2.10: The Visual Studio Configure your new project screen

4. On the next screen, select **.NET 7.0 (Standard Term Support)** from the dropdown.

5. In this dialog box, two new choices that were not available in the Blazor Server template appear. The first option is **ASP.NET Core hosted**, which will create an ASP.NET backend project and will host the WebAssembly app, which is good if you want to host web APIs for your app to access; you should check this box.

6. The second option is **Progressive Web Application**, which will create a `manifest.json` file and a `service-worker.js` file that will make your app available as a **Progressive Web Application (PWA)**. Make sure the **Progressive Web Application** option is checked as well, and then press **Create**:

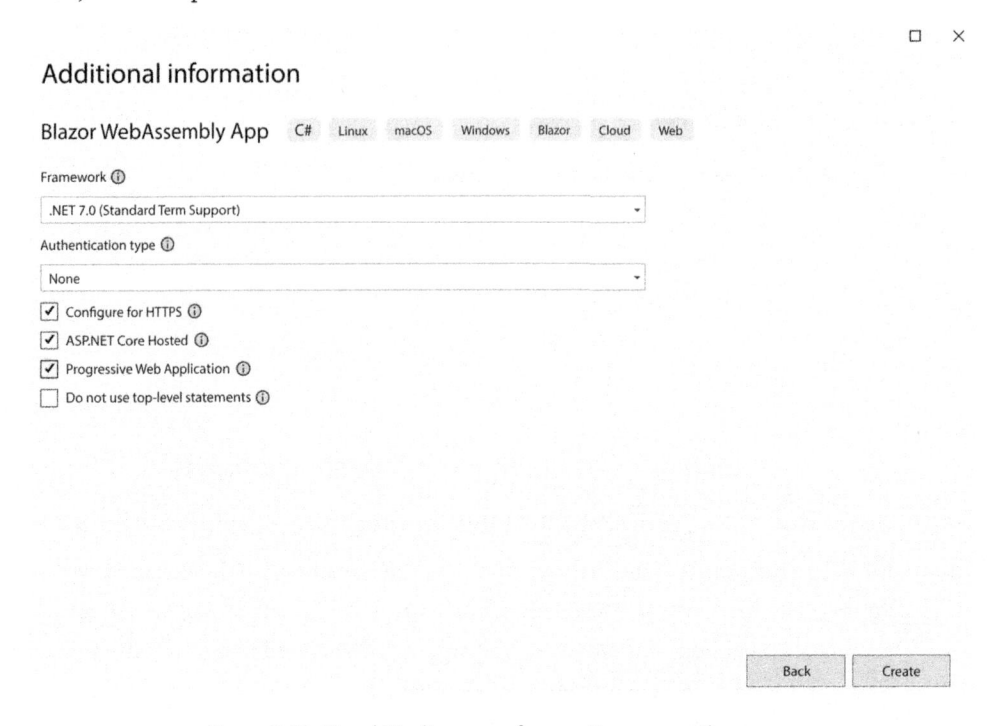

Figure 2.11: Visual Studio screen for creating a new Blazor app

7. Right-click on the **WebAssembly.Server** project and select **Set as Startup Project**.

> **NOTE:**
>
> It can be confusing that this project also has Server in the name.
>
> Since we chose **ASP.NET Core hosted** when we created the project, we are hosting the backend for our client-side (WebAssembly) in **WebAssembly.Server,** and it is not related to Blazor Server.
>
> Remember that if you want to run the WebAssembly app, you should run the **WebAssembly.Server** project; that way, we know the backend ASP.NET Core project will also run.

8. Run the app by pressing *Ctrl + F5* (start without debugging).

Congratulations! You have just created your first Blazor WebAssembly application, as shown in *Figure 2.12*:

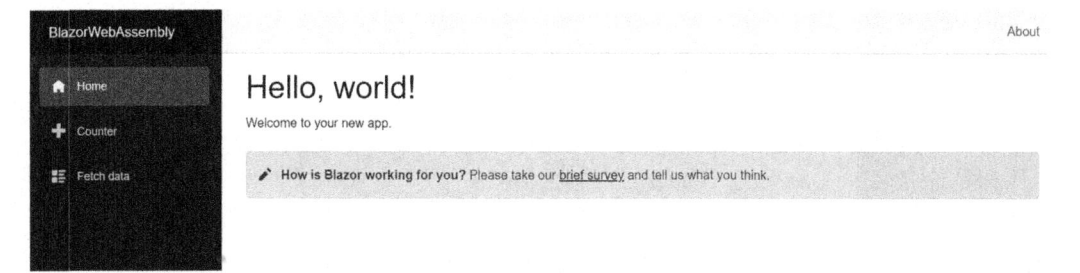

Figure 2.12: A new Blazor WebAssembly app

Explore the site by clicking the **Counter** and **Fetch data** links. The app should behave in the same way as the Blazor Server version.

Press *F12* in your browser (to access the developer tools), switch to the **Network** tab, and reload the page (*F5*); you'll see all the files downloaded to the browser.

In *Figure 2.13*, you can see some of the files that got downloaded:

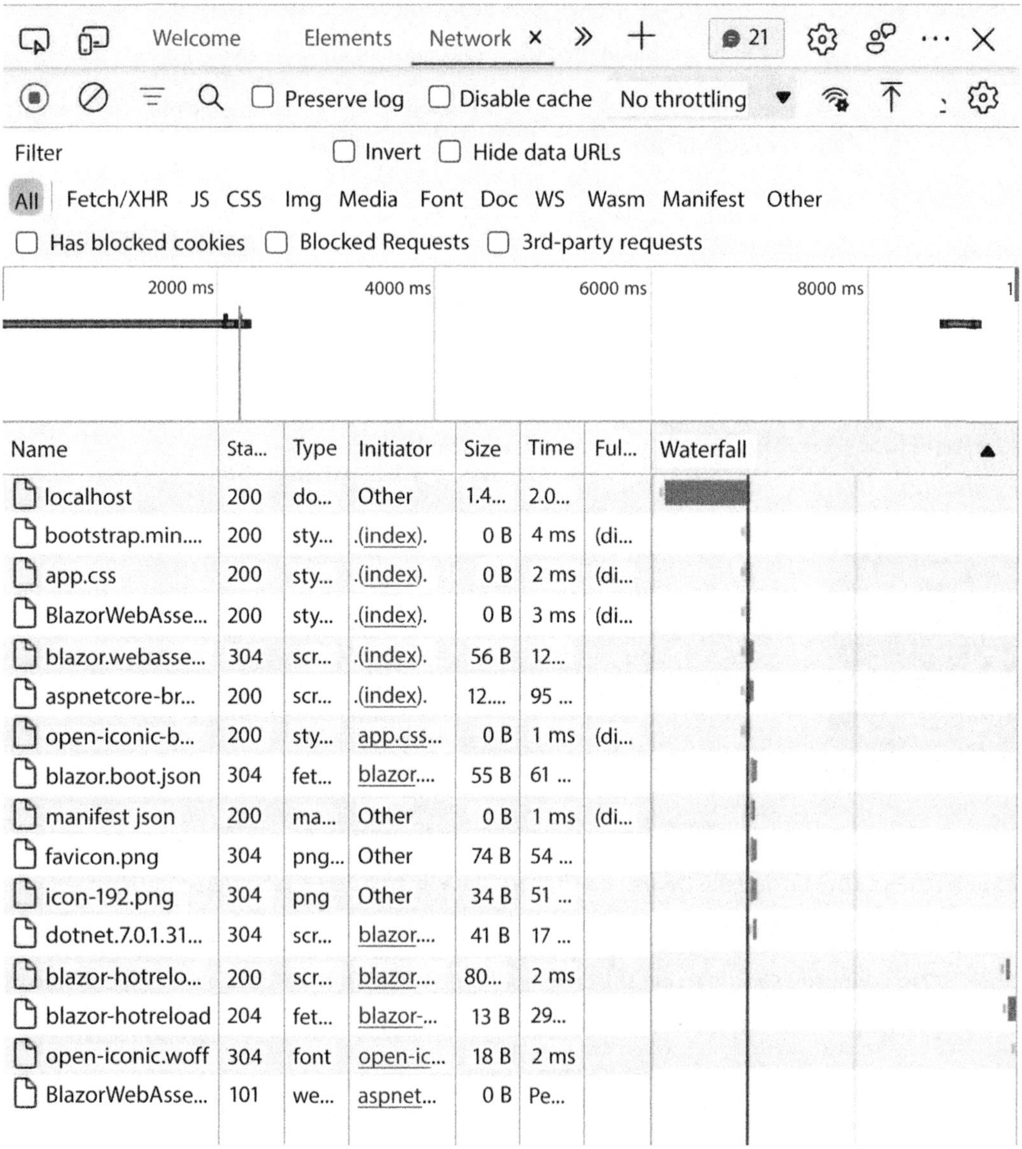
Welcome
Elements
Network
21
Preserve log
Disable cache
No throttling
Filter
Invert
Hide data URLs
All
Fetch/XHR
JS
CSS
Img
Media
Font
Doc
WS
Wasm
Manifest
Other
Has blocked cookies
Blocked Requests
3rd-party requests
2000 ms
4000 ms
6000 ms
8000 ms
Name
Sta...
Type
Initiator
Size
Time
Ful...
Waterfall
localhost 200 do... Other 1.4... 2.0...
bootstrap.min.... 200 sty... .(index). 0 B 4 ms (di...
app.css 200 sty... .(index). 0 B 2 ms (di...
BlazorWebAsse... 200 sty... .(index). 0 B 3 ms (di...
blazor.webasse... 304 scr... .(index). 56 B 12...
aspnetcore-br... 200 scr... .(index). 12.... 95 ...
open-iconic-b... 200 sty... app.css... 0 B 1 ms (di...
blazor.boot.json 304 fet... blazor.... 55 B 61 ...
manifest json 200 ma... Other 0 B 1 ms (di...
favicon.png 304 png... Other 74 B 54 ...
icon-192.png 304 png Other 34 B 51 ...
dotnet.7.0.1.31... 304 scr... blazor.... 41 B 17 ...
blazor-hotrelo... 200 scr... blazor.... 80... 2 ms
blazor-hotreload 204 fet... blazor-... 13 B 29...
open-iconic.woff 304 font open-ic... 18 B 2 ms
BlazorWebAsse... 101 we... aspnet... 0 B Pe...

Figure 2.13: The Network tab in Microsoft Edge

In this case, when the page gets downloaded, it will trigger a download of the `blazor.webassembly.js` file. Then, `blazor.boot.json` gets downloaded. *Figure 2.14* shows an example of part of `blazor.boot.json`:

```json
{
  "cacheBootResources": true,
  "config": [ ],
  "debugBuild": true,
  "entryAssembly": "BlazorWebAssembly.Client",
  "icuDataMode": 0,
  "linkerEnabled": false,
  "resources": {
    "assembly": {
      "Microsoft.AspNetCore.Authorization.dll": "sha256-slDjDcX+jWHK37C+TcMSiNdKjR4Lf+sFS2PdJocVk6U=",
      "Microsoft.AspNetCore.Components.dll": "sha256-SVqESV3aJFKOkvmnDOFkvktvfEc45ZUYwu8bUNegy1k=",
      "Microsoft.AspNetCore.Components.Forms.dll": "sha256-HHOtjws+9ItTGHLV1WO5wEcobrA+Qyj85eko5TVrHEE=",
      "Microsoft.AspNetCore.Components.Web.dll": "sha256-uyN0L7t6VFUm3ZbOUfdqsL1B2B5zztk6NdoJzbyZKdY=",
      "Microsoft.AspNetCore.Components.WebAssembly.dll": "sha256-ecggAD0m8Nfz7rxgDHriZVSqjAmNHqoTT6xHnRx\/pwU=",
      "Microsoft.AspNetCore.Metadata.dll": "sha256-XWZE0MPVLuLPVAegFKQPS09aa94oGNnImQsjzL5VH0o=",
      "Microsoft.Extensions.Configuration.dll": "sha256-PqQvp77oZ4+uuy2E1Xk8AU9I6RfZSf18UGTrd4rulOo=",
      "Microsoft.Extensions.Configuration.Abstractions.dll": "sha256-CnS3b9EMFQmETBUVEgtcron4DBsfFdcVt3zfCP6Uflg=",
      "Microsoft.Extensions.Configuration.Binder.dll": "sha256-em\/Vt\/2aV1DQPuXI8gSU7RHK2If1CprFUyVvpA0UefI=",
      "Microsoft.Extensions.Configuration.FileExtensions.dll": "sha256-S86mGNxJnkVJ\/qolp6cBN7xwXQ\/YVtHy7QTaPO93AIA=",
      "Microsoft.Extensions.Configuration.Json.dll": "sha256-k525Vc8hbMpPjxYUYZNPuzJIuy+E1Is2XRTMFbUm1pE=",
      "Microsoft.Extensions.DependencyInjection.dll": "sha256-\/+vk9BsQP4bCVt1Y6aXakSztSMA1i200ER6untxHLBg=",
      "Microsoft.Extensions.DependencyInjection.Abstractions.dll": "sha256-jrAm+30mcWoI54hsUTOr+RMOzHIq+zO8ZuRBVrBvCoo=",
      "Microsoft.Extensions.FileProviders.Abstractions.dll": "sha256-Zt60Y6gg\/1Tzt9oFOQBkezPvUVkFK4dyM6Pfk+MTUvg=",
      "Microsoft.Extensions.FileProviders.Physical.dll": "sha256-9xkIbIienaRj9Td2MyWYzL9JmVx6CKbGCPrvJ1Pxfn8=",
```

Figure 2.14: Part of the blazor.boot.json file

The most important thing `blazor.boot.json` contains is the entry assembly, which is the name of the DLL the browser should start executing. It also includes all the framework DLLs the app needs to run. Now our app knows what it needs to start up.

The JavaScript will then download `dotnet.7.0.*.js`, which will download all the resources mentioned in `blazor.boot.json`: this is a mix of your code compiled to a .NET Standard DLL, Microsoft .NET Framework code, and any community or third-party DLLs you might use. The JavaScript then downloads `dotnet.wasm`, the Mono runtime compiled to WebAssembly, which will start booting up your app.

If you watch closely, you might see some text when you reload your page saying **Loading**. Between **Loading** showing up and the page finishing loading, JSON files, JavaScript, WebAssembly, and DLLs are downloaded, and everything boots up. According to Microsoft Edge, it takes 1.8 seconds to run in debug mode and with unoptimized code.

Now we have the base for our project, including a Blazor WebAssembly version and a Blazor Server version. Throughout this book, we will use Visual Studio, but there are other ways to run your Blazor site, such as using the command line. The command line is a super powerful tool, and in the next section, we will take a look at how to set up a project using the command line.

Using the command line

With .NET 5, we got a super powerful tool called `dotnet.exe`. Developers that have used .NET Core before will already be familiar with the tool, but with .NET 5, it is no longer exclusively for .NET Core developers.

It can do many things Visual Studio can do, for example, creating projects, adding and creating NuGet packages, and much more. In the following example, we will create a Blazor Server and a Blazor WebAssembly project.

Creating projects using the command line

The following steps are to demonstrate the power of using the command line. We will not use this project later in the book, so if you don't want to try it, go ahead and skip this section. To create a solution with Blazor server and Blazor WebAssembly projects like the one we just did, we can run this command:

```
dotnet new blazorserver -o BlazorServer
dotnet new blazorwasm -o BlazorWebAssembly --pwa –hosted
```

Here, dotnet is the command. To create a new project, we use the new parameter.

blazorserver is the template's name, and -o is the output folder (in this case, the project will be created in a subfolder called BlazorServer).

The second line uses the template blazorwasm that created a Blazor WebAssembly project, and it uses the pwa flag to make it a Progressive web app and the hosted flag to get an ASP.NET hosted backend.

We also need to create a solution for our projects, and we can do that from the command line by using the template sln.

```
dotnet new sln --name MyBlog
```

We also need to add the projects we created, which are one Blazor Server project and 3 Blazor WebAssembly projects.

```
dotnet sln MyBlog.sln add ./BlazorWebAssembly\Server\BlazorWebAssembly.Server.csproj
dotnet sln MyBlog.sln add ./BlazorWebAssembly\Client\BlazorWebAssembly.Client.csproj
dotnet sln MyBlog.sln add .\BlazorWebAssembly\Shared\BlazorWebAssembly.Shared.csproj
dotnet sln MyBlog.sln add .\BlazorServer\BlazorServer.csproj
```

The dotnet command is super powerful; for some scenarios, it makes sense to use it. I mostly use the UI in Visual Studio, but it's important to know we have the dotnet tool we can use.

> **NOTE: THE .NET CLI**
>
> The idea is that you should be able to do everything from the command line. If you prefer working with the command line, you should check out the .NET CLI; you can read more about the .NET CLI here: https://docs.microsoft.com/en-us/dotnet/core/tools/.

Let's go back to the Blazor template, which has added a lot of files for us. In the next section, we will look at what Visual Studio has generated for us.

Figuring out the project structure

Now it's time to look at the different files and how they may differ in different projects. Take a look at the code in the two projects we just created (in the *Creating our first Blazor app* section) while we go through them.

Program.cs

Program.cs is the first class that gets called. It also differs between Blazor Server and Blazor WebAssembly.

WebAssembly Program.cs

In the WebAssembly.Client project, there is a file called Program.cs, and it looks like this:

```
var builder = WebAssemblyHostBuilder.CreateDefault(args);
builder.RootComponents.Add<App>("#app");
builder.RootComponents.Add<HeadOutlet>("head::after");
builder.Services.AddScoped(sp => new HttpClient { BaseAddress = new Uri(builder.HostEnvironment.BaseAddress) });
await builder.Build().RunAsync();
```

Program.cs uses top-level statements without any classes or methods. By using top-level statements, C# understands that this is the application's entry point. It will look for a div with the ID "app" and add (render) the App component inside the div, and the whole single-page application site will be rendered inside of the App component (we will get back to that component later in the chapter).

It adds a component called HeadOutlet and this component is for handling changing the head tag. Things that are located in the head tag are Title and head tags (to name a few). The Headoutlet gives us the ability to change the title of our page as well as meta tags.

It adds HttpClient as a scoped dependency. In *Chapter 3, Managing State – Part 1*, we will dig deeper into dependency injection, but for now, it is a way to abstract the creation of objects and types by injecting objects (dependencies), so we don't create objects inside a page. The objects get passed into the page/classes instead, making testing easier, and the classes don't have any dependencies we don't know about.

The WebAssembly version is running in the browser, so it can only get data by making external calls (to a server, for example); therefore, we need to be able to access HttpClient. WebAssembly is not allowed to make direct calls to download data. Therefore, HttpClient is a special implementation for WebAssembly that will make JavaScript interop calls to download data.

As I mentioned before, WebAssembly is running in a sandbox, and to be able to communicate outside of this sandbox, it needs to go through appropriate JavaScript/browser APIs.

Blazor Server Program.cs

Blazor Server projects look a bit different (but do pretty much the same thing). In the BlazorServer project, the Program.cs file looks like this:

```
var builder = WebApplication.CreateBuilder(args);
builder.Services.AddRazorPages();
builder.Services.AddServerSideBlazor();
builder.Services.AddSingleton<WeatherForecastService>();
var app = builder.Build();

// Configure the HTTP request pipeline.
if (!app.Environment.IsDevelopment())
{
    app.UseExceptionHandler("/Error");
    app.UseHsts();
}

app.UseHttpsRedirection();
app.UseStaticFiles();
app.UseRouting();
app.MapBlazorHub();
```

```
app.MapFallbackToPage("/_Host");
app.Run();
```

In .NET 6, Microsoft removed the Startup.cs file and put all the startup code in Program.cs.

There are a few things worthy of mentioning here. It starts with adding all the dependencies we need in our application. In this case, we add RazorPages, the pages that run Blazor (these are the .cshtml files). Then we add ServerSideBlazor, giving us access to all the objects we need to run Blazor Server. Then we add WeatherForcastService, which is used when you navigate to the **Forecast** page.

It also configures **HTTP Strict Transport Security (HSTS)**, forcing your application to use HTTPS, and will make sure that your users don't use any untrusted resources or certificates. We also ensure that the site redirects to HTTPS to secure the site.

UseStaticFiles enables downloading static files such as CSS or images.

The different Use* methods add request delegates to the request pipeline or middleware pipeline. Each request delegate (DeveloperException, httpRedirection, StaticFiles, and so on) is called consecutively from the top to the bottom and back again.

This is why the exception handler is the first one to be added.

If there is an exception in any of the request delegates that follow, the exception handler will still be able to handle it (since the request travels back through the pipeline), as shown in *Figure 2.15*:

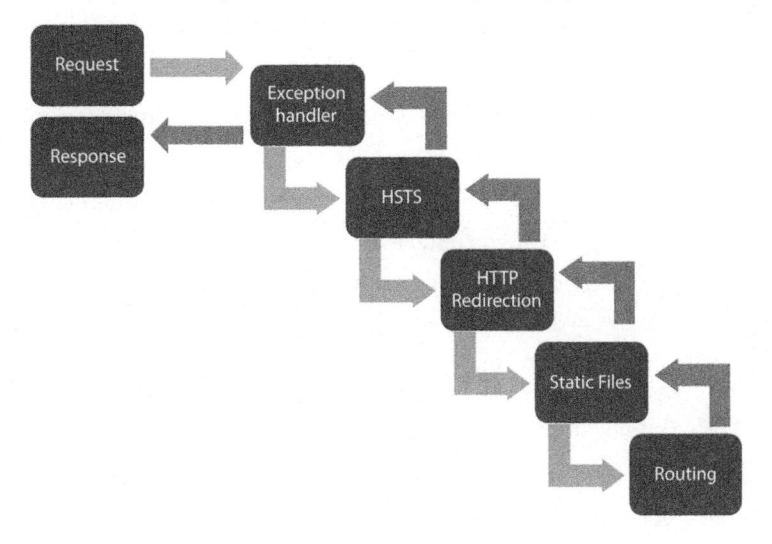

Figure 2.15: The request middleware pipeline

If any of these request delegates handle the request in the case of a static file, for example, there is no need to involve routing, and the remaining request delegates will not get called. There is no need to involve routing if the request is for a static file. Sometimes, it is essential to add the request delegated in the correct order.

> **NOTE:**
>
> There is more information about this here if you want to dig even further: `https://docs.microsoft.com/en-us/aspnet/core/fundamentals/middleware/?view=aspnetcore-7.0`.

At the end of the class, we hook up routing and add endpoints. We create an endpoint for the Blazor SignalR hub, and if we don't find anything to return, we make sure that we will call the _host file that will handle routing for the app. When _host has triggered, the first page of the app will get loaded.

Index/_Host

The next thing that happens is that the Index or _host file runs, and it contains the information to load the necessary JavaScript.

_Host (Blazor Server)

The Blazor Server project has a `_Host.cshtml` file that is located in the pages folder. It is a Razor page, which is not the same thing as a Razor component:

- A **Razor page** is a way to create views or pages. It can use Razor syntax but not as a component (a component can be used as part of a page and inside of another component).
- A **Razor component** is a way to build reusable views (called **components**) that you can use throughout your app. You can build a Grid component (for example, a component that renders a table) and use it in your app, or package it as a library for others to use. However, a component can be used as a page by adding an @page directive to your component, and it can be called a page (more on that later).

For most Blazor Server applications, you should only have one `.cshtml` page; the rest should be Razor components.

At the top of the page, you will find some @ directives (such as page, namespace, and addTagHelper):

```
@page "/"
```

```
@using Microsoft.AspNetCore.Components.Web
@namespace BlazorServer.Pages
@addTagHelper *, Microsoft.AspNetCore.Mvc.TagHelpers

<!DOCTYPE html>
<html lang="en">
<head>
    ...
    <component type="typeof(HeadOutlet)" render-mode="ServerPrerendered" />
</head>
<body>
    <component type="typeof(App)" render-mode="ServerPrerendered" />
```

There are a couple of aspects of this file that are worth noting. The @ directives make sure to set the URL for the page, add a namespace, add a tag helper, and that we are using a Layout page. We will cover directives in *Chapter 4, Understanding Basic Blazor Components*.

Then we have the component tag:

```
<component type="typeof(App)" render-mode="ServerPrerendered" />
```

This is where the entire application will be rendered. The App component handles that. This is also how you would add a Blazor component to your existing non-Blazor app using the component tag helper.

It will render a component called App. There are five different render modes:

- The first one is the default ServerPrerendered mode, which will render all the content on the server and deliver it as part of the content when the page gets downloaded for the first time. Then it will hook up the Blazor SignalR hub and make sure your changes will be pushed to and from the server; however, the server will make another render and push those changes over SignalR. Typically, you won't notice anything, but if you are using certain events on the server, they may get triggered twice and make unnecessary database calls, for example.
- The second option is Server, which will send over the whole page and add placeholders for the components. It then hooks up SignalR and lets the server send over the changes when it is done (when it has retrieved data from the database, for example).

- The third option is Static, which will render the component and then disconnect, which means that it will not listen to events and won't update the component any longer. This can be a good option for static data.
- The fourth option is WebAssembly, which will render a marker for the WebAssembly application but not output anything from the component.
- The fifth option is WebAssemblyPrerendered, which will render the component into static HTML and bootstrap the WebAssembly app into that space. We will explore this scenario in *Chapter 5, Creating Advanced Blazor Components*.

ServerPrerendered is technically the fastest way to get your page up on the screen; if you have a page that loads quickly, this is a good option. If you want your page to have a perceived fast loading time that shows you content fast and loads the data when the server gets the data from a database, then Server is a better option, in my opinion.

I prefer the Server option because the site should feel fast. Switching to Server is the first thing I change when creating a new Blazor Server site; I'd much rather have the data pop up a couple of milliseconds later because the page will feel like it loads faster.

Close to the top of the page, we have the base tag:

```
<base href="~/" />
```

The base tag allows Blazor to find the site's root. Without the base tag, Blazor won't be able to find any static resources like images, JavaScript, and CSS.

Then we have CSS. By default, there are two static CSS files, one for Bootstrap and one for the site.

```
<link rel="stylesheet" href="css/bootstrap/bootstrap.min.css" />
<link href="css/site.css" rel="stylesheet" />
<link href="BlazorServer.styles.css" rel="stylesheet" />
```

There is also the one called BlazorServer.styles.css, a generated file with all the isolated CSS. CSS and Isolated CSS is something we will cover more in-depth in *Chapter 9, Sharing Code and Resources*.

We also have a component that gets rendered. This is the HeadOutlet component, which makes it possible to change the head metadata like the title and meta tags:

```
<component type="typeof(HeadOutlet)" render-mode="ServerPrerendered" />
```

We will use this component in *Chapter 5, Creating Advanced Blazor Components*, to add metadata and change the title.

There is a small part of the UI that will show if there are any error messages:

```
<div id="blazor-error-ui">
    <environment include="Staging,Production">
        An error has occurred. This application may no longer respond
until reloaded.
    </environment>
    <environment include="Development">
        An unhandled exception has occurred. See browser dev tools for
details.
    </environment>
    <a href="" class="reload">Reload</a>
    <a class="dismiss">🗙</a>
</div>
```

I would recommend keeping this error UI (or a variation) if we changed the layout completely because JavaScript is involved in updating the UI. Sometimes, your page may break, the JavaScript will stop running, and the SignalR connection will fail. You will get a nice error message in the JavaScript console if that happens. But by having the error UI pop up, you'll know that you need to check the console.

The last thing we will cover on this page is also where all the magic happens, the JavaScript responsible for hooking everything up:

```
<script src="_framework/blazor.server.js"></script>
```

The script will create a SignalR connection to the server and is responsible for updating the DOM from the server and sending triggers back to the server.

Index (WebAssembly)

The WebAssembly project looks pretty much the same.

In the `BlazorWebAssembly.Client` project, open the `wwwroot/index.html` file. This file is HTML only, so there are no directives at the top like in the Blazor Server version.

Just like the Blazor Server version, you will find a base tag:

```
<base href="/" />
```

When hosting a Blazor WebAssembly site on, for example, GitHub Pages, we need to change the base tag to make the site work since it is served from a subfolder.

Instead of a `component` tag (as with Blazor Server), you'll find a `div` tag here. Instead, there was a line in `Program.cs` that connects the `App` component to the `div` tag (see the previous *Program.cs* section):

```
<div id="app">Loading...</div>
```

You can replace `Loading...` with something else if you want to – this is the content shown while the app is starting.

The error UI looks a bit different as well. There is no difference between development and production as in Blazor Server. Here, you only have one way of displaying errors:

```
<div id="blazor-error-UI">
    An unhandled error has occurred.
    <a href="" class="reload">Reload</a>
    <a class="dismiss">✖</a>
</div>
```

Lastly, we have a `script` tag that loads JavaScript. This makes sure to load all the code needed for the WebAssembly code to run:

```
<script src="_framework/blazor.webassembly.js"></script>
```

Like how the Blazor Server script communicates with the backend server and the DOM, the WebAssembly script communicates between the WebAssembly .NET runtime and the DOM.

At this point, the app is starting up running the Razor component. These components are the same in both projects.

App

The App component is the same for both Blazor WebAssembly and Blazor Server. It contains a `Router` component:

```
<Router AppAssembly="@typeof(App).Assembly">
    <Found Context="routeData">
        <RouteView RouteData="@routeData" DefaultLayout="@typeof(MainLayout)" />
        <FocusOnNavigate RouteData="@routeData" Selector="h1" />
    </Found>
```

```
    <NotFound>
        <PageTitle>Not found</PageTitle>
        <LayoutView Layout="@typeof(MainLayout)">
            <p role="alert">Sorry, there's nothing at this address.</p>
        </LayoutView>
    </NotFound>
</Router>
```

This file handles the routing, finding the suitable component to show (based on the @page directive). It shows an error message if the route can't be found. In *Chapter 8, Authentication and Authorization*, we will make changes to this file when we implement authentication.

The `App` component also includes a default layout. We can override the layout per component, but usually, you'll have one layout page for your site. In this case, the default layout is called `MainLayout`.

MainLayout

MainLayout contains the default layout for all components when viewed as a page. The `MainLayout` contains a couple of `div` tags, one for the sidebar and one for the main content:

```
@inherits LayoutComponentBase

<PageTitle>BlazorServer</PageTitle>

<div class="page">
    <div class="sidebar">
        <NavMenu />
    </div>

    <main>
        <div class="top-row px-4">
            <a href="https://docs.microsoft.com/aspnet/" target="_blank">About</a>
        </div>

        <article class="content px-4">
            @Body
        </article>
    </main>
</div>
```

The only things you need in this document are @inherits LayoutComponentBase and @Body; the rest is just Bootstrap. The @inherits directive inherits from LayoutComponentBase, which contains all the code to use a layout. @Body is where the component will be rendered (when viewed as a page).

Bootstrap

Bootstrap is one of the most popular CSS frameworks for developing responsive and mobile-first websites.

We can find a reference to Bootstrap in the wwwroot/index.html file.

It was created by and for Twitter. You can read more about Bootstrap here: https://getbootstrap.com/.

At the top of the layout, you can see <NavMenu>, a Razor component. It is located in the Shared folder and looks like this:

```
<div class="top-row ps-3 navbar navbar-dark">
    <div class="container-fluid">
        <a class="navbar-brand" href="">BlazorServer</a>
        <button title="Navigation menu" class="navbar-toggler" @onclick="ToggleNavMenu">
            <span class="navbar-toggler-icon"></span>
        </button>
    </div>
</div>

<div class="@NavMenuCssClass nav-scrollable" @onclick="ToggleNavMenu">
    <nav class="flex-column">
        <div class="nav-item px-3">
            <NavLink class="nav-link" href="" Match="NavLinkMatch.All">
                <span class="oi oi-home" aria-hidden="true"></span> Home
            </NavLink>
        </div>
        <div class="nav-item px-3">
            <NavLink class="nav-link" href="counter">
                <span class="oi oi-plus" aria-hidden="true"></span> Counter
            </NavLink>
```

```
            </div>
            <div class="nav-item px-3">
                <NavLink class="nav-link" href="fetchdata">
                    <span class="oi oi-list-rich" aria-hidden="true"></span> Fetch data
                </NavLink>
            </div>
        </nav>
    </div>

    @code {
        private bool collapseNavMenu = true;

        private string? NavMenuCssClass => collapseNavMenu ? "collapse" : null;

        private void ToggleNavMenu()
        {
            collapseNavMenu = !collapseNavMenu;
        }
    }
```

It contains the left-side menu and is a standard Bootstrap menu. It also has three menu items and logic for a hamburger menu (if viewed on a phone). This type of nav menu is usually done with JavaScript, but this one is done solely with CSS and C#.

You will find another component, `NavLink`, which is built into the framework. It will render an anchor tag but will also check the current route. If you are currently on the same route/URL as the nav link, it will automatically add a CSS class called `active` to the tag.

We will run into a couple more built-in components that will help us along the way. There are also some pages in the template, but we will leave them for now and go through them in the next chapter when we go into components.

CSS

In the `Shared` folder, there are two CSS files as well: `NavMenu.razor.css` and `MainLayout.razor.css`.

These files are CSS styles that affect only the specific component (the first part of the name). We will return to a concept called isolated CSS in *Chapter 9, Sharing Code and Resources*.

Summary

In this chapter, we got the development environment up and running, and we created our first Blazor app for both Blazor WebAssembly and Blazor Server. You learned in what order classes, components, and layouts are called, making it easier to follow the code. We also covered some differences between a Blazor Server project and a Blazor WebAssembly project.

In the next chapter, we will take a break from Blazor to look at managing state and set up a repository to store our blog posts.

3
Managing State – Part 1

In this chapter, we will start looking at managing state. There is also a continuation of this chapter in *Chapter 11, Managing State – Part 2*.

There are many different ways of managing state or persisting data. Since this book focuses on Blazor, we will not explore how to connect to databases but create a simple JSON storage instead.

In the repo on GitHub, you can find more examples of storing data in databases such as RavenDB or MSSQL.

We will use a common pattern called the **repository pattern**.

We will also create an API to access the data from the JSON repository.

By the end of this chapter, we will have learned how to create a JSON repository and an API.

We will cover the following main topics:

- Creating a data project
- Adding the API to Blazor

Technical requirements

Make sure you have followed the previous chapters or use the Chapter02 folder as the starting point.

You can find the source code for this chapter's result at https://github.com/PacktPublishing/Web-Development-with-Blazor-Second-Edition/tree/main/Chapter03.

Creating a data project

There are many ways of persisting data: document databases, relational databases, and files, to name a few. To remove complexity from the book, we will use the simplest way of creating blog posts by storing them as JSON in a folder.

The data will be accessible from both our Blazor WebAssembly project and the Blazor Server project, so we want to create a new project (not just put the code in one of the projects we created previously).

To save our blog posts, we will use JSON files stored in a folder, and to do so, we need to create a new project.

Creating a new project

We can also create a new project from within Visual Studio (to be honest, that's how I would do it), but to get to know the .NET CLI, let's do it from the command line instead.

To create a new project, follow these steps:

1. Open a PowerShell prompt.
2. Navigate to the MyBlog folder.
3. Create a class library (classlib) by typing the following command:

   ```
   dotnet new classlib -o Data
   ```

   The dotnet tool should now have created a folder called Data.

4. We also need to create a project where we can put our models:

   ```
   dotnet new classlib -o Data.Models
   ```

5. Add the new projects to our solution by running the following command:

   ```
   dotnet sln add Data
   dotnet sln add Data.Models
   ```

   It will look for any solution in the current folder.

We call the projects Data and Data.Models so their purpose will be easy to understand and they will be easy to find.

The default project has a class1.cs file – feel free to delete the file.

The next step is to create data classes to store our information.

Creating data classes

Now we need to create a class for our blog post. To do that, we will go back to Visual Studio:

1. Open the `MyBlog` solution in Visual Studio (if it is not already open).

   We should now have a new project called `Data` in our solution. We might get a popup asking if we want to reload the solution; click **Reload** if so.

2. Now we need to create three data classes. Right-click on `Data.Models` and select **Add | New Folder**. Name the folder `Models`.

3. Right-click on the `Models` folder and select **Add | Class**. Name the class `BlogPost.cs` and press **Add**.

4. Right-click on the `Models` folder and select **Add | Class**. Name the class `Category.cs` and press **Add**.

5. Right-click on the `Models` folder and select **Add | Class**. Name the class `Tag.cs` and press **Add**.

6. Open `Category.cs` and replace the content with the following code:

   ```
   namespace Data.Models;
   public class Category
   {
       public string? Id { get; set; }
       public string Name { get; set; } = string.Empty;
   }
   ```

   The `Category` class contains `Id` and `Name`. It might seem strange that the `Id` property is a string, but this is because we will support multiple data storage types, including MSSQL, RavenDB, and JSON.

   A string is a great datatype to support all of these. `Id` is also nullable, so if we create a new `Category` we send in null as an `Id`.

7. Open `Tag.cs` and replace the content with the following code:

   ```
   namespace Data.Models;
   public class Tag
   {
       public string? Id { get; set; }
       public string Name { get; set; } = string.Empty;
   }
   ```

The `Tag` class contains an `Id` and `Name`.

8. Open `BlogPost.cs` and replace the content with the following code:

```
namespace Data.Models;

public class BlogPost
{
    public string? Id { get; set; }
    public string Title { get; set; } = string.Empty;
    public string Text { get; set; } = string.Empty;
    public DateTime PublishDate { get; set; }
    public Category? Category { get; set; }
    public List<Tag> Tags { get; set; } = new();
}
```

In this class, we define the content of our blog post. We need an `Id` to identify the blog post, a title, some text (the article), and the publishing date. We also have a `Category` property in the class, which is of the `Category` type. In this case, a blog post can have only one category, and A blog post can contain zero or more tags. We define the `Tag` property with `List<Tag>`.

By now, we have created a couple of classes that we will use. I have kept the complexity of these classes to a minimum since we are here to learn about Blazor.

Next, we will create a way to store and retrieve the information.

Creating an interface

In this section, we will create an API. Since we are currently working with Blazor Server, we can access the database directly, so the API we create here will have a direct connection to the database:

1. Right-click on the **Data.Models** project and select **Add | New Folder** and name it `Interfaces`.
2. Right-click in the `Interfaces` folder and select **Add | Class**.
3. In the list of different templates, select **Interface** and name it `IBlogApi.cs`.
4. Open `IBlogApi.cs` and replace its content with the following:

```
namespace Data.Models.Interfaces;

public interface IBlogApi
{
```

```csharp
    Task<int> GetBlogPostCountAsync();
    Task<List<BlogPost>?> GetBlogPostsAsync(int numberofposts, int startindex);
    Task<List<Category>?> GetCategoriesAsync();
    Task<List<Tag>?> GetTagsAsync();
    Task<BlogPost?> GetBlogPostAsync(string id);
    Task<Category?> GetCategoryAsync(string id);
    Task<Tag?> GetTagAsync(string id);
    Task<BlogPost?> SaveBlogPostAsync(BlogPost item);
    Task<Category?> SaveCategoryAsync(Category item);
    Task<Tag?> SaveTagAsync(Tag item);
    Task DeleteBlogPostAsync(string id);
    Task DeleteCategoryAsync(string id);
    Task DeleteTagAsync(string id);
    Task InvalidateCacheAsync();
}
```

The interface contains all the methods we need to get, save, and delete blog posts, tags, and categories.

Now we have an interface for the API with the methods we need to list blog posts, tags, and categories, as well as save (create/update) and delete them. Next, let's implement the interface.

Implementing the interface

The idea is to create a class that stores our blog posts, tags, and categories as JSON files on our filesystem.

To implement the interface for the Blazor Server implementation, follow these steps:

1. First, we need to add a reference to our **Data** models. Expand the Data project and right-click on the **Dependencies** node. Select **Add Project reference** and check the Data.Models project. Click **OK**.

2. Right-click on the **Dependencies** node once again, but select **Manage NuGet Packages**. Search for Microsoft.Extensions.Options and click **Install**.

3. Next, we need to create a class. Right-click on the **Data** project, select **Add | Class**, and name the class BlogApiJsonDirectAccess.cs.

4. Open `BlogApiJsonDirectAccess.cs` and replace the code with the following:

```
using Data.Models.Interfaces;
using Microsoft.Extensions.Options;
using System.Text.Json;
using Data.Models;

namespace Data;
public class BlogApiJsonDirectAccess: IBlogApi
{

}
```

The error list should contain many errors since we haven't implemented the methods yet. We are inheriting from the `IBlogApi`, so we know what methods to expose.

5. We need a class to hold our settings.

   In the **Data** project, add a new class called `BlogApiJsonDirectAccessSetting.cs` and replace its content with:

```
namespace Data;

public class BlogApiJsonDirectAccessSetting
{
    public string BlogPostsFolder { get; set; } = string.Empty;
    public string CategoriesFolder { get; set; } = string.Empty;
    public string TagsFolder { get; set; } = string.Empty;
    public string DataPath { get; set; } = string.Empty;
}
```

`IOptions` is configured in program during the configuration of dependencies and is injected into all the classes that ask for a specific type.

6. To be able to read settings, we also add a way to inject `IOptions`. By getting the settings this way we don't have to add any code – it can come from a database, a setting file, or even be hard coded. This is my favorite way to get settings because this part of the code itself doesn't know how to do it – instead, we add all our configurations by using dependency injection.

Add the following code to the `BlogApiJsonDirectAccess` class:

```
    BlogApiJsonDirectAccessSetting _settings;
    public
BlogApiJsonDirectAccess(IOptions<BlogApiJsonDirectAccessSetting>
option)
    {
        _settings = option.Value;
        if (!Directory.Exists(_settings.DataPath))
        {
            Directory.CreateDirectory(_settings.DataPath);
        }
        if (!Directory.Exists($@"{_settings.DataPath}\{_settings.
BlogPostsFolder}"))
        {
            Directory.CreateDirectory($@"{_settings.DataPath}\{_
settings.BlogPostsFolder}");
        }
        if (!Directory.Exists($@"{_settings.DataPath}\{_settings.
CategoriesFolder}"))
        {
            Directory.CreateDirectory($@"{_settings.DataPath}\{_
settings.CategoriesFolder}");
        }
        if (!Directory.Exists($@"{_settings.DataPath}\{_settings.
TagsFolder}"))
        {
            Directory.CreateDirectory($@"{_settings.DataPath}\{_
settings.TagsFolder}");
        }
    }
```

We get the injected setting and ensure we have the correct folder structure for our data.

7. We need a couple of private variables where we can store the data. Add the following code in the `BlogApiJsonDirectAccess` class:

```
private List<BlogPost>? _blogPosts;
private List<Category>? _categories;
private List<Tag>? _tags;
```

8. Now it's time to implement the API, but first, we need a couple of helper methods that can load the data from our filesystem and cache them. Let's start with the methods for loading data from our filesystem by adding the following code to our class:

```csharp
private void Load<T>(ref List<T>? list, string folder)
{
    if (list == null)
    {
        list = new();
        var fullpath = $@"{_settings.DataPath}\{folder}";
        foreach (var f in Directory.GetFiles(fullpath))
        {
            var json = File.ReadAllText(f);
            var bp = JsonSerializer.Deserialize<T>(json);
            if (bp != null)
            {
                list.Add(bp);
            }
        }
    }
}
private Task LoadBlogPostsAsync()
{
    Load<BlogPost>(ref _blogPosts, _settings.BlogPostsFolder);
    return Task.CompletedTask;
}
private Task LoadTagsAsync()
{
    Load<Tag>(ref _tags, _settings.TagsFolder);
    return Task.CompletedTask;
}
private Task LoadCategoriesAsync()
{
    Load<Category>(ref _categories, _settings.CategoriesFolder);
    return Task.CompletedTask;
}
```

The Load method is a generic method that allows us to load blog posts, tags, and categories using the same method.

It will only load data from the filesystem if we don't already have any data. We also add separate methods that load each type: LoadBlogpostsAsync, LoadCategoriesAsync, and LoadTagsAsync.

9. Next, we will add a couple of methods to help manipulate the data, namely SaveAsync and DeleteAsync. Add the following methods:

```csharp
private async Task SaveAsync<T>(List<T>? list, string folder, string filename, T item)
{
    var filepath = $@"{_settings.DataPath}\{folder}\{filename}";
    await File.WriteAllTextAsync(filepath, JsonSerializer.Serialize<T>(item));
    if (list == null)
    {
        list = new();
    }
    if (!list.Contains(item))
    {
        list.Add(item);
    }
}
private void DeleteAsync<T>(List<T>? list, string folder, string id)
{
    var filepath = $@"{_settings.DataPath}\{folder}\{id}.json";
    try
    {
        File.Delete(filepath);
    }
    catch { }
}
```

These methods are also generic to share as much code as possible and avoid repeating the code for every type of class (BlogPost, Category, and Tag).

10. Next, it's time to implement the API by adding the methods to get blog posts. Add the following code:

```csharp
public async Task<List<BlogPost>?> GetBlogPostsAsync(int
numberofposts, int startindex)
{
    await LoadBlogPostsAsync();
    return _blogPosts ?? new();
}
public async Task<BlogPost?> GetBlogPostAsync(string id)
{
    await LoadBlogPostsAsync();
    if (_blogPosts == null)
        throw new Exception("Blog posts not found");
    return _blogPosts.FirstOrDefault(b => b.Id == id);
}
public async Task<int> GetBlogPostCountAsync()
{
    await LoadBlogPostsAsync();
    if (_blogPosts == null)
        return 0;
    else
        return _blogPosts.Count();
}
```

The GetBlogPostsAsync method takes a couple of parameters we will use later for paging. We execute the LoadBlogPostsAsync at the start of each method to ensure we have loaded any data from our filesystem. This method will only be executed while the _blogposts list (in this case) is null.

We also have a method that returns the current blog post count, which we will also use for paging.

11. Now we need to add the same methods for categories, add the following code:

```csharp
public async Task<List<Category>?> GetCategoriesAsync()
{
    await LoadCategoriesAsync();
    return _categories ?? new();
}
```

```csharp
public async Task<Category?> GetCategoryAsync(string id)
{
    await LoadCategoriesAsync();
    if (_categories == null)
        throw new Exception("Categories not found");
    return _categories.FirstOrDefault(b => b.Id == id);
}
```

The Category methods don't have any support for paging. Otherwise, they should look familiar as they do almost the same as the blog post methods.

12. Now it's time to do the same thing for tags. Add the following code:

    ```csharp
    public async Task<List<Tag>?> GetTagsAsync()
    {
        await LoadTagsAsync();
        return _tags ?? new();
    }
    public async Task<Tag?> GetTagAsync(string id)
    {
        await LoadTagsAsync();
        if (_tags == null)
            throw new Exception("Tags not found");
        return _tags.FirstOrDefault(b => b.Id == id);
    }
    ```

    As we can see, the code for tags is basically a copy of the one for categories.

13. We also need a couple of methods for saving the data, so next up we'll add methods for saving, blog posts, categories, and tags.

    Add the following code:

    ```csharp
    public async Task<BlogPost?> SaveBlogPostAsync(BlogPost item)
    {
        if (item.Id == null)
        {
            item.Id = Guid.NewGuid().ToString();
        }
        await SaveAsync<BlogPost>(_blogPosts, _settings.BlogPostsFolder, $"{item.Id}.json", item);
    ```

```csharp
        return item;
    }
    public async Task<Category?> SaveCategoryAsync(Category item)
    {
        if (item.Id == null)
        {
            item.Id = Guid.NewGuid().ToString();
        }
        await SaveAsync<Category>(_categories, _settings.CategoriesFolder, $"{item.Id}.json", item);
        return item;
    }
    public async Task<Tag?> SaveTagAsync(Tag item)
    {
        if (item.Id == null)
        {
            item.Id = Guid.NewGuid().ToString();
        }
        await SaveAsync<Tag>(_tags, _settings.TagsFolder, $"{item.Id}.json", item);
        return item;
    }
```

The first thing we do is to check that the `id` of the item is not null. If it is, we create a new `Guid`. This is the `id` of the new item. And this is also going to be the name of the JSON files stored on the filesystem.

14. We now have a method for saving items as well as getting items. But sometimes things don't go as planned and we need a way to delete the items that we have created. Next up, we will add some delete methods. Add the following code:

```csharp
public Task DeleteBlogPostAsync(string id)
{
    DeleteAsync(_blogPosts, _settings.BlogPostsFolder, id);
    if (_blogPosts != null)
    {
        var item = _blogPosts.FirstOrDefault(b => b.Id == id);
        if (item != null)
        {
```

```
                    _blogPosts.Remove(item);
                }
            }
            return Task.CompletedTask;
        }
        public Task DeleteCategoryAsync(string id)
        {
            DeleteAsync(_categories, _settings.CategoriesFolder, id);
            if (_categories != null)
            {
                var item = _categories.FirstOrDefault(b => b.Id == id);
                if (item != null)
                {
                    _categories.Remove(item);
                }
            }
            return Task.CompletedTask;
        }
        public Task DeleteTagAsync(string id)
        {
            DeleteAsync(_tags, _settings.TagsFolder, id);
            if (_tags != null)
            {
                var item = _tags.FirstOrDefault(b => b.Id == id);
                if (item != null)
                {
                    _tags.Remove(item);
                }
            }
            return Task.CompletedTask;
        }
```

The code we just added calls the DeleteAsync method that deletes the item and will also remove the item from the collection.

15. Since we are updating the collections as we go, they should always be updated, but for good measure, let's add a method for clearing the cache.

Add the following method:

```
public Task InvalidateCacheAsync()
{
    _blogPosts = null;
    _tags = null;
    _categories = null;
    return Task.CompletedTask;
}
```

Our JSON storage is done!

In the end, there will be three folders stored on the filesystem, one for blog posts, one for categories, and one for tags.

The next step is to add and configure the Blazor project to use our new storage.

Adding the API to Blazor

We now have a way to access JSON files stored on our filesystem. In the repo on GitHub, you can find more ways of storing our data with RavenDB or SQL server, but be mindful to keep the focus on what is important (Blazor).

Now it's time to add the API to our Blazor Server project:

1. In the **BlazorServer** project, **add a project reference** to the Data project. Open Program.cs and add the following namespaces:

    ```
    using Data;
    using Data.Models.Interfaces;
    ```

2. Add the following code:

    ```
    builder.Services.AddOptions<BlogApiJsonDirectAccessSetting>()
        .Configure(options =>
        {
            options.DataPath = @"..\..\..\Data\";
            options.BlogPostsFolder = "Blogposts";
            options.TagsFolder = "Tags";
            options.CategoriesFolder = "Categories";
        });
    builder.Services.AddScoped<IBlogApi, BlogApiJsonDirectAccess>();
    ```

The snippet of code is the setting for where we want to store our files. You can change the data path property to where you want to store the files. Whenever we ask for `IOptions<BlogApiJsonDirectAccessSetting>`, the dependency injection will return an object populated with the information we have supplied above. This is an excellent place to load configuration from our .NET configuration, a key vault, or a database.

We are also saying that when we ask for an `IBlogAPI` we will get an instance of `BlogApiJsonDirectAccess` back from our dependency injection. We will return to dependency injection in *Chapter 4, Understanding Basic Blazor Components*.

Now we can use our API to access the database in our Blazor Server project.

Summary

This chapter taught us how to create a simple JSON repository for our data. We also learned that other alternatives could be found in the GitHub repo if you want to look at other options.

We also created an interface to access the data, which we will use more throughout the book.

In the next chapter, we will learn about components, particularly the built-in components in Blazor templates. We will also create our first component using the API and repository we made in this chapter.

4

Understanding Basic Blazor Components

In this chapter, we will look at the components that come with the Blazor template and start to build our own components. Knowing the different techniques used for creating Blazor websites will help us when we start building our components.

Blazor uses components for most things, so we will use the knowledge from this chapter throughout the book.

We will start this chapter with theory and end by creating a component to show some blog posts using the API we created previously in *Chapter 3, Managing State – Part 1*.

In this chapter, we will cover the following topics:

- Exploring components
- Learning Razor syntax
- Understanding dependency injection
- Figuring out where to put the code
- Lifecycle events
- Parameters
- Writing our first component

Technical requirements

Make sure you have followed the previous chapters or use the Chapter03 folder as the starting point.

You can find the source code for this chapter's result at https://github.com/PacktPublishing/Web-Development-with-Blazor-Second-Edition/tree/main/Chapter04.

For this chapter, we will work with the Blazor Server project, so make sure to right-click on the **BlazorServer** project and select **Set as Startup Project**.

Exploring components

In Blazor, a **component** is a .razor file containing a small, isolated functionality (code and markup) or it can be used as a page. A component can host other components as well. This chapter will show us how components work and how to use them.

There are three different ways we can create a component:

- Using Razor syntax, with the code and HTML sharing the same file
- Using a code-behind file together with a .razor file
- Using only a code-behind file

We will go through the different options. The templates we will go through next all use the first option, .razor files, where we have a mix of code and HTML in the same file.

The components in the template are as follows:

- **Counter**
- **FetchData**

Counter

The **counter** page shows a button and a counter; if we press the button, the counter increases. We will now break the page apart, making it easier to understand.

At the top of the page is the @page directive, which makes it possible to route to the component directly, as we can see in this code:

```
@page "/counter"
```

If we start the **BlazorServer** project and add /counter to the end of the URL, we see that we can directly access the component by using its route. We can also make the route take parameters, but we will return to that later.

Next, let's explore the code. To add code to the page, we use the @code statement, and within that statement, we can add ordinary C# code, as shown:

```
@code {
    private int currentCount = 0;
    private void IncrementCount()
    {
        currentCount++;
    }
}
```

In the preceding code block, we have a private currentCount variable set to 0. Then we have a method called IncrementCount(), which increments the currentCount variable by 1.

We show the current value by using the @ sign. In Razor, the @ sign indicates that it is time for some code:

```
<p role="status">Current count: @currentCount</p>
```

As we can see, Razor is very smart because it understands when the code stops and the markup continues, so there is no need to add something extra to transition from the code to the markup (more on that in the next section).

As we can see in the preceding example, we are mixing HTML tags with @currentCount, and Razor understands the difference. Next, we have a button that is the trigger for changing the value:

```
<button class="btn btn-primary" @onclick="IncrementCount">Click me</button>
```

This is an HTML button with a **Bootstrap** class (to make it look a bit nicer). @onclick binds the button's onclick event to the IncrementCount() method. If we were to use onclick without the @, it would refer to the JavaScript event and not work.

So, when we press the button, it will call the IncrementCount() method (depicted by **1** in *Figure 4.1*), the method increments the variable (depicted by **2**), and due to changing the variable, the UI will automatically be updated (depicted by **3**), as shown in *Figure 4.1*:

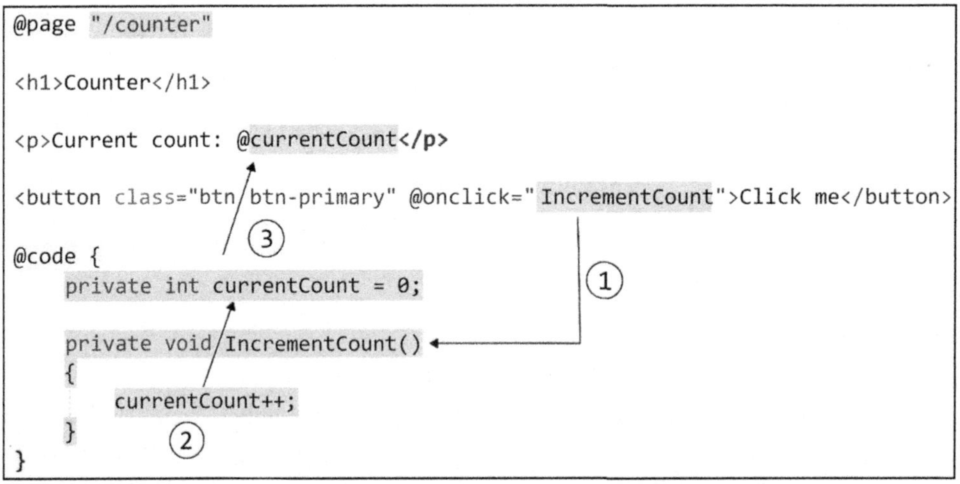

```
@page "/counter"

<h1>Counter</h1>

<p>Current count: @currentCount</p>

<button class="btn btn-primary" @onclick=" IncrementCount">Click me</button>

@code {
    private int currentCount = 0;

    private void IncrementCount()
    {
        currentCount++;
    }
}
```

Figure 4.1: The flow of the counter component

The counter component is implemented similarly for both Blazor WebAssembly and Blazor Server. The **FetchData** component has two different implementations simply because the Blazor Server project can access the server data directly and Blazor WebAssembly needs to access it through a web API.

We use the same approach with our API to get a feel for how we can leverage **Dependency Injection (DI)** and connect to a database directly when we use Blazor Server.

FetchData

The next component we will take a look at is the **FetchData** component. It's located in the Pages/FetchData.razor folder.

The main implementation of the **FetchData** component looks similar in both Blazor WebAssembly and Blazor Server. The top rows of the files and the way it gets data differ in the two versions. For Blazor Server, it looks like this:

```
@page "/fetchdata"
@using BlazorServer.Data
@inject WeatherForecastService ForecastService
```

It defines a route, adds a namespace, and injects a service. We can find the service in the **Data** folder in the **BlazorServer** project.

The service is a class that creates some random forecast data; the code looks like this:

```
public class WeatherForecastService
{
    private static readonly string[] Summaries = new[]
    {
        "Freezing", "Bracing", "Chilly", "Cool", "Mild", "Warm", "Balmy", "Hot", "Sweltering", "Scorching"
    };
    public Task<WeatherForecast[]> GetForecastAsync(DateOnly startDate)
        {
            return Task.FromResult(Enumerable.Range(1, 5).Select(index => new WeatherForecast
            {
                Date = startDate.AddDays(index),
                TemperatureC = Random.Shared.Next(-20, 55),
                Summary = Summaries[Random.Shared.Next(Summaries.Length)]
            }).ToArray());
    }
}
```

As we can see, it generates summaries and randomizes temperatures.

In the **code** section of the **FetchData** component, we will find the code that calls the service:

```
private WeatherForecast[] forecasts;
protected override async Task OnInitializedAsync()
{
    forecasts = await ForecastService.GetForecastAsync(DateTime.Now);
}
```

The code will get the data from the service and populate an array of **WeatherForecast** called forecasts.

In the BlazorWebAssembly.Client project, things look a bit different. First of all, the top rows of the file look like this:

```
@page "/fetchdata"
```

```
@using BlazorWebAssembly.Shared
@inject HttpClient Http
```

The code defines a route using a **page** directive, adds @using reference to our shared library namespace, and injects HttpClient instead of the service. HttpClient is used to get the data from the server, which is a more realistic real-world scenario.

HttpClient is defined in the Program.cs file and has the same base address as the BlazorWebAssembly.Server project, since the server project is hosting the client project.

Getting the data looks like this:

```
private WeatherForecast[] forecasts;
protected override async Task OnInitializedAsync()
{
    forecasts = await Http.GetFromJsonAsync<WeatherForecast[]>("WeatherForecast");
}
```

The code will get the data and populate an array of **WeatherForecast** called **forecasts**. But instead of getting the data from the service, we are making a call to the "WeatherForecast" URL. We can find the web API in the BlazorWebAssembly.Server project.

Notice that we are using the same **WeatherForecast** class on both the server and the client. This is one of the things I really like with Blazor.

The controller (Controllers/WeatherForcastController.cs) looks like this (with many similarities to the service):

```
[ApiController]
[Route("[controller]")]
public class WeatherForecastController : ControllerBase
{
    private static readonly string[] Summaries = new[]
    {
        "Freezing", "Bracing", "Chilly", "Cool", "Mild", "Warm", "Balmy", "Hot", "Sweltering", "Scorching"
    };
    private readonly ILogger<WeatherForecastController> logger;
    public WeatherForecastController(ILogger<WeatherForecastController> logger)
```

```
    {
        this.logger = logger;
    }
    [HttpGet]
    public IEnumerable<WeatherForecast> Get()
    {
        var rng = new Random();
        return Enumerable.Range(1, 5).Select(index => new WeatherForecast
        {
            Date = DateTime.Now.AddDays(index),
            TemperatureC = rng.Next(-20, 55),
            Summary = Summaries[rng.Next(Summaries.Length)]
        })
        .ToArray();
    }
}
```

It looks the same as the service but is implemented as a web API. As the data looks the same in both versions, getting the data (in both cases) will populate an array with weather forecast data.

In Pages/FetchData.razor, the code for showing the weather data looks like this in both Blazor WebAssembly and Blazor Server:

```
<h1>Weather forecast</h1>
<p>This component demonstrates fetching data from a service.</p>
@if (forecasts == null)
{
    <p><em>Loading...</em></p>
}
else
{
    <table class="table">
        <thead>
            <tr>
                <th>Date</th>
                <th>Temp. (C)</th>
                <th>Temp. (F)</th>
                <th>Summary</th>
            </tr>
```

```
            </thead>
            <tbody>
                @foreach (var forecast in forecasts)
                {
                    <tr>
                        <td>@forecast.Date.ToShortDateString()
                        </td>
                        <td>@forecast.TemperatureC</td>
                        <td>@forecast.TemperatureF</td>
                        <td>@forecast.Summary</td>
                    </tr>
                }
            </tbody>
        </table>
}
```

As we can see, by using the Razor syntax, we are seamlessly mixing code with HTML. The code checks whether there is any data – if yes, it will render the table; if not, it will show a loading message. We have full control over the HTML, and Blazor will not add anything to the generated HTML.

There are component libraries that can make this process a bit simpler, which we will look at in the next chapter, *Chapter 5, Creating Advanced Blazor Components*.

Now that we know how the sample template is implemented, it is time to dive deeper into the Razor syntax.

Learning Razor syntax

One of the things I like about the Razor syntax is that it is easy to mix code and HTML tags. By having the code close to the markup, it is, in my opinion, easier to follow and understand. The syntax is very fluid; the razor parser understands when the code stops and markup begins, which means we don't need to think about it that much. It is also not a new language; instead, we can leverage our existing C# and HTML knowledge to create our components. This section will be a lot of theory to help us understand the Razor syntax.

To transition from HTML to code (C#), we use the @ symbol. There are a handful of ways we can add code to our file:

- Razor code blocks
- Implicit Razor expressions

- Explicit Razor expressions
- Expression encoding
- Directives

Razor code blocks

We have already seen some code blocks. A code block looks like this:

```
@code {
    //your code here
}
```

If we wish, we can skip the **code** keyword like so:

```
@{
    //your code here
}
```

Inside those curly braces, we can mix HTML and code like this:

```
@{
    void RenderName(string name)
    {
        <p>Name: <strong>@name</strong></p>
    }
    RenderName("Steve Sanderson");
    RenderName("Daniel Roth");
}
```

Notice how the `RenderName()` method transitions from code into the paragraph tags and back to code; this is an implicit transition.

If we want to output text without having an HTML tag, we can use the text tag instead of using the paragraph tags, as shown in the following example:

```
<text>Name: <strong>@name</strong></text>
```

This would render the same result as the previous code but without the paragraph tags, and the text tag won't be rendered.

Implicit Razor expressions

Implicit Razor expressions are when we add code inside HTML tags.

We have already seen this in the **FetchData** example:

```
<td>@forecast.Summary</td>
```

We start with a `<td>` tag, then use the @ symbol to switch to C#, and switch back to HTML with the end tag. We can use the **await** keyword together with a method call, but other than that, implicit Razor expressions cannot contain any spaces.

We cannot call a generic method using implicit expressions since <> would be interpreted as HTML. Hence, to solve this issue, we can use explicit expressions.

Explicit Razor expressions

We can use explicit Razor expressions if we want to use spaces in the code. Write the code with the @ symbol followed by parentheses ( ). So, it would look like this: @( ).

In this sample, we subtract **7** days from the current date:

```
<td>@(DateTime.Now - TimeSpan.FromDays(7))</td>
```

We can also use explicit Razor expressions to concatenate text; for example, we can concatenate text and code like this:

```
<td>Temp@(forecast.TemperatureC)</td>
```

The output would then be `<td>Temp42</td>`.

Using explicit expressions, we can easily call generic methods by using this syntax:

```
<td>@(MyGenericMethod<string>())</td>
```

The Razor engine knows whether we are using code or not. It also makes sure to encode strings to HTML when outputting it to the browser, called **expression encoding**.

Expression encoding

If we have HTML as a string, it will be escaped by default. Take this code, for example:

```
@("<span>Hello World</span>")
```

The rendered HTML would look like this:

```
&lt;span&gt;Hello World&lt;/span&gt;
```

To output the actual HTML from a string (something we want to do later on), you can use this syntax:

```
@((MarkupString)"<span>Hello World</span>")
```

Using `MarkupString`, the output will be HTML, showing the HTML tag span. In some cases, one line of code isn't enough; then, we can use code blocks.

Directives

There are a bunch of directives that change the way a component gets parsed or can enable functionality. These are reserved keywords that follow the @ symbol. We will go through the most common and useful ones.

I find that it is pretty nice to have the layout and the code inside of the same .razor file.

Note that we can use code-behind to write our code to get a bit more separation between the code and layout. Later in this chapter, we will look at how to use code-behind instead of Razor syntax for everything. For now, the following examples will look at how we would do the same directives using both Razor syntax and code-behind.

Adding an attribute

To add an attribute to our page, we can use the `attribute` directive:

```
@attribute [Authorize]
```

If we were using a code-behind file, we would use the following syntax instead:

```
[Authorize]
```

Adding an interface

To implement an interface (`IDisposable` in this case), we would use the following code:

```
@implements IDisposable
```

Then we would implement the methods the interface needs in a `@code{}` section.

To do the same in a code-behind scenario, we would add the interface after the class name, as shown in the following example:

```
public partial class SomeClass : IDisposable {}
```

Inheriting

To inherit another class, we should use the following code:

```
@inherits TypeNameOfClassToInheritFrom
```

To do the same in a code-behind scenario, we would add the class we want to inherit from after the class name:

```
public class SomeClass : TypeNameOfClassToInheritFrom {}
```

Generics

We can define our component as a generic component.

Generics allow us to define the data type, so the component works with any data type.

To define a component as a generic component, we add the @typeparam directive; then, we can use the type in the code of the component like this:

```
@typeparam TItem
@code
{
    [Parameter]
    public List<TItem> Data { get; set; }
}
```

Generics are super-powerful when creating reusable components, and we will return to generics in *Chapter 6, Building Forms with Validation*.

Changing the layout

If we want to have a specific layout for a page (not the default one specified in the App.razor file), we can use the @layout directive:

```
@layout AnotherLayoutFile
```

This way, our component will use the specified layout file (this only works for components with the @page directive).

Setting a namespace

By default, the component's namespace will be the name of the default namespace of our project, plus the folder structure. If we want our component to be in a specific namespace, we can use the following:

```
@namespace Another.NameSpace
```

Setting a route

We have already touched on the @page directive. If we want our component to be directly accessed using a URL, we can use the @page directive:

```
@page "/theurl"
```

The URL can contain parameters, subfolders, and much more, which we will return to later in this chapter.

Adding a using statement

To add a namespace to our component, we can use the @using directive:

```
@using System.IO
```

If there are namespaces that we use in several of our components, then we can add them to the _Imports.razor file instead. This way, they will be available in all the components we create.

Now we know more about how Razor syntax works. Don't worry; we will have plenty of time to practice it. There is one more directive that I haven't covered in this section, and that is inject. We have seen it a couple of times already, but to cover all the bases, we first need to understand what DI is and how it works, which we will see in the next section.

Understanding dependency injection

DI is a software pattern and a technique to implement **Inversion of Control (IoC)**.

IoC is a generic term that means we can indicate that the class needs a class instance instead of letting our classes instantiate an object. We can say that our class wants either a specific class or a specific interface. The creation of the class is somewhere else, and it is up to IoC what class it will create.

When it comes to DI, it is a form of IoC when an object (class instance) is passed through constructors, parameters, or service lookups.

Here is a great resource if you want to dive deeper into DI in .NET: https://learn.microsoft.com/en-us/dotnet/core/extensions/dependency-injection.

In Blazor, we can configure DI by providing a way to instantiate an object. In Blazor, this is a key architecture pattern that we should use. We have already seen a couple of references to it, for example, in Startup.cs:

```
services.AddSingleton<WeatherForecastService>();
```

Here, we say that if any class wants WeatherForecastService, the application should instantiate an object of the WeatherForecastService type. In this case, we don't use an interface; instead, we could create an interface and configure it like this:

```
services.AddSingleton<IWeatherForecastService, WeatherForecastService>();
```

In this case, if a class asks for an instance of IWeatherForecastService, the app will instantiate a WeatherForecastService object and return it. We did this in the previous chapter, *Chapter 3, Managing State – Part 1*. We created an *IBlogApi* interface that returned an instance of BlogApiJsonDirectAccess; when we implement the WebAssembly version, DI will return another class instead.

There are many advantages to using DI. Our dependencies are loosely coupled, so we don't instantiate another class in our class. Instead, we ask for an instance, which makes it easier to write tests and change implementations depending on platforms.

Any external dependencies will be much more apparent since we must pass them into the class. We also can set the way we should instantiate the object in a central place. We configure the DI in **Program.cs**.

We can configure the creation of objects in different ways, such as the following:

- Singleton
- Scoped
- Transient

Singleton

When we use a singleton, the object will be the same for all site users. The object will only be created once.

To configure a singleton service, use the following:

```
services.AddSingleton<IWeatherForecastService, WeatherForecastService>();
```

We should use a singleton when we want to share our object with all the users of our site, but beware that the state is shared, so do not store any data connected to one particular user or user preference because it will affect all the users.

Scoped

When we use scoped, a new object will be created once for each connection, and since Blazor Server needs a connection to work, it will be the same object as long as the user has a connection. WebAssembly does not have the concept of scoped, since there is no connection, so all the code runs inside the user's web browser. If we use scoped, it will work the same way as a singleton for Blazor WebAssembly, since we only have one user and everything running inside the browser. The recommendation is still to use scoped if the idea is to scope a service to the current user. This makes it easier to move code between Blazor Server and Blazor WebAssembly and gives a bit more context on how the service is supposed to be used.

To configure a scoped service, use the following:

```
services.AddScoped<IWeatherForecastService, WeatherForecastService>();
```

We should use scoped if we have data that belongs to the user. We can keep the user's state by using scoped objects. More on that in *Chapter 11, Managing State – Part 2*.

Transient

When we use transient, a new object will be created every time we ask for it.

To configure a transient service, use the following:

```
services.AddTransient<IWeatherForecastService, WeatherForecastService>();
```

We should use transient if we don't need to keep any state, and we don't mind the object being created every time we ask for it.

Now that we know how to configure a service, we need to start using the service by injecting it.

Injecting the service

There are three ways to inject a service.

We have already seen the first method in the **FetchData** component code. We can use the @inject directive in the Razor file:

```
@inject WeatherForecastService ForecastService
```

This will make sure we have access to `WeatherForecastService` in our component.

The second way is to create a property by adding the `Inject` attribute if we are using code-behind:

```
[Inject]
public WeatherForecastService ForecastService { get; set; }
```

The third way is if we want to inject a service into another service, then we need to inject the services using the constructor:

```
public class MyService
{
    public MyService(WeatherForecastService
      weatherForecastService)
    {
    }
}
```

Now we know how DI works and why we should use it.

In this chapter, we have mentioned code-behind a couple of times. In the next section, we will look at how we can use code-behind with Razor files and skip the Razor files altogether.

Figuring out where to put the code

We have seen examples of writing code directly in the Razor file. I prefer doing that unless the code gets too complicated. I always lean in favor of readability.

There are four ways we can write our components:

- In the Razor file
- In a partial class
- Inheriting a class
- Only code

Let's go through each item on this list in more detail.

In the Razor file

If we are writing a file that is not that complex, it would be nice not to switch files when writing components. As we already covered in this chapter, we can use the @code directive to add code directly to our Razor file.

If we want to move the code to a code-behind file, then it is only the directives that we need to change. For the rest of the code, we can just move to the code-behind class. When I started with Blazor, writing code and markup in the same file felt strange, but I suggest you try it out when developing your web apps.

At work, we started using code-behind but switched to writing code in the .razor file instead, and we haven't looked back since.

But many developers prefer code-behind, separating code from the layout. For that, we can use a partial class.

In a partial class

We can create a partial class with the same filename as the Razor file and just add .cs.

If you have downloaded the source code (or you can check the code on GitHub) for *Chapter 3, Managing State – Part 1*, you can look at FetchDataWithCodeBehind.razor.cs in the **BlazorServer** project. I have moved all the code to the code-behind file; the result when compiling this will be the same as if we kept the code in the Razor file. It is just a matter of preference.

The code-behind looks like this:

```
public partial class FetchDataWithCodeBehind
{
    private WeatherForecast[]? forecasts;
    [Inject]
    public WeatherForecastService? ForecastService { get; set; }
    protected override async Task OnInitializedAsync()
    {
        if (ForecastService != null)
        {
            forecasts = await ForecastService.GetForecastAsync(DateOnly.FromDateTime(DateTime.Now));
        }
    }
}
```

As we can see, instead of using @inject, we are using [Inject] like this:

```
[Inject]
public WeatherForecastService ForecastService { get; set; }
```

Other than that, I have just copied the code from the Razor file.

This is not the only way to use a code-behind file; we can also inherit from a code-behind file.

Inheriting a class

We can also create a completely different class (the common pattern is to call it the same thing as the Razor file and add **Model** at the end) and inherit it in our Razor file. For that to work, we need to inherit from **ComponentBase**. In the case of a partial class, the class already inherits from **ComponentBase**, since the Razor file does that.

Fields must be protected or public (not private) for the page to access the fields. I recommend using the partial class if we don't need to inherit from our base class.

This is a snippet of the code-behind class declaration:

```
public class FetchDataWithInheritsModel:ComponentBase
```

We'll need to inherit from ComponentBase or from a class that inherits from ComponentBase.

In the Razor file, we will use the @inherits directive:

```
@inherits FetchDataWithInheritsModel
```

The Razor file will now inherit from our code-behind class (this was the first available way to create code-behind classes).

Both the partial and inherit options are simple ways of moving the code to a code-behind file. But another option is to entirely skip the Razor file and use only code.

Only code

Visual Studio will use source generators to convert the Razor code into C#. We will dig deeper into source generators in *Chapter 17, Examining Source Generators*. The Razor file will generate code at compile time. We can skip the Razor step if we want to and write our layout completely in code.

This file (CounterWithoutRazor.cs) is available on GitHub.

The counter sample would look like this:

```
using Microsoft.AspNetCore.Components;
using Microsoft.AspNetCore.Components.Rendering;
using Microsoft.AspNetCore.Components.Web;
namespace BlazorServer.Pages
{
```

```
    [Route("/CounterWithoutRazor")]
    public class CounterWithoutRazor: ComponentBase
    {
        protected override void BuildRenderTree
          (RenderTreeBuilder builder)
        {
            builder.AddMarkupContent(0, "<h1>Counter</h1>\r\n\r\n");
            builder.OpenElement(1, "p");
            builder.AddContent(2, "Current count: ");
            builder.AddContent(3,currentCount);
            builder.CloseElement();
            builder.AddMarkupContent(4, "\r\n\r\n");
            builder.OpenElement(5, "button");
            builder.AddAttribute(6, "class","btn btn-primary");
            builder.AddAttribute(7,"onclick", EventCallback.Factory.
Create<MouseEventArgs>(this,IncrementCount));
            builder.AddContent(8, "Click me");
            builder.CloseElement();
        }
        private int currentCount = 0;
        private void IncrementCount()
        {
            currentCount++;
        }
    }
}
```

The Razor file will first be converted in to something roughly the same as the previous code, and then the code is compiled. It adds the elements one by one, which, in the end, will render the HTML.

The numbers in the code are how Blazor keeps track of each element in the render tree. Some prefer to write the code as in the previous code block rather than using the Razor syntax; there are even efforts in the community to simplify the process of manually writing the BuildRenderTree() function.

Some of Microsoft's built-in components are built in this way.

I recommend never writing this manually, but I've kept it in the book because it shows how Razor files get compiled. Now that we know how to use code-behind let's look at the life cycle events of Blazor and when they get executed.

Lifecycle events

We can use a couple of lifecycle events to run our code. In this section, we will go through them and see when we should use them. Most life cycle events have two versions – synchronous and asynchronous.

OnInitialized and OnInitializedAsync

The first time the component is loaded, `OnInitialized()` is called, then `OnInitializedAsync()`. This is a great method to load any data, as the UI has not yet been rendered. If we are doing long-running tasks (such as getting data from a database), we should put that code in the `OnInitializedAsync()` method.

These methods will only run once. If we want to update the UI when a parameter changes, see `OnParametersSet()` and `OnParametersSetAsync()`.

OnParametersSet and OnParametersSetAsync

`OnParametersSet()` and `OnParametersSetAsync()` are called when the component is initialized (after `OnInitialized()` and `OnInitializedAsync()`) and whenever we change the value of a parameter.

If we, for example, load data in the `OnInitialized()` method but it does use a parameter, the data won't be reloaded if the parameter is changed, since `OnInitialized()` will only run once. We need to trigger a reload of the data in `OnParametersSet()` or `OnParametersSetAsync()`, or move the loading to that method.

OnAfterRender and OnAfterRenderAsync

After the component renders, the `OnAfterRender()` and `OnAfterRenderAsync()` methods are called. When the methods are being called, all the elements are rendered, so if we want/need to call any JavaScript code, we have to do that from these methods (we will get an error if we try to make a JavaScript interop from any of the other lifecycle event methods). We also have access to a `firstRender` parameter, so we can only run our code on the first render.

ShouldRender

`ShouldRender()` is called when our component is re-rendered; if it returns `false`, the component will not be rendered again. It will always render once; it is only when it is re-rendered that the method runs.

`ShouldRender()` does not have an asynchronous option.

Now we know when the different lifecycle events happen and in what order. A component can also have parameters, and that way, we can reuse them but with different data.

Parameters

A **parameter** makes it possible to send a value to a component. To add a parameter to a component, we use the [Parameter] attribute on the public property:

```
@code {
    [Parameter]
    public int MyParameter { get; set; }
}
```

We can also do the same using a code-behind file. We can add a parameter using the @page directive by specifying it in the route:

```
@page "/parameterdemo/{MyParameter}"
```

In this case, we have to have a parameter specified with the same name as the name inside the curly braces. To set the parameter in the @page directive, we go to /parameterdemo/THEVALUE.

There are cases where we want to specify another type instead of a string (string is the default). We can add the data type after the parameter name like this:

```
@page "/parameterdemo/{MyParameter:int}"
```

This will match the route only if the data type is an integer. We can also pass parameters using cascading parameters.

Cascading parameters

If we want to pass a value to multiple components, we can use a cascading parameter.

Instead of using [Parameter], we can use [CascadingParameter] like this:

```
[CascadingParameter]
public int MyParameter { get; set; }
```

To pass a value to the component, we surround it with a CascadingValue component like this:

```
<CascadingValue Value="MyProperty">
    <ComponentWithCascadingParameter/>
</CascadingValue>
@code {
```

```
    public string MyProperty { get; set; } = "Test Value";
}
```

`CascadingValue` is the value we pass to the component, and `CascadingParameter` is the property that receives the value.

As we can see, we don't pass any parameter values to the `ComponentWithCascadingParameter` component; the cascading value will match the parameter with the same data type. If we have multiple parameters of the same type, we can specify the name of the parameter in the component with the cascading parameter like this:

```
[CascadingParameter(Name = "MyCascadingParameter")]
```

We can also do so for the component that passes `CascadingValue`, like this:

```
<CascadingValue Value="MyProperty" Name="MyCascadingParameter">
    <ComponentWithCascadingParameter/>
</CascadingValue>
```

If we know that the value won't change, we can specify that by using the `IsFixed` property:

```
<CascadingValue Value="MyProperty" Name="MyCascadingParameter" IsFixed="True">
    <ComponentWithCascadingParameter/>
</CascadingValue>
```

This way, Blazor won't look for changes. The cascading values/parameters cannot be updated upward but are updated only downward. This means that to update a cascading value, we need to implement it in another way; updating it from inside the component won't change any components that are higher in the hierarchy.

In *Chapter 5*, *Creating Advanced Blazor Components*, we will look at events, which are one way to solve the problem of updating a cascading value.

Phew! This has been an information-heavy chapter, but now we know the basics of Blazor components. Now it is time to build one!

Writing our first component

The first component we will build shows all the blog posts on a site. To be fair, we haven't written any blog posts yet, but we will temporarily solve that so we can start doing something fun.

Chapter 4 85

In *Chapter 3, Managing State – Part 1*, we created a JSON repository and an API (or interface); now, it is time to use them.

Components with or without a page directive can be shared across different projects. By the end of this book, we will have built a blog in both Blazor Server and Blazor WebAssembly that share code.

There is a whole chapter on sharing (*Chapter 9, Sharing Code and Resources*) but let's start now.

Creating a components library

The first thing we need to do is to create a new project and then add our components to that project.

To create our first component, follow these instructions:

1. Right-click on the **MyBlog** solution and select **Add | New Project**.
2. Find the template **Razor Class Library** and click **Next**.
3. Name the project Components and click **Next**.
4. Select **.NET 7.0 (Standard Term Support)** and click **Create**.
5. We now have a project called **Components**, where we can add all the components we want to share. Remove the Component1.razor and ExampleJsInterop.cs that are created by default.
6. In the **Components** project, add a project reference to **Data.Models**.
7. In the **BlazorServer** project, in the Pages folder, delete all .razor files.
8. In the **BlazorServer** project, delete the Shared folder completely.
9. Now, we will move some of the files from the **BlazorWebAssembly.Client** project. These are the files we can share between the projects.

    That would be the files in the Pages folder and Shared folder. In the **BlazorWebAssembly.Client** project, cut the Pages and Shared folders, and paste them into the **Components** project.

10. Since FetchData has a bit of a different implementation, let's delete that one as well.

    In the Components project, delete Pages/FetchData.razor.

11. In the **Components** project, open _Imports.razor and add the following lines:

    ```
    @using System.Net.Http
    @using Microsoft.AspNetCore.Authorization
    @using Microsoft.AspNetCore.Components.Forms
    ```

```
@using Microsoft.AspNetCore.Components.Routing
@using Microsoft.AspNetCore.Components.Web
@using Microsoft.AspNetCore.Components.Web.Virtualization
@using Microsoft.JSInterop
@using Components.Pages
@using Components.Shared
```

We have a new project, moved components, and cleaned up the **BlazorServer** and **BlazorWebAssembly** projects.

Next, we will put the components to use.

Using our components library

We have a nice library, and can start using the components right now, but we also want to trigger the routes. We want our site to get the Index component if we navigate to "/".

To do that, we need to follow a couple of steps:

1. In the **BlazorServer** project, add a project reference to the **Components** project.

2. Open App.razor and add the following property to the **Router** component:

   ```
   <Router AppAssembly="@typeof(App).Assembly"
   AdditionalAssemblies="new[] { typeof(Components.Pages.Index).Assembly}">
   ```

   We are telling Blazor to look for Razor components inside the assembly where the app component lives.

   This means the BlazorServer assembly in this case.

   We also want Blazor to look for components in the assembly where the Index component is located, which is the components assembly.

3. Open _Imports.razor and add the following:

   ```
   @using Components.Pages
   @using Components.Shared
   ```

4. Remove the @using BlazorServer.Shared since that namespace doesn't exist now we have moved our files.

   Now we need to do the same thing for our WebAssembly project.

Chapter 4

5. In the **BlazorWebAsesembly.Client** project, add a project reference to the **Components** project.

6. Open App.razor and add the following property to the **Router** component.

   ```
   <Router AppAssembly="@typeof(App).Assembly"
   AdditionalAssemblies="new[] { typeof(Components.Pages.Index).
   Assembly}">
   ```

   Just as with Blazor Server, we are telling Blazor that it should look for Razor components inside the assembly where the app component lives.

   This means the **BlazorWebAssembly.Client** assembly in this case.

   We also want Blazor to look for components in the assembly where the Index component is located, which is the components assembly.

7. Open _Imports.razor and add the following:

   ```
   @using Components.Pages
   @using Components.Shared
   ```

8. Remove the @using BlazorWebAssembly.Client.Shared since that namespace doesn't exist after we moved our files.

Great! we have all our components in a separate library and are sharing the components between the **BlazorServer** and the **BlazorWebAssembly** projects.

Creating our own component

Now it's time to start adding our own component!

OK, this is not completely true because we will reuse Index.razor. Let's start by creating a component that lists our blog posts:

1. In the **Components** project, open **Pages/Index.razor**.

2. Replace the contents of that file with the following code:

   ```
   @page "/"
   @using Data.Models.Interfaces
   @using Data.Models
   @inject IBlogApi _api
   @code{
   }
   ```

If we start from the top, we can see a page directive. It will ensure that the component is shown when the route is "/". Then, we have three @using directives, bringing in the namespaces so we can use them in the Razor file.

Then we inject our API (using DI) and name the instance _api.

3. Add a variable that holds all our posts. In the code section, add the following:

   ```
   protected List<BlogPost> posts = new List<BlogPost>();
   ```

4. Now we need to load the data.

   To load posts, add the following in the code section:

   ```
   protected override async Task OnInitializedAsync()
   {
       posts = await _api.GetBlogPostsAsync(10, 0);
       await base.OnInitializedAsync();
   }
   ```

5. Now, when the page loads, the posts will be loaded as well: 10 posts and page 0 (the first page).

6. Under the @inject row, add the following code:

   ```
   <ul>
       @foreach (var p in posts)
       {
           <li>@p.Title</li>
       }
   </ul>
   ```

We add an **Unordered List** (**UL**); inside that, we loop over **blog posts** and show the title.

Now we can run the application by pressing *Ctrl + F5* (**Debug** | **Start Without Debugging**). Make sure you have the **BlazorServer** selected as the startup project.

Since we don't have any blog posts, this would take us to an empty page. Luckily there is a folder in the repo called **Example data.**; if you download that, put those files in the **Data** folder, and reload the web, you should see a couple of posts.

Great job, we have created our first component!

There are a few noteworthy things; the **Components** project knows nothing about the JSON repository implementation and only knows about the **IBlogApi** interface.

The **Index** component asks for an instance of **IBlogApi,** and the **BlazorServer** project knows it should return an instance of **BlogApiJsonDirectAccess**. This is one of the things I love about Blazor; we can create components that only consume an interface and know nothing about the implementation.

We will come back to this when we implement a web API for WebAssembly in *Chapter 7, Creating an API*.

Summary

In this chapter, we learned a lot about Razor syntax – something we will use throughout the book. We learned about DI, directives, and parameters and, of course, created our first component. This knowledge will help us understand how to create and reuse components.

In the next chapter, we will look at more advanced component scenarios.

Join our community on Discord

Join our community's Discord space for discussions with the author and other readers:

https://packt.link/WebDevBlazor2e

5

Creating Advanced Blazor Components

In the last chapter, we learned all the basics of creating a component. This chapter will teach us how to take our components to the next level.

This chapter will focus on some of the features that will make our components reusable, which will enable us to save time and also give us an understanding of how to use reusable components made by others.

We will also look at some built-in components that will help you by adding additional functionality (compared to using HTML tags) when you build your Blazor app.

In this chapter, we will cover the following topics:

- Exploring binding
- Actions and EventCallback
- Using RenderFragment
- Exploring the new built-in components

Technical requirements

In this chapter, we will start building our components. For this, you'll need the code we developed in *Chapter 4, Understanding Basic Blazor Components*. You are good to go if you followed the instructions in the previous chapters. If not, then make sure you clone/download the repo. The starting point for this chapter can be found in the chapter04 folder, and the finished chapter is in chapter05.

You can find the source code for this chapter's result at https://github.com/PacktPublishing/Web-Development-with-Blazor-Second-Edition/tree/main/Chapter05.

Exploring binding

When building applications, data is important, and we can use binding to show or change data. Using binding, you can connect variables within a component (so that it updates automatically) or by setting a component attribute. Perhaps the most fantastic thing is that by using binding, Blazor understands when it should update the UI and the variable (if the data changes in the UI).

In Blazor, there are two different ways that we can bind values to components, as follows:

- One-way binding
- Two-way binding

By using binding, we can send information between components and make sure we can update a value when we want to.

One-way binding

We have already **discussed one-way binding** in *Chapter 4, Creating Basic Blazor Components*. Let's look at the component again and continue building on it in this section.

In this section, we will combine parameters and binding.

The **Counter.razor** example looks like this:

```
@page "/counter"
<PageTitle>Counter</PageTitle>
<h1>Counter</h1>
<p role="status">Current count: @currentCount</p>
<button class="btn btn-primary" @onclick="IncrementCount">Click me</button>

@code {
    private int currentCount = 0;
    private void IncrementCount()
    {
        currentCount++;
    }
}
```

The component will show the current count and a button that will increment the current count. This is one-way binding. Even though the button can change, the value of currentCount only flows in one direction.

Since this part is designed to demonstrate the functionality and theory and is not part of the finished project we are building, you don't have to write or run this code. The source code for these components is available on GitHub.

We can add a parameter to the Counter component. The code will then look like this:

```
@page "/counterwithparameter"
<h1>Counter</h1>
<p>Current count: @CurrentCount</p>
<button class="btn btn-primary" @onclick="IncrementCount">Click me</button>
@code {
    [Parameter]
    public int IncrementAmount { get; set; } = 1;
    [Parameter]
    public int CurrentCount { get; set; } = 0;
    private void IncrementCount()
    {
        CurrentCount+=IncrementAmount;
    }
}
```

The code sample has two parameters, one for CurrentCount and one for IncrementAmount. By adding parameters to the components, we can change their behavior. This sample is, of course, a bit silly. The chances are that you won't have any use for a component like this, but it illustrates the idea very well.

We can now take the component and add it to another component. This is how we can create a reusable component and change its behavior by changing the value of the parameters.

We change its behavior like this:

```
@page "/parentcounter"
<CounterWithParameter IncrementAmount="@incrementamount" CurrentCount="@currentcount"></CounterWithParameter>
The current count is: @currentcount
@code {
```

```
        int incrementamount = 10;
        int currentcount = 0;
}
```

In this sample, we have two variables, `incrementamount` and `currentcount`, that we pass into our `CounterWithParameter` component.

If we were to run this, we would see a `Counter` component that counts in increments of **10**. However, the `currentcount` variable will not be updated since it is only a one-way binding (one direction).

To help us with that, we can implement two-way binding so that our parent component will be notified of any changes.

Two-way binding

Two-way binding binds values in both directions, and our `Counter` component will be able to notify our parent component of any changes. In the next chapter, *Chapter 6, Building Forms with Validation*, we will talk even more about two-way binding.

To make our `CounterWithParameter` component bind in two directions, we need to add `EventCallback`. The name must consist of the parameter's name followed by `Changed`. This way, Blazor will update the value if it changes. In our case, we would need to name it `CurrentCountChanged`. The code would then look like this:

```
[Parameter]
public EventCallback<int> CurrentCountChanged { get; set; }
private async Task IncrementCount()
{
    CurrentCount += IncrementAmount;
    await CurrentCountChanged.InvokeAsync(CurrentCount);
}
```

By merely using that naming convention, Blazor knows that `CurrentCountChanged` is the event that will get triggered when a change to `CurrentCount` occurs.

`EventCallback` cannot be `null`, so there is no reason to do a null check (more on that in the next section).

We also need to change how we listen for changes:

```
<CounterWithParameterAndEvent IncrementAmount="@incrementamount" @bind-CurrentCount="currentcount"/>
```

We need to add @bind- before the CurrentCount binding. You can also use the following syntax to set the name of the event:

```
<CounterWithParameterAndEvent IncrementAmount="@incrementamount" @bind-
CurrentCount="currentcount" @bind-CurrentCount:event="CurrentCountChang
ed"/>
```

By using :event, we can tell Blazor exactly what event we want to use; in this case, the CurrentCountChanged event.

In the next chapter, *Chapter 6, Building Forms with Validation*, we will continue to look at binding with input/form components.

We can, of course, create events as well using **EventCallback**.

Actions and EventCallback

To communicate changes, we can use **EventCallback**, as shown in the *Two-way binding* section. EventCallback<T> differs a bit from what we might be used to in .NET. EventCallback<T> is a class that is specially made for Blazor to be able to have the event callback exposed as a parameter for the component.

In .NET, in general, you can add multiple listeners to an event (multi-cast), but with EventCallback<T>, you will only be able to add one listener (single-cast).

It is worth mentioning that you can use events the way you are used to from .NET in Blazor. However, you probably want to use EventCallback<T> because there are many upsides to using EventCallback over traditional .NET events.

.NET events use classes, and EventCallback uses structs. This means that in Blazor, we don't have to perform a null check before calling EventCallback because a struct cannot be null.

EventCallback is asynchronous and can be awaited. When EventCallback has been called, Blazor will automatically execute StateHasChanged on the consuming component to ensure the component updates (if it needs to be updated).

So, if you require multiple listeners, you can use Action<T>. Otherwise, it would be best if you used EventCallback<T>.

Some event types have event arguments that we can access. They are optional, so you don't need to add them in most cases.

You can add them by specifying them in a method, or you can use a lambda expression like this:

```
<button @onclick="@((e)=>message=$"x:{e.ClientX} y:{e.ClientY}")">Click me</button>
```

When the button is clicked, it will set a variable called message to a string containing the mouse coordinates. The lambda has one parameter, e, of the MouseArgs type. However, you don't have to specify the type, and the compiler understands what type the parameter is.

Now that we have added actions and used **EventCallback** to communicate changes, we will see how we can execute **RenderFragment** in the next section.

Using RenderFragment

To make our components even more reusable, we can supply them with a piece of Razor syntax. In Blazor, you can specify **RenderFragment**, which is a fragment of Razor syntax that you can execute and show.

Now that we have added actions and used **EventCallback** to communicate changes, we will see how we can execute **RenderFragment** in the next section.

There are two types of render elements, RenderFragment and RenderFragment<T>. RenderFragment is simply a Razor fragment without any input parameters, and RenderFragment<T> has an input parameter that you can use inside the Razor fragment code by using the context keyword. We won't go into depth about how to use this now, but later in this chapter, we will talk about a component (**Virtualize**) that uses RenderFragment<T> and, in the next chapter, *Chapter 6*, *Building Forms with Validation*, we will implement a component using RenderFragment<T>.

We can make RenderFragment the default content inside of the component tags as well as giving it a default value. We will explore this next and build a component using these features.

> **GRID COMPONENT**
>
> If you want to dig deeper into render fragments, please check out **Blazm.Components**, which have a grid component that heavily uses RenderFragment<T>. Where I currently work, we use this component, and it has been developed using real-world scenarios.
>
> You can find it on GitHub here: https://github.com/EngstromJimmy/Blazm.Components.

ChildContent

By naming the render fragment `ChildContent`, Blazor will automatically use whatever is between the component tags as content. This only works, however, if you are using a single render fragment; if you are using more than one, you will have to specify the `ChildComponent` tag as well.

Default value

We can supply `RenderFragment` with a default value or set it in code by using an **@** symbol:

```
@<b>This is a default value</b>;
```

Building an alert component

To better understand how to use render fragments, let's build an alert component. The built-in templates use Bootstrap, so we will do the same for this component. Bootstrap has many components that are easy to import to Blazor. When working on big projects with multiple developers, building components is an easy way to ensure that everyone in one team is writing code the same way.

Let's build a simple alert component based on Bootstrap:

1. Create a folder by right-clicking on **Components project** | **Add** | **New folder** and name the folder `RazorComponents`.
2. Create a new Razor component and name it `Alert.razor`.
3. Replace the content with the following code in the `Alert.razor` file:

   ```
   <div class="alert alert-primary" role="alert">
       A simple primary alert—check it out!
   </div>
   ```

   The code is taken from Bootstrap's web page, `http://getbootstrap.com`, and it shows an alert that looks like this:

   > A simple primary alert—check it out!

   Figure 5.1: The default look of a Bootstrap alert component

   There are two ways in which we could customize this `alert` component. We could add a `string` parameter for the message.

However, since this is a section on render fragments, we will explore the second option, yes, you guessed it, *render fragments*.

1. Add a code section with a `RenderFragment` property called `ChildContent` and replace the alert text with the new property:

    ```
    <div class="alert alert-primary" role="alert">
        @ChildContent
    </div>
    @code{
        [Parameter]
        public RenderFragment ChildContent { get; set; } =@<b>This is a default value</b>;
    }
    ```

    Now we have a `RenderFragment` and set a default value, displaying the fragment between the `div` tags. We also want to add an enum for the different ways you can style the alert box.

2. In the code section, add an enum containing the different styles available:

    ```
    public enum AlertStyle
    {
        Primary,
        Secondary,
        Success,
        Danger,
        Warning,
        Info,
        Light,
        Dark
    }
    ```

3. Add a parameter/property for the enum style:

    ```
    [Parameter]
    public AlertStyle Style { get; set; }
    ```

4. The final step is to update the `class` attribute for `div`. Change the `class` attribute to look like this:

    ```
    <div class="@($"alert alert-{Style.ToString().ToLower()}")" role="alert">
    ```

5. In the Pages folder, add a new **Razor component**, and name it `AlertTest.razor`.

   Replace the code with the following snippet:

   ```
   @page "/alerttest"
   @using Components.RazorComponents
   <Alert Style="Alert.AlertStyle.Danger">
       This is a test
   </Alert>
   <Alert Style="Alert.AlertStyle.Success">
       <ChildContent>
           This is another test
       </ChildContent>
   </Alert>
   <Alert Style="Alert.AlertStyle.Success"/>
   ```

   The page shows three alert components:

   The first one has the `Danger` style, and we are not specifying what property to set for the `This is a test` text, but by convention, it will use the property called `ChildContent`.

   In the second one, we have specified the `ChildContent` property. If you use more render fragments in your component, you must set them like this, with full names.

   In the last one, we didn't specify anything that will give the property the default render fragment we specified in the component.

6. Run the BlazorServer project and navigate to `/AlertTest` to see the test page:

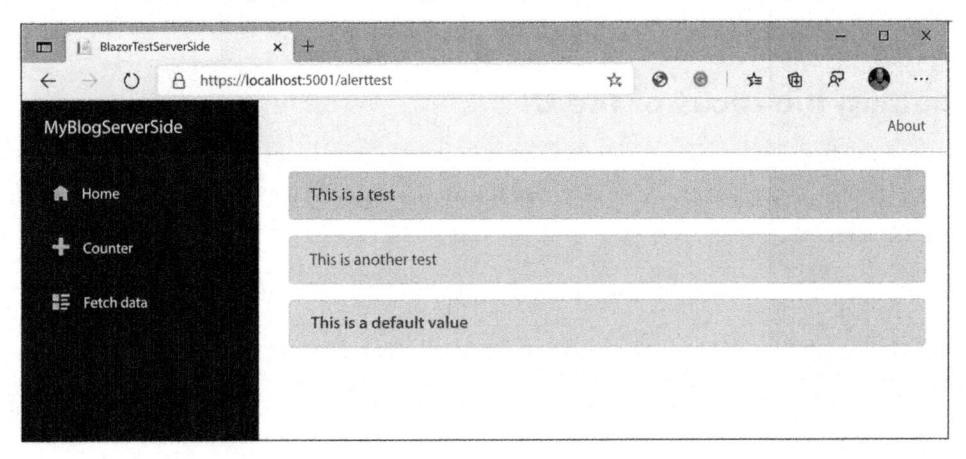

Figure 5.2: Screenshot of the test page

We have finished our first reusable component!

Creating reusable components is how I prefer to make my Blazor sites because I don't have to write the same code twice. This becomes even more apparent if you are working in a larger team. It makes it easier for all developers to produce the same code and end result, and with that, they can get a higher code quality and require fewer tests.

When we upgraded to the latest Bootstrap version, a few CSS classes were deprecated and replaced by others. Thankfully, we followed this approach by making reusable components, so we only had to change a handful of places. There were a couple of places where we still had some old code base (not using components), and it became very apparent that creating components was worth the effort.

Blazor has a bunch of built-in components. In the next section, we will dig deeper into what they are and how to use them.

Exploring the new built-in components

When Blazor first came out, there were a couple of things that were hard to do, and, in some cases, we needed to involve JavaScript to solve the challenge. In this section, we will look at some of the new components we got in .NET 5 and .NET 6.

We will take a look at the following new components or functions:

- Setting the focus of the UI
- Influencing the HTML head
- Component virtualization
- Error boundaries

Setting the focus of the UI

One of my first Blazor blog posts was about how to set the focus on a UI element, but now this is built into the framework. The previous solution involved JavaScript calls to change the focus on a UI element.

By using `ElementReference`, you can now set the focus on the element.

Let's build a component to test the behavior of this new feature:

1. In the **Components** project, in the Pages folder, add a new **Razor component**, and name it `SetFocus.razor`.

2. Open SetFocus.razor and add a page directive:

   ```
   @page "/setfocus"
   ```

3. Add an element reference:

   ```
   @code {
       ElementReference textInput;
   }
   ```

   `ElementReference` is precisely what it sounds like, a reference to an element. In this case, it is an input textbox.

4. Add the textbox and a button:

   ```
   <input @ref="textInput" />
   <button @onclick="() => textInput.FocusAsync()">Set focus</button>
   ```

   Using `@ref`, we specify a reference to any type of component or tag that we can use to access the input box. The `button onclick` method will execute the `FocusAsync()` method and set the focus on the textbox.

5. Press *F5* to run the project and then navigate to /setfocus.
6. Press the **Set focus** button and notice how the textbox gets its focus.

It could seem like a silly example since this only sets the focus, but it is a handy feature, and the autofocus HTML attribute won't work for Blazor.

In my blog post, I had another approach. My goal was to set the focus of an element without having to use code. In the upcoming chapter, *Chapter 6, Building Forms with Validation*, we will implement the autofocus feature from my blog post but use the new .NET features instead.

The release of .NET 5 solves many things we previously had to write with JavaScript; setting the focus is one example. In .NET 6, we have a way to influence the HTML head.

Influencing the HTML head

Sometimes, we want to set our page's title or change the social network meta tags. The head tag is located in _host.cshtml (Blazor Server) and index.html (Blazor WebAssembly), and that part of the page isn't reloaded/rerendered (only the components within the app component are rerendered). In previous versions of Blazor, you had to write code for that yourself using JavaScript.

But .NET has a new component called **HeadOutlet** that can solve that.

To use these components, we will create a page to view one of our blog posts. And we will use many of the techniques we have learned:

1. In the **Components** project, open **Pages/Index.razor**.

2. Change the `foreach` loop to look like this:

   ```
   <li><a href="/Post/@p.Id">@p.Title</a></li>
   ```

   We added a link to the title to look at one blog post. Notice how we can use the @ symbol inside the `href` attribute to get the ID of the post.

3. In the Pages folder, add a **Razor component**, and name it `Post.razor`.

4. In the code section, add a parameter that will hold the ID of the post:

   ```
   [Parameter]
   public string BlogPostId { get; set; }
   ```

   This will hold the ID of the blog post that comes from the URL.

5. Add a page directive to get the set, the URL, and the ID:

   ```
   @page "/post/{BlogPostId}"
   ```

   The page directive will set the URL for our blog post to `/post/`, followed by the ID of the post. We don't have to add a `using` statement to all our components. Instead, open `_Imports.razor` and add the following namespaces:

   ```
   @using Data.Models.Interfaces
   @using Data.Models
   ```

   This will ensure that all our components will have these namespaces by default.

6. Open `Post.razor` again and, just beneath the page directive, inject the API (the namespace is now supplied from `_Imports.razor`):

   ```
   @inject IBlogApi _api
   @inject NavigationManager _navman
   ```

   Our API will now be injected into the component, and we can retrieve our blog post. We also have access to a navigation manager.

Chapter 5 103

7. In the code section, add a property for our blog post:

   ```
   public BlogPost? BlogPost { get; set; }
   ```

   This will contain the blog post we want to show on the page.

8. To load the blog post, add the following code:

   ```
   protected async override Task OnParametersSetAsync()
   {
       BlogPost=await _api.GetBlogPostAsync(BlogPostId);
       await base.OnParametersSetAsync();
   }
   ```

   In this case, we are using the `OnParametersSetAsync()` method. This is to make sure that the parameter is set when we get data from the database and that the content updates when the parameter changes.

9. We must also show the post and add the necessary meta tags. To do that, add the following code just above the code section:

   ```
   @if (BlogPost != null)
   {
       <PageTitle>@BlogPost.Title</PageTitle>
       <HeadContent>
       <meta property="og:title"
         content="@BlogPost.Title" />
       <meta property="og:description" content="@(new
         string(BlogPost.Text.Take(100).ToArray()))" />
       <meta property="og:image" content=
         "@($"{_navman.BaseUri}/pathtoanimage.png")" />
       <meta property="og:url" content="@_navman.Uri" />
       <meta name="twitter:card" content="@(new string(BlogPost.Text.
   Take(100).ToArray()))" />
       </HeadContent>

       <h2>@BlogPost.Title</h2>
       @((MarkupString)BlogPost.Text)

   }
   ```

When the page is first loaded, the `BlogPost` parameter can be null, so we first need to check whether we should show the content at all.

By adding the `Title` component, Blazor will set the title of our site to, in this instance, the title of our blog post.

According to the information I gathered on **Search Engine Optimization** (**SEO**), the meta tags we have added are the bare minimum to use with Facebook and Twitter. We don't have an image for each blog post, but we can have one that is site-wide (for all blog posts) if we would like. Just change `Pathtoanimage.png` to the name of the image and put the image in the `wwwroot` folder.

If the blog post is loaded, then show an **H3** tag with the title and the text beneath that. You might remember **MarkupString** from *Chapter 4, Understanding Basic Blazor Components*. This will output the string from our blog post without changing the HTML (not escaping the HTML).

10. Run the project by pressing *F5* and navigate to a blog post to see the title change:

Figure 5.3: Blog post screenshot

Our blog is starting to take form. We have a list of blog posts, and can view a single post; we are far from done but we're well on our way.

Component virtualization

Virtualize is a component in Blazor that will make sure that it only renders the components or rows that can fit the screen. If you have a large list of items, rendering all of them will have a big impact on memory.

Many third-party component vendors offer grid components with the same virtualization function. The **Virtualize** component is, in my opinion, the most exciting thing in the .NET 5 release.

The **Virtualize** component will calculate how many items can fit on the screen (based on the size of the window and the height of an item). Blazor will add a div tag before and after the content list if you scroll the page, ensuring that the scrollbar is showing the correct position and scale (even though there are no items rendered).

The Virtualize component works just like a foreach loop.

The following is the code we currently have in our Index.razor file:

```
<ul>
    @foreach (var p in posts)
    {
        <li><a href="/Post/@p.Id">@p.Title</a></li>
    }
</ul>
```

Right now, it will show all our blog posts in our database in a long list. Granted, we only have a few right now, but we might have many posts one day.

We can change the code (don't change the code just yet) to use the new Virtualize component by changing it to the following:

```
<Virtualize Items="posts" Context="p">
    <li><a href="/Post/@p.Id">@p.Title</a></li>
</Virtualize>
```

Instead of the foreach loop, we use the **Virtualize** component and add a render fragment that shows how each item should be rendered. The **Virtualize** component uses RenderFragment<T>, which, by default, will send in an item of type T to the render fragment. In the case of the **Virtualize** component, the object will be one blog post (since items are List<T> of blog posts). We access each post with the variable named context. However, we can use the **Context** property on the **Virtualize** component to specify another name, so instead of context, we are now using p.

The **Virtualize** component is even more powerful than this, as we will see in the next feature that we implement:

1. In the **Components** project, open **Pages/Index.razor**.
2. Delete the OnInitializedAsync method and protected List<BlogPost> posts = new List<BlogPost>(); we don't need them anymore.

3. Change the loading of the post to `Virtualize`:

   ```
   <ul>
       <Virtualize ItemsProvider="LoadPosts" Context="p">
           <li><a href="/Post/@p.Id">@p.Title</a></li>
       </Virtualize>
   </ul>
   ```

   In this case, we are using the `ItemsProvider` delegate, which will take care of getting posts from our API.

   We pass in a method called `LoadPosts`, which we also need to add to the file.

4. Now, let's add the `LoadPosts` method by adding the following code:

   ```
   public int totalBlogposts { get; set; }
   private async ValueTask<ItemsProviderResult<BlogPost>> 
   LoadPosts(ItemsProviderRequest request)
   {
       if (totalBlogposts == 0)
       {
           totalBlogposts = await _api.GetBlogPostCountAsync();
       }
       var numblogposts = Math.Min(request.Count, totalBlogposts - 
   request.StartIndex);
       var blogposts= await _api.
   GetBlogPostsAsync(numblogposts,request.StartIndex);
       return new ItemsProviderResult<BlogPost>(blogposts, 
   totalBlogposts);
   }
   ```

   We add a `totalBlogposts` property where we store how many posts we currently have in our database. The `LoadPost` method returns `ValueTask` with `ItemsProviderResult<Blogpost>`. The method has `ItemsProviderRequest` as a parameter, which contains the number of posts the **Virtualize** component wants and how many it wants to skip.

   If we don't know how many total posts we have, we need to retrieve that information from our API by calling the `GetBlogPostCountAsync` method. Then, we need to figure out how many posts we should get; either we get as many posts as we need, or we get all the remaining posts (whatever value is the smallest).

Chapter 5 107

Then, we call our API to get the actual posts by calling `GetBlogPostsAsync` and returning `ItemsProviderResult`.

Now we have implemented a **Virtualize** component that will load and render only the number of blog posts needed to fill the screen.

Error boundaries

In .NET 6, we got a very handy component to handle errors called **ErrorBoundary**.

We can surround the component with an `ErrorBoundary` component; if an error occurs, it will show an error message instead of the whole page failing:

```
<ErrorBoundary>
    <ComponentWithError />
</ErrorBoundary>
```

We can also supply a custom error message like this:

```
<ErrorBoundary>
    <ChildContent>
        <ComponentWithError />
    </ChildContent>
    <ErrorContent>
        <h1 style="color: red;">Oops... something broke</h1>
    </ErrorContent>
</ErrorBoundary>
```

This is a great component to extend and create your own functionality. You can get access to the exception by using the context parameter (as we did with `virtualize`):

```
<ErrorBoundary Context=ex>
    <ChildContent>
        <p>@(1/zero)</p>
    </ChildContent>
    <ErrorContent>
        An error occurred
        @ex.Message
    </ErrorContent>
</ErrorBoundary>
@code {
```

```
        int zero = 0;
}
```

This is a great way to handle errors in the UI.

Summary

In this chapter, we looked at more advanced scenarios for building components. Building components is what Blazor is all about. Components also make it easy to make changes along the way because there is only one point where you must implement the change. We also implemented our first reusable component, which will help maintain the same standard across the team and reduce duplicated code.

We also used some Blazor features to load and display data.

In the next chapter, we will look at forms and validation to start building the administration part of our blog.

6
Building Forms with Validation

In this chapter, we will learn about creating forms and validating them, which is an excellent opportunity to build our admin interface where we can manage our blog posts. We will also build multiple reusable components and learn about some of the new functionalities in Blazor.

This chapter will be super fun, and we will use a lot of the things we have learned up until now.

In this chapter, we will cover the following topics:

- Exploring form elements
- Adding validation
- Custom validation class attributes
- Looking at bindings
- Building an admin interface

Technical requirements

Make sure you have followed the previous chapters or use the Chapter05 folder as a starting point.

You can find the source code for this chapter's result at https://github.com/PacktPublishing/Web-Development-with-Blazor-Second-Edition/tree/main/Chapter06.

Exploring form elements

There are many form elements in HTML, and we can use them all in Blazor. In the end, what Blazor will output is HTML.

Blazor does have components that will add to the functionality, so we can and should try to use those components instead of HTML elements. The built-in components will give us great functionality for free; we will return to this later in this chapter.

Blazor offers the following components:

```
EditForm
InputBase<>
InputCheckbox
InputDate<TValue>
InputNumber<TValue>
InputSelect<TValue>
InputText
InputTextArea
InputRadio
InputRadioGroup
ValidationMessage
ValidationSummary
```

Let's go through them all in the next sections.

EditForm

EditForm renders as a `form` tag, but it has a lot more functionalities.

First, we will not have an action or method like traditional `form` tags; Blazor will handle all of that.

EditForm will create an EditContext instance as a cascading value so that all the components you put inside of EditForm will access the same EditContext. EditContext will track the metadata regarding the editing process, such as what fields have been edited, and keep track of any validation messages.

You need to assign either a model (a class you wish to edit) or an EditContext instance.

For most use cases, assigning a model is the way to go, but for more advanced scenarios, you might want to be able to trigger EditContext.Validate(), for example, to validate all the controls connected to EditContext.

EditForm has the following events that you can use to handle form submissions:

- OnValidSubmit gets triggered when the data in the form validates correctly (we will come back to validation in just a bit).

- `OnInvalidSubmit` gets triggered if the form does not validate correctly.
- `OnSubmit` gets triggered when the form is submitted, regardless of whether the form validates correctly or not. Use `OnSubmit` if you want to control the validation yourself.

Let's take a look at an example.

Consider a class that holds a person; the class has a name and an age for that person and looks like this:

```
public class Person
{
    public string Name { get; set; }
    public int Age { get; set; }
}
```

`EditForm` for this class would look like this (without any other elements for now):

```
<EditForm Model="personmodel" OnValidSubmit="validSubmit">
    ...
    <button type="submit">Submit</button>
</EditForm>
@code {
    Person personmodel = new Person();
    private Task validSubmit()
    {
        //Do database stuff
        return Task.CompletedTask;
    }
}
```

`EditForm` specifies a model (in this case, `personmodel`), and we are listening to the `OnValidSubmit` event.

The `Submit` button is a regular HTML button that is not a specific Blazor component.

InputBase<>

All the Blazor input classes derive from the `InputBase` class. It has a bunch of things we can use for all the `input` components; we will go through the most important ones.

`InputBase` handles `AdditionalAttributes`, which means that if we add any other attributes to the tag, they will automatically get transferred to the output. This means that the components derived from this class can leverage any HTML attributes since they will be part of the output.

`InputBase` has properties for `Value`, which we can bind to, and an event callback for when the value changes called `ValueChanged`.

We can also change `DisplayName` so that the automated validation messages will reflect the correct name and not the property's name, which is the default behavior.

All controls do not support the `DisplayName` property. Some properties are only used inside the component, and we will return to those in a bit.

InputCheckbox

The `InputCheckbox` component will render as `<input type="checkbox">`.

InputDate<TValue>

The `InputDate` component will render as `<input type="date">`. We can use `DateTime` and `DateTimeOffset` as values for the `InputDate` component.

There is no way to format the date; it will use the web browser's current setting. This behavior is by design and is part of the HTML5 spec.

InputNumber<TValue>

The `InputNumber` component will render as `<input type="number">`. We can use `Int32`, `Int64`, `Single`, `Double`, and `Decimal` as values for the `InputNumber` component.

InputSelect<TValue>

The `InputSelect` component will render as `<select>`. We will create `InputSelect` later in this chapter, so I won't go into further detail here.

InputText

The `InputText` component will render as `<input type="text">`.

InputTextArea

The `InputSelect` component will render as `<textarea>`. In this chapter, we will build our own version of this control.

InputRadio

The `InputRadio` component will render as `<input type="radio">`.

InputRadioGroup

The `InputRadioGroup` component will render as `<Input type="radio">`.

InputFile

The `InputFile` component will render as `<Input type="file">`. This component will make it easier to get the file data. It will supply us with a stream for each file's content.

As we can see, there is a Blazor component for almost all the HTML form controls with some added functionality such as validation, which we will see in the next section.

Adding validation

We have already touched on validation; there are some built-in functionalities in the `input` components and `EditForm` to handle validation.

One way to add validation to our form is to use `DataAnnotations`. Using data annotations, we don't have to write any custom logic to ensure the data in the form is correct; instead, we can add attributes to the data model and let `DataAnnotationsValidator` take care of the rest.

There are a bunch of `DataAnnotations` instances in .NET already that we can use; we can also build our own annotations.

Some of the built-in data annotations are as follows:

- `Required`: Makes the field required.
- `Email`: Will check that the entered value is an email address.
- `MinLength`: Will check that the number of characters is not fewer than the value specified.
- `MaxLength`: Will check that the number of characters is not exceeded.
- `Range`: Will check that the value is within a specific range.

There are many more annotations that can help us validate our data. To test this out, let's add data annotations to our data classes:

1. In the **Data.Models** project, open `Models/BlogPost.cs`.
2. At the top of the file, add a using statement for `System.ComponentModel.DataAnnotations`:

    ```
    using System.ComponentModel.DataAnnotations;
    ```

3. Add the `Required` and `MinLength` attributes to the `Title` property:

    ```
    [Required]
    ```

```
[MinLength(5)]
public string Title { get; set; } = string.Empty;
```

The `Required` attribute will ensure we can't leave the title empty, and `MinLength` will make sure it has at least 5 characters.

4. Add the `Required` attribute to the `Text` property:

```
[Required]
public string Text { get; set; } = string.Empty;
```

The `Required` attribute will ensure the `Text` property cannot be empty, which makes sense – why would we create an empty blog post?

5. Open `Models/Category.cs`, and at the top of the file, add a using statement for `System.ComponentModel.DataAnnotations`.

6. Add the `Required` attribute to the `Name` property:

```
[Required]
public string Name { get; set; }="";
```

The `Required` attribute will make sure we can't leave the name empty.

7. Open `Models/Tag.cs`, and at the top of the file, add a using statement for `System.ComponentModel.DataAnnotations`.

8. Add the `Required` attribute to the `Name` property:

```
[Required]
public string Name { get; set; }="";
```

The `Required` attribute will make sure we can't leave the name empty.

Great, now our data models have validation built into them. We need to give our users feedback on what went wrong with the validation.

We can do that by using the `ValidationMessage` or `ValidationSummary` components.

ValidationMessage

The `ValidationMessage` component can show us individual error messages for a specific property. We want to use this component to show validation errors under a form element.

To add a `ValidationMessage` component, we have to specify the `For` property with the name of the property we want to show the validation errors for:

```
<ValidationMessage For="@(() => model.Name)"/>
```

ValidationSummary

The `ValidationSummary` component will show all the validation errors as a list for the entire `EditContext`.

I prefer to show the error close to the problem so it's apparent to the user where the issue is. But we also have the option to show the validation errors as a list using `ValidationSummary`.

To ensure our input controls match the Bootstrap theme (or whatever theme we might use), we can create our **custom validation class**.

Custom validation class attributes

By simply using the edit form, input components, and `DataAnnotationValidator`, the framework will automatically add classes to the components when it's valid and not.

By default, these classes are `.valid` and `.invalid`. In .NET 5, we are given a way to customize these class names ourselves.

When using Bootstrap, the default class names are `.is-valid` and `.is-invalid`, and the class names must also have `.form-control` to get the proper styles.

The next component we build will help us get the proper Bootstrap styling on all our form components.

We will create our own `FieldCssClassProvider` to customize what classes Blazor will use:

1. In the **Components** project, inside the **RazorComponents** folder, add a new class called `BootstrapFieldCssClassProvider.cs`.
2. Open the new class and add the following code:

   ```
   using Microsoft.AspNetCore.Components.Forms;
   namespace Components;
   public class BootstrapFieldCssClassProvider : FieldCssClassProvider
   ```

```
{
    public override string GetFieldCssClass(EditContext editContext,
in FieldIdentifier fieldIdentifier)
    {
        var isValid = !editContext.
GetValidationMessages(fieldIdentifier).Any();
        var isModified = editContext.IsModified(fieldIdentifier);
        return (isModified, isValid) switch
        {
            (true, true) => "form-control modified is-valid",
            (true, false) => "form-control modified is-invalid",
            (false, true) => "form-control",
            (false, false) => "form-control"
        };
    }
}
```

BootstrapFieldCssClassProvider needs an EditContext instance to work.

The code will check whether the form (or EditContext to be specific) is valid and whether or not it has been modified. Based on that, it returns the correct CSS classes.

It returns the form control for all elements; that way, we don't have to add it to every element in the form. We could validate an untouched form as valid or invalid, but we don't want it to show that the form is OK just because it hasn't been changed yet.

Without the code we are about to build, we need to get the EditContext instance from our EditForm and then set FieldCssClassProvider on EditContext as follows:

```
CurrentEditContext.SetFieldCssClassProvider(provider);
```

Next, we will do that more elegantly (in my humble opinion) with the CustomCssClassProvider we will create next.

Earlier in this chapter, I mentioned that EditForm is exposing its EditContext as CascadingValue.

That means we will build a component that we can just put inside of our EditForm and access EditContext that way:

1. In the **Components** project, inside the **RazorComponents** folder, add a new class and name it CustomCssClassProvider.cs.

2. Open the new file and replace the content with the following code:

```
using Microsoft.AspNetCore.Components;
using Microsoft.AspNetCore.Components.Forms;
namespace Components;

public class CustomCssClassProvider<ProviderType> : ComponentBase
where ProviderType : FieldCssClassProvider, new()
{
    [CascadingParameter]
    EditContext? CurrentEditContext { get; set; }
    public ProviderType Provider { get; set; } = new ProviderType();
    protected override void OnInitialized()
    {
        if (CurrentEditContext == null)
        {
            throw new
InvalidOperationException($"{nameof(CustomCssClassProvider
<ProviderType>)} requires a cascading parameter of
type {nameof(EditContext)}. For example, you can use
{nameof(CustomCssClassProvider<ProviderType>)} inside an
EditForm.");
        }
        CurrentEditContext.SetFieldCssClassProvider
          (Provider);
    }
}
```

This generic component takes a type value, in this case, the type of Provider.

We specified that type must inherit from FieldCssClassProvider and must have a constructor without parameters.

The component inherits from ComponentBase, which makes it possible to place the component inside a Blazor component.

In this case, we are writing our component with C# only, but it is not rendering anything.

We have a Cascading parameter that will be populated from EditForm. We throw an exception if EditContext is missing for some reason (for example, if we place the component outside of EditForm.

Finally, we set FieldCssClassProvider on EditContext.

To use the component, we have to add the following code inside of our EditForm (don't worry, we will create an EditForm soon):

```
<CustomCssClassProvider ProviderType="BootstrapFieldCssClassProvider"/>
```

We provide our CustomCssClassProvider component with the right ProviderType: BootstrapFieldCssClassProvider.

This is one way of implementing components, to help us encapsulate functionality. We could have written the code this way:

```
<EditForm Model="personmodel" @ref="CurrentEditContext">
...
</EditForm>
@code {
    public EditContext CurrentEditContext { get; set; }
    protected override Task OnInitializedAsync()
    {
        CurrentEditContext.SetFieldCssClassProvider(new BootstrapFieldCssClassProvider())
        return base.OnInitializedAsync();
    }
}
```

But with the new CustomCssClassProvider component, we can write the same thing like this:

```
<EditForm Model="personmodel">
<CustomCssClassProvider ProviderType="BootstrapFieldCssClassProvider" />
</EditForm>
```

If we are doing something with an EditContext we can always create a component like this since it is a cascading parameter.

Now, we have a component that will make our form controls look like Bootstrap controls. Next, it's time to put that into practice and create a couple of forms by building our admin interface.

Looking at bindings

In this chapter, we are using bindings to bind data to our form controls. We briefly discussed bindings in *Chapter 5*, *Creating Advanced Blazor Components*, but it's time to dig deeper into bindings.

Binding to HTML elements

With HTML elements we can use @bind to bind to the element. We are not binding to a property; therefore, we don't have to supply a name.

So if we are binding to a textbox, we would do it like this:

```
<input type="text" @bind="Variable"/>
```

@bind and @bind-value both work and do the same thing. Note the lower v in value.

By default, the value in the variable will change when we leave the textbox. But we can change that behavior by adding a @bind:event attribute like this:

```
<input type="text" @bind="Variable" @bind:event="oninput"/>
```

We can even take full control over what is happening by using the @bind:get and @bind:set attributes like this:

```
<input type="text" @bind:get="SomeText" @bind:set="SetAsync" />
```

These are doing the same thing as @bind, so we can't use them together with @bind. The @bind:set attribute has another nice feature. We can run asynchronous methods when we set a value.

There is also a way for us to run a method after the value is set by using @bind:after like this:

```
<input type="text" @bind="SomeText" @bind:after="AfterAsync" />
```

This gives us great flexibility when it comes to binding to HTML elements.

On top of that, we can also set the culture using @bind:culture. Both date and number fields use invariant culture and will use the appropriate browser formatting, but if we use a text field, we can change the behavior like this:

```
<input type="text" @bind="SomeNumber" @bind:culture="GBCulture" />
```

Lastly, we can set the format using `@bind:format`. This is only implemented for `DateTime` at his point:

```
<input type="text" @bind="SomeDate" @bind:format="MM/dd/yyyy" />
<input type="text" @bind="SomeDate" @bind:format="yyyy-MM-dd" />
```

We now know how we can bind to HTML elements. Next, we will take a look at binding to components.

Binding to components

When binding to components `Get`, `Set`, and `After` will also work. `Culture`, `Event`, and `Format` will work on some components.

When binding to a component, we use `@bind-{ParameterName}`, so for the parameter `Value` it would look like this:

```
<InputText @bind-Value="text" />
```

In the background, `@bind-Value` will affect two other parameters, `ValueExpression` and `ValueChanged`. This means you will not be able to set them manually if you use `@bind-Value`. When we change the value, `ValueChanged` will get triggered, and we can listen to the event and make things happen when it changes.

We can also use `Get` and `Set` like this:

```
<InputText @bind-Value:get="text" @bind-Value:set="(value) => {text=value;
}" />
<InputText @bind-Value:get="text" @bind-Value:set="Set" />
<InputText @bind-Value:get="text" @bind-Value:set="SetAsync" />
```

We must always supply both a `Get` and a `Set`. These samples use `InputText`, a built-in Blazor component, but this concept works with any parameter on any component. The same thing goes for `After`. It can be used with any component like this:

```
<InputText @bind-Value="text" @bind-Value:after="() => { }" />
<InputText @bind-Value="text" @bind-Value:after="After" />
<InputText @bind-Value="text" @bind-Value:after="AfterAsync" />
```

We have access to some nice binding features, and they work when binding to components as well as HTML elements.

Next, we will build an admin interface using bindings.

Building an admin interface

Now it's time to build a simple admin interface for our blog.

We need to be able to do the following:

- List categories
- Edit categories
- List tags
- Edit tags
- List blog posts
- Edit blog posts

If we look at the preceding list, we might notice that some of the things seem similar – perhaps we can build components for those. Categories and tags are very similar; they have names, and the name is the only thing we should be able to edit.

Let's make a component for that. The component is going to be responsible for listing, adding, deleting, and updating the object.

Since the object we are working with is either Category or Tag, we need to be able to call different APIs depending on the object, so our component needs to be generic:

1. In the **Components** project, in the **RazorComponents** folder, add a new Razor component and call it ItemList.razor.

2. Open the newly created file and at the top of the file, add:

    ```
    @typeparam ItemType
    ```

    @typeparam is to make the component generic, and the variable holding the generic type is called ItemType.

3. In the code section, add the following lines of code:

    ```
    [Parameter]
    public List<ItemType> Items { get; set; } = new();
    [Parameter, EditorRequired]
        public required RenderFragment<ItemType> ItemTemplate { get; set; }
    ```

4. We need two parameters: a list where we can add all the items and an `ItemTemplate` instance that we can use to change how we want the item to be shown.

   In this case, we are using `RenderFragment<T>`, which will give us access to the item inside the template (things will become clearer as soon as we implement it).

5. We also need a couple of events; add the following code to the code section:

   ```
   [Parameter]
   public EventCallback<ItemType> DeleteEvent { get; set; }
   [Parameter]
   public EventCallback<ItemType> SelectEvent { get; set; }
   ```

   We added two events; the first is when we delete a tag or a category. We will send an event to the parent component where we can add the code needed to delete the item.

   The second one is when we select an item so that we can edit the item.

6. Now it's time to add the UI; replace the top of the file below the @typeparam to the code tag with:

   ```
   @using System.Collections.Generic
   <h3>List</h3>
   <table>
       <Virtualize Items="@Items" Context="item">
           <tr>
               <td>
                   <button class="btn btn-primary" @onclick="@(()=>
   {SelectEvent.InvokeAsync(item); })"> Select</button>
               </td>
               <td>@ItemTemplate(item)</td>
               <td>
                   <button class="btn btn-danger" @onclick="@(()=>
   {DeleteEvent.InvokeAsync(item);})"> Delete</button>
               </td>
           </tr>
       </Virtualize>
   </table>
   ```

   If we look back to *Step 3*, we'll notice that we used the variable for the lists and `RenderFragment`.

Then, we use the new `Virtualize` component to list our items; to be fair, we might not have that many categories or tags, but why not use it when we can? We set the `Items` property to `"Items"` (which is the name of our list) and the `Context` parameter to `"item"`.

We can give it whatever name we want; we're only going to use it inside of the `Virtualize` render template.

We added two buttons that simply invoke the `EventCallback` instance we added in *Step 4*. Between those buttons, we added `@ItemTemplate(item)`; we want Blazor to render the template, but we also send the current item in the loop.

That means we have access to the item's value inside our template.

Listing and editing categories

With our new component, it's now time to create a component for listing and editing our categories:

1. In the **Components** project, right-click on the **Pages** folder, select **Add** | **New folder**, and name the folder `Admin`.
2. In the **Pages/Admin** folder, add a new Razor component and name it `CategoryList.razor`.
3. At the top of the component, replace `<h3>CategoryList</h3>` with the following code:

   ```
   @page "/admin/categories"
   @using Components.RazorComponents
   @inject IBlogApi _api
   <h3>Categories</h3>
   ```

   We started with the `@page` directive, telling Blazor that if we navigate to the URL `"admin/categories"`, we will get to the `CategoryList.Razor` component.

   We will add a `using` statement and then inject our API.

4. The next step is adding a form to edit the categories. Add the following code under the code from the previous step:

   ```
   <EditForm OnValidSubmit="Save" Model="Item">
       <DataAnnotationsValidator />
       <CustomCssClassProvider
   ProviderType="BootstrapFieldCssClassProvider" />
       <InputText @bind-Value="@Item.Name" />
       <ValidationMessage For="@(()=>Item.Name)" />
   ```

```
        <button class="btn btn-success" type="submit">Save</button>
</EditForm>
```

We added `EditForm`, which will execute the `Save` method if the form validates OK. For validation, we added `DataAnnotationsValidator`, which will validate the supplied data against the annotations we added to the `Tag` and `Category` classes.

Since we are using Bootstrap, we want our form controls to look the same, so we added `CustomCssClassProvider`, which we created earlier in this chapter.

We added `InputText` and connected it to a `Category` object called `Item` (which we will add in just a second).

Below that, we added `ValidationMessage`, which will show any errors for the name property, and then a `Submit` button.

5. Now it's time to add our `ItemList` component; under the code we added in the previous step, add this code:

```
<ItemList Items="Items" DeleteEvent="@Delete" SelectEvent="@Select"
ItemType="Category">
    <ItemTemplate>
        @{
            var item = context as Category;
            if (item != null)
            {
                @item.Name
            }
        }
    </ItemTemplate>
</ItemList>
```

We added our component, and we bind the `Items` property to a list of items (we will create that list in the next step).

We bind the `Select` and `Delete` events to methods and we specify the type of the list in the `ItemType` property. Then, we have `ItemTemplate`. Since we are using `RenderFragment<T>`, we now have access to a variable called `context`.

We convert that variable to a category and print out the name of the category. This is the template for each item that will be shown on the list.

6. Finally, we add the following code to the code section:

```
@code {
    private List<Category> Items { get; set; } = new();
    public Category Item { get; set; } = new();
    protected async override Task OnInitializedAsync()
    {
        Items = (await _api.GetCategoriesAsync()) ?? new();
        await base.OnInitializedAsync();
    }

    private async Task Delete(Category category)
    {
        try
        {
            await _api.DeleteCategoryAsync(category.Id!);
            Items.Remove(category);
        }
        catch { }
    }

    private async Task Save()
    {
        try
        {
            await _api.SaveCategoryAsync(Item);
            if (!Items.Contains(Item))
            {
                Items.Add(Item);
            }
            Item = new Category();
        }
        catch { }
    }

    private Task Select(Category category)
    {
        try
```

```
            {
                Item = category;
            }
            catch { }
            return Task.CompletedTask;
        }
    }
}
```

We added a list to hold all our categories and a variable that holds one item (the item currently being edited). We use `OnInitializedAsync` to load all the categories from the API.

The `Delete` and `Save` methods call the API's corresponding method, and the `Select` method takes the provided item and puts it into the item variable (ready to be edited).

We check if we already have the item in the list before we add it to the list. This is because in the Blazor Server version it will be added automatically (cached), and in the Blazor WebAssembly version, it will not be added automatically.

7. Run the project (`BlazorServer`) and navigate to /admin/categories.
8. Try to add, edit, and delete a category, as shown in *Figure 6.1*:

Categories

Save

List

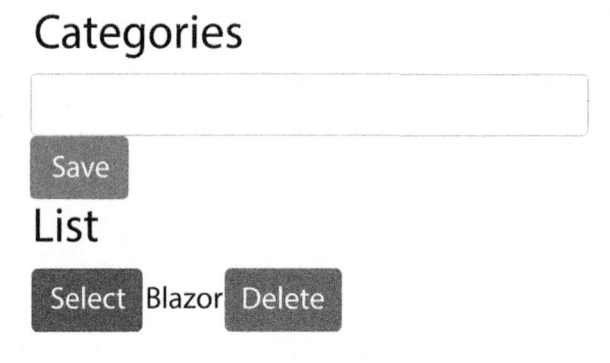

Select Blazor Delete

Figure 6.1: The edit category view

Now we need a component for listing and editing tags as well – it is pretty much the same thing, but we need to use `Tag` instead of `Category`.

Listing and editing tags

We just created a component for listing and editing categories, now we need to create a component to list and edit tags:

1. In the **Pages/Admin** folder, add a new Razor component called `TagList.razor`.

2. At the top of the component, replace <h3>TagList</h3> with the following code:

   ```
   @page "/admin/tags"
   @using Components.RazorComponents
   @inject IBlogApi _api
   <h3>Tags</h3>
   ```

   We started with the @page directive telling Blazor that if we navigate to the URL "admin/tags", we will get to the TagList.Razor component.

   We add a using statement and then inject our API.

3. The next step is adding a form to edit the tags. Add the following code under the code from the previous step:

   ```
   <EditForm OnValidSubmit="Save" Model="Item">
       <DataAnnotationsValidator />
       <CustomCssClassProvider
         ProviderType="BootstrapFieldCssClassProvider" />
       <InputText @bind-Value="@Item.Name" />
       <ValidationMessage For="@(()=>Item.Name)" />
       <button class="btn btn-success" type="submit">Save</button>
   </EditForm>
   ```

   We added EditForm, which will execute the Save method if the form validates OK. For validation, we added DataAnnotationsValidator, which will validate the supplied data against the annotations we added to the Tag and Category classes.

   Since we are using Bootstrap, we want our form controls to look the same, so we added CustomCssClassProvider, which we created earlier in this chapter.

   We added InputText and connected it to a Tag object called Item (which we will add in a moment).

   Below, we add a ValidationMessage instance that will show any errors for the name property and then a Submit button.

4. Now it's time to add our ItemList component. Under the code we added in the previous step, add this code:

   ```
   <ItemList Items="Items" DeleteEvent="@Delete" SelectEvent="@Select" ItemType="Tag">
       <ItemTemplate>
   ```

```
        @{
            var item = context as Tag;
            if (item != null)
            {
                @item.Name
            }
        }
    </ItemTemplate>
</ItemList>
```

We added our component and bound the Items property to a list of items (we will create that list in the next step). We bind the Select and Delete events to methods and specify the List type in the ItemType property.

Then we have ItemTemplate; since we are using RenderFragment<T>, we now have access to a variable called context. We convert that variable to a tag and print out the tag's name.

This is the template for each item shown in the list.

5. Finally, we add the following code under the code section:

```
@code {
    private List<Tag> Items { get; set; } = new List<Tag>();
    public Tag Item { get; set; } = new Tag();
    protected async override Task OnInitializedAsync()
    {
        Items = (await _api.GetTagsAsync())??new();
        await base.OnInitializedAsync();
    }

    private async Task Delete(Tag tag)
    {
        try
        {
            await _api.DeleteTagAsync(tag.Id!);
            Items.Remove(tag);
        }
        catch { }
    }
```

```csharp
            private async Task Save()
            {
                try
                {
                    await _api.SaveTagAsync(Item);
                    if (!Items.Contains(Item))
                    {
                        Items.Add(Item);
                    }
                    Item = new Tag();
                }
                catch { }
            }

            private Task Select(Tag tag)
            {
                try
                {
                    Item = tag;
                }
                catch { }
                return Task.CompletedTask;
            }
```

We added a list to hold all our tags and a variable that holds one item (the item currently being edited). We use `OnInitializedAsync` to load all the tags from the API.

The `Delete` and `Save` methods call the API's corresponding method and the `Select` method takes the provided item and puts it into the `Item` variable (ready to be edited).

We check if we already have the item in the list before we add it to the list. This is because in the Blazor Server version, it will be added automatically (cached), and in the Blazor WebAssembly version, it will not be added automatically.

6. Run the project and navigate to /admin/tags.

7. Try to add, edit, and delete a tag, as shown in *Figure 6.2*:

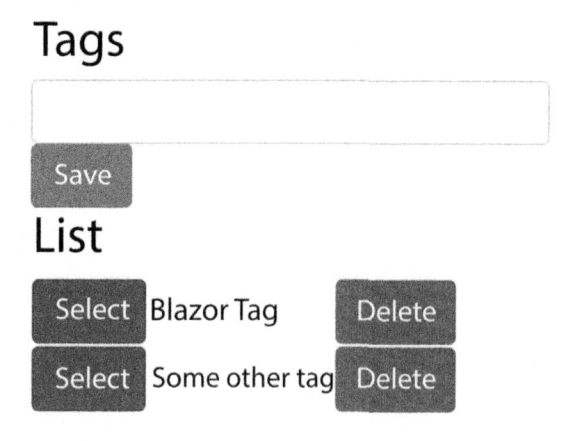

Figure 6.2: The edit tag view

Now we only have two things left: we need ways to list and edit blog posts.

Listing and editing blog posts

Let's start with listing and editing blog posts:

1. In the **Pages/Admin** folder, add a new Razor component called `BlogPostList.razor`.
2. At the top of the `BlogPostList.razor` file, replace `<h3>BlogPostList</h3>` with the following code:

```
@page "/admin/blogposts"
@inject IBlogApi _api
<a href="/admin/blogposts/new">New blog post</a>
<ul>
    <Virtualize ItemsProvider="LoadPosts" Context="p">
        <li>@p.PublishDate
          <a href="/admin/blogposts/@p.Id">@p.Title</a>
        </li>
    </Virtualize>
</ul>
```

We added a page directive, injected our API, and listed the blog posts using the `Virtualize` component.

We also linked the posts to a URL with the `Id` instance of the blog.

3. Replace the code section with the following code:

```
@code {
    public int TotalBlogposts { get; set; }
    private async ValueTask<ItemsProviderResult<BlogPost>> LoadPosts(ItemsProviderRequest request)
    {
        if (TotalBlogposts == 0)
        {
            TotalBlogposts = await
               _api.GetBlogPostCountAsync();
        }
        var numblogposts = Math.Min(request.Count, TotalBlogposts - request.StartIndex);
        List<BlogPost> posts = (await _api.GetBlogPostsAsync(numblogposts, request.StartIndex))??new();
        return new ItemsProviderResult<BlogPost> (posts, TotalBlogposts);
    }
}
```

We added a method that can load posts from the database. This code is identical to the code we have on our **Index** page. Now there is only one thing left in the chapter: adding the page where we can edit the blog post.

A very popular way of writing blog posts is using Markdown; our blog engine will support that. Since Blazor supports any .NET Standard DLLs, we will add an existing library called Markdig.

This is the same engine that Microsoft uses for their docs site.

We can extend Markdig with different extensions (as Microsoft has done), but let's keep this simple and only add support for Markdown without all the fancy extensions:

1. Under the **Components** project, right-click on the **Dependencies** node in the Solution Explorer and select **Manage NuGet Packages**.
2. Search for Markdig and click **Install**.
3. Right-click on the **RazorComponents** folder and select **Add | Class**, then name the component InputTextAreaOnInput.cs.

4. Open the new file and replace its contents with the following code:

```
using System.Diagnostics.CodeAnalysis;
using Microsoft.AspNetCore.Components.Rendering;
namespace Microsoft.AspNetCore.Components.Forms;
    public class InputTextAreaOnInput :
      InputBase<string?>
    {
        protected override void BuildRenderTree(RenderTreeBuilder builder)
        {
            builder.OpenElement(0, "textarea");
            builder.AddMultipleAttributes(1, AdditionalAttributes);
            builder.AddAttribute(2, "class", CssClass);
            builder.AddAttribute(3, "value", BindConverter.FormatValue(CurrentValue));
            builder.AddAttribute(4, "oninput", EventCallback.Factory.CreateBinder <string?>(this, __value => CurrentValueAsString = __value, CurrentValueAsString));
            builder.CloseElement();
        }
        protected override bool TryParseValueFromString(string? value, out string? result, [NotNullWhen(false)] out string? validationErrorMessage)
        {
            result = value;
            validationErrorMessage = null;
            return true;
        }
    }
```

The preceding code is taken from Microsoft's GitHub repository; it is how they implement the InputTextArea component.

In their build system, they can't handle .razor files, so that's why they implement the code this way. I made one change in Microsoft's code, and that is oninput, which used to say OnChange.

Chapter 6 133

For most cases, OnChange will be just fine, which means when I leave the textbox, the value will be updated (and trigger validations). But in our case, we want the preview of the HTML to be updated in real time, which is why we had to implement our own.

One option could have been not to use the InputTextArea component and instead use the TextArea tag, but we would lose the validation highlighting. This is the way to go if we ever need to customize the behavior on an input control.

I recommend using .razor files over .cs files if you make many changes to the implementation.

5. In the **Pages/Admin** folder, add a new Razor component called BlogPostEdit.razor.

6. At the top of the BlogPostEdit.razor file, replace `<h3>BlogPostEdit</h3>` with the following code:

```
@page "/admin/blogposts/new"
@page "/admin/blogposts/{Id}"
@inject IBlogApi _api
@inject NavigationManager _manager
@using Components.RazorComponents
@using Markdig;
```

We add two different page directives because we want to be able to create a new blog post as well as supply an ID to edit an already existing one. If we do not supply an ID, the Id parameter will be null (or the default).

We inject our API and NavigationManager as well as adding using statements.

7. Now we need to add the form; add the following code:

```
<EditForm Model="Post" OnValidSubmit="SavePost">
    <DataAnnotationsValidator />
    <CustomCssClassProvider
 ProviderType="BootstrapFieldCssClassProvider" />
    <InputText @bind-Value="Post.Title"/>
    <ValidationMessage For="()=>Post.Title"/>
    <InputDate @bind-Value="Post.PublishDate"/>
    <ValidationMessage For="()=>Post.PublishDate"/>
    <InputSelect @bind-Value="selectedCategory">
        <option value="0" disabled>None selected</option>
        @foreach (var category in Categories)
```

```
                {
                    <option value="@category.Id">@category.Name </option>
                }
            </InputSelect>
            <ul>
                @foreach (var tag in Tags)
                {
                <li>
                    @tag.Name
                    @if (Post.Tags.Any(t => t.Id == tag.Id))
                    {
                        <button type="button" @onclick="@(() => {Post.Tags.
Remove(Post.Tags.Single(t=>t.Id==tag.Id)); })">Remove</button>
                    }
                    else
                    {
                        <button type="button" @onclick="@(()=> { Post.Tags.
Add(tag); })">Add</button>
                    }
                </li>
                }
            </ul>
            <InputTextAreaOnInput @bind-Value="Post.Text" @
onkeyup="UpdateHTML"/>
            <ValidationMessage For="()=>Post.Text"/>
            <button type="submit" class="btn btn-success">Save</button>
        </EditForm>
```

We add an `EditForm`, and when we submit the form (if it is valid), we execute the `SavePost` method. We add `DataAnnotationValidator`, which will validate our model against the data annotations in the class.

We add `CustomCssClassProvider` so that we get the correct Bootstrap class names. Then, we add boxes for the title, publish date, category, tags, and, last but not least, the text (the blog post's content).

Finally, we add the text using the component we created in *Step 4* (the component that updates for each keystroke).

We also hook up the @onkeyup event to update the preview for each keystroke.

8. We also need to add our SavePost method. Add the following code in the code section:

```
public async Task SavePost()
{
    if (!string.IsNullOrEmpty(selectedCategory) && Categories != null)
    {
        var category = Categories.FirstOrDefault(c =>c.Id == selectedCategory);
        if (category != null)
        {
            Post.Category = category;
        }
    }
    await _api.SaveBlogPostAsync(Post);
    _manager.NavigateTo("/admin/blogposts");
}
```

9. Now it's time to show the preview. Add the following code just below EditForm:

```
@((MarkupString)markDownAsHTML)
```

We use MarkupString to make sure Blazor outputs the HTML code without escaping the characters. You might remember that from *Chapter 4, Understanding Basic Blazor Components*.

10. We also need some variables. Add the following code in the code section:

```
[Parameter]
public string? Id { get; set; }
BlogPost Post { get; set; } = new();
List<Category> Categories { get; set; }=new();
List<Tag> Tags { get; set; }= new();
string? selectedCategory = null;
string? markDownAsHTML { get; set; }
```

We added a parameter for the blog post ID (if we want to edit one), a variable to hold the post we are editing, one that holds all the categories, and one that holds all the tags. We also added a variable that holds the currently selected category and one that holds the Markdown converted to HTML.

11. Now it is time to set up `Markdig`. Add the following code somewhere in the code section:

    ```
    MarkdownPipeline pipeline = default!;
    protected override Task OnInitializedAsync()
    {
        pipeline = new MarkdownPipelineBuilder()
                    .UseEmojiAndSmiley()
                    .Build();
        return base.OnInitializedAsync();
    }
    ```

    To configure `Markdig`, we need to create a pipeline. As I mentioned earlier in the chapter, this is the engine Microsoft uses for their Docs site. It has many extensions available, including source code highlighting and emoticons.

    We also added emoticons to the pipeline to make it a little more fun.

12. We must also add code to load the data (blog post, categories, and tags). Add the following methods in the code section:

    ```
    protected void UpdateHTML()
    {
        markDownAsHTML = Markdig.Markdown.ToHtml(Post.Text, pipeline);
    }
    bool hasTag(Tag tag)
    {
        return Post.Tags.Contains(tag);
    }
    protected override async Task OnParametersSetAsync()
        {
            if (Id != null)
            {
                var p = await _api.GetBlogPostAsync(Id);
                if (p != null)
                {
                    Post = p;
                    if (Post.Category != null)
                    {
                        selectedCategory = Post.Category.Id;
                    }
    ```

```
                UpdateHTML();
            }
        }
        Categories = (await _api.GetCategoriesAsync())??new();
        Tags = (await _api.GetTagsAsync())?? new();
        base.OnParametersSet();
    }
```

13. Now run the site, navigate to /admin/blogposts, click on a blog post to edit it, and test the new Markdown support. *Figure 6.4* shows the **Edit** page with Markdown support:

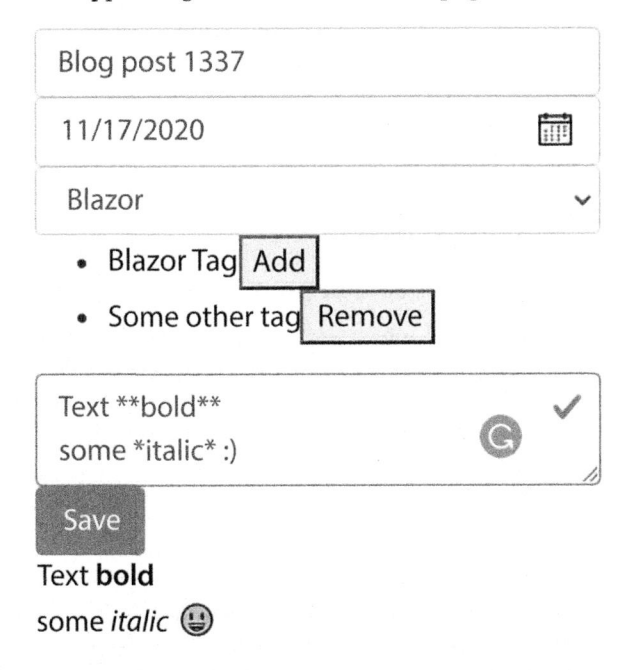

Figure 6.4: Edit page with Markdown support

We still have one more thing to do: we need to ensure that the blog post page shows a converted HTML version of the Markdown.

14. Open /Pages/Post.razor and add the following using statement at the top of the file:

    ```
    @using Markdig;
    ```

15. Add the following code to the code section:

    ```
    MarkdownPipeline pipeline;
    protected override Task OnInitializedAsync()
    ```

```
    {
        pipeline = new MarkdownPipelineBuilder()
                .UseEmojiAndSmiley()
                .Build();
        return base.OnInitializedAsync();
    }
```

16. Replace the following row:

    ```
    @((MarkupString)BlogPost.Text)
    ```

    Replace it with this:

    ```
    @((MarkupString)Markdig.Markdown.ToHtml(BlogPost.Text, pipeline))
    ```

Great job! Now we have an admin interface up and running so that we can start writing blog posts.

Before we summarize this chapter, we have one more component to build.

In .NET 7, we got a new component called `NavigationLock`. Right now if we write a blog post and click somewhere in the menu, our changes will be lost. The same thing happens if we change the URL and press *Enter*. With `NavigationLock` we can prevent that from happening.

`NavigationLock` can prevent us from leaving the page and navigating to another page inside our site. In that case, we can show a custom message using JavaScript. If we navigate to another site, it can trigger a warning, but we don't have control over the message shown. This functionality is built into the browser.

We will implement this in the same way we did with the `FieldCssClassProvider`, as a reusable component. We want to check if our `EditContext` has any changes made so we can trigger the navigation lock:

1. In the **Components** project, in the **RazorComponents** folder, add a new Razor component and name it `BlogNavigationLock.razor`.

2. In the code section, add the following code:

    ```
    [CascadingParameter]
    public required EditContext CurrentEditContext { get; set; }
    public string InternalNavigationMessage { get; set; } = "You are
    about to loose changes, are you sure you want to navigate away?";
    ```

    We have a `CascadingParameter` that gets the current `EditContext`, just as we did with `FieldCssClassProvider`.

Chapter 6 139

We also added a string that is the message shown when we try to navigate from the page.

3. At the top of the component (outside the code section), add the following code:

   ```
   @inject IJSRuntime JSRuntime
   @implements IDisposable
   ```

   We inject an `IJSRuntime` to make JavaScript calls. We will return to JavaScript interop in *Chapter 10, JavaScript Interop*.

   We also implement the `IDisposable` interface.

4. When a change happens in the `EditContext` we need to update the component and make sure it locks the navigation. Add the following code:

   ```
   protected override Task OnInitializedAsync()
   {
       CurrentEditContext.OnFieldChanged += OnFieldChangedAsync;
       return base.OnInitializedAsync();
   }

   private async void OnFieldChangedAsync(object? sender, FieldChangedEventArgs args)
       {
           await InvokeAsync(StateHasChanged);
       }
   void IDisposable.Dispose()
   {
           CurrentEditContext.OnFieldChanged -= OnFieldChangedAsync;
       }
   ```

   We start to listen for field changes, and if a field changes, we call the `StateHasChanged` method to update the component.

   `InvokeAsync` is needed since the call comes from another thread.

   We also override the `Dispose` method and remove the event listener.

5. In the code section, add the following code:

   ```
   private async Task OnBeforeInternalNavigation
   (LocationChangingContext context)
   ```

```
{
    if (CurrentEditContext.IsModified() && CheckNavigation)
    {
        var isConfirmed = await JSRuntime.
InvokeAsync<bool>("confirm",
            InternalNavigationMessage);

        if (!isConfirmed)
        {
            context.PreventNavigation();
        }
    }
}
```

This method will make a JavaScript call, if there are changes in the EditContext (or model), showing a confirm dialog and the message we added. If we do not confirm, the navigation will be prevented.

6. Now we can add the NavigationLock component. Just under the directives, add the following code:

```
<NavigationLock ConfirmExternalNavigation="@
(CurrentEditContext.IsModified() && CheckNavigation)"
OnBeforeInternalNavigation="OnBeforeInternalNavigation" />
```

This NavigationLock component will prevent external navigation (navigating to another site) and internal navigation (navigating to another page in our blog). It checks if the EditContext (model) has any changes and prevents external navigation. On internal navigation, it will execute the OnBeforeInternalNavigation method, which checks if the EditContext has been changed.

Now we only have one more thing to do.

7. In Pages/Admin/BlogPostEdit.razor add the new Razor component we created just below the CustomCssClassProvider:

```
<BlogNavigationLock @ref="NavigationLock"/>
```

This will get the EditContext from the cascading value, and execute the code we just wrote.

8. In the code section add:

   ```
   BlogNavigationLock? NavigationLock { get; set; }
   ```

9. In the `Save` method, just before navigating to admin/blogposts, add:

   ```
   NavigationLock?.CurrentEditContext.MarkAsUnmodified();
   ```

   When saving the object, the `EditContext` doesn't know that, so we are telling the `EditContext` that the model is now unmodified, so the navigation should not be stopped.

10. Run the site, navigate to **Admin/BlogPosts**, and click a blog post.

    Try to navigate to another site (it should work).

    Try to navigate to another page (it should work).

    Change the blog post.

    Try navigating to another site (it should show a message box).

    Try navigating to another page (it should show a message box).

Awesome! We have implemented another reusable component.

Summary

This chapter taught us how to create forms and make API calls to get and save data.

We built custom input controls and got Bootstrap styling on our controls. Most business apps use forms, and by using data annotations, we can add logic close to the data.

We also created multiple reusable components and used many of the things we discussed in previous chapters. We even touched on JavaScript interop, which we will go into more depth about in *Chapter 10, JavaScript Interop*.

The functionality that Blazor offers when it comes to validation and input controls will help us build amazing applications and give our users a great experience. You may notice that, right now, the admin pages are wide open. We need to secure our blog with login, but we will come to that in *Chapter 8, Authentication and Authorization*.

In the next chapter, we will create a web API to get data in our Blazor WebAssembly project.

7
Creating an API

Blazor WebAssembly needs to be able to retrieve data and also change our data. For that to work, we need an API to access the data. In this chapter, we will create a Web API using **Minimal API**.

When using Blazor Server, the API will be secured with the page (if we add an **Authorize** attribute), so we get that for free. But with WebAssembly, everything will be executed in the browser, so we need something that WebAssembly can communicate with to update the data on the server.

To do this, we will need to cover the following topics:

- Creating the service
- Creating the client

Technical requirements

Make sure you have read the previous chapters or use the Chapter06 folder as a starting point.

You can find the source code for this chapter's end result at https://github.com/PacktPublishing/Web-Development-with-Blazor-Second-Edition/tree/main/Chapter07.

Creating the service

There are many ways to create a service, such as via REST or perhaps gRPC. In this book, we will cover REST.

For those who haven't worked with REST before, **REST** stands for **REpresentational State Transfer**. Simply put, it is a way for machines to talk to other devices using HTTP.

With REST, we use different HTTP verbs for different operations. They could look something like this:

URI	Verb	Action
`/BlogPosts`	Get	Gets a list of blog posts
`/BlogPosts`	Post	Creates a new blog post
`/BlogPosts/{id}`	Get	Gets a blog post with a specific ID
`/BlogPost/{id}`	Put	Replaces a blog post
`/BlogPost/{id}`	Patch	Updates a blog post
`/BlogPost/{id}`	Delete	Deletes a blog post

Figure 7.1: Rest calls

We will implement an API for **tags**, **categories**, and **blog posts**.

Since the API takes care of whether the *post* should be created, we'll cheat and only implement Put (replace) because we don't know whether we are creating or updating the data.

The API will only be used by Blazor WebAssembly, so we will implement the API in the **BlazorWebAssembly.Server** project. Blazor Server has direct data access.

Adding data access

For our API to get data from our repository, we need to add the `BlogApiJsonDirectAccessSetting` class to the dependency injection.

Execute the following steps to provide database access:

1. In the **BlazorWebAssembly.Server** project, open `Program.cs`.
2. Add the following lines just above `var app = builder.Build();`:

    ```
    builder.Services.AddOptions<BlogApiJsonDirectAccessSetting>()
        .Configure(options =>
        {
            options.DataPath = @"..\..\..\..\Data\";
            options.BlogPostsFolder = "Blogposts";
            options.TagsFolder = "Tags";
            options.CategoriesFolder = "Categories";
        });
    builder.Services.AddScoped<IBlogApi, BlogApiJsonDirectAccess>();
    ```

This is the same database configuration as with the **BlazorServer** project.

We are even pointing to the same folder, but since the folder structure is one level deeper for the Blazor WebAssembly project, we use ..\..\..\..\Data to reach the existing data.

3. Add a reference to the **Data** project by right-clicking **Dependencies** beneath the **Blazor-WebAssembly.Server** project and selecting **Add project reference**.
4. Check **Data** and click **OK**.
5. Add the following namespaces:

    ```
    using Data;
    using Data.Models.Interfaces;
    ```

    Now we have added access to the classes we have in the **Data** project.

    We have configured it so that if we ask for an instance of **IBlogApi**, we will get an instance of the `BlogApiJsonDirectAccess` class. This is because we are on the server side, so the API can directly access the database.

Now, let's create the API. For this, we will use Minimal API. The idea is that it should be easy to add without the need to add a lot of files.

Learning about Minimal APIs

Before we jump into implementing the Minimal API, let's take a moment to learn about it. Back in November 2019 when one of the members of the **Distributed Application Runtime (Dapr)** team wrote a couple of tutorials on how to build a distributed calculator using different languages.

They had examples using Go, Python, Node.js, and .NET Core. The code showed how much harder it was to write a distributed calculator in C# compared with the other languages.

Microsoft asked various non-.NET developers what their perception was of C#. Their response wasn't great. Then Microsoft asked them to complete a tutorial using an early version of Minimal APIs.

After the tutorial, they were asked about their perception now, and their response had shifted and was now more positive; it felt like home.

The goal of Minimal APIs was to reduce complexity and ceremony and embrace minimalism. I thought that "minimal" meant that I wouldn't be able to do everything but digging deeper into the code, I soon realized that was not the case.

From my point of view, Minimal APIs are a much nicer way to code APIs. The idea is that if we need to, we can grow our API, and as soon as we feel like it, we can move our code into a controller to get more structure. At my workplace, we switched to Minimal APIs because we think the syntax is much nicer.

A very simple sample of adding a Minimal API would be just adding this line in `Program.cs`:

```
app.MapGet("/", () => "Hello world!");
```

We say that if we navigate to a URL without specifying any route, just a "/", we return a string with "Hello World".

This is of course, the simplest example possible, but it is possible to implement more complex things as well, as we will see in the next section.

Adding the API controllers

We have three data models: blog posts, tags, and categories.

Let's create three different files, one for each data model, to demonstrate that there are friendly ways to add more complex APIs using Minimal APIs. For a small project, it would probably make more sense to add everything in `Program.cs`.

Adding APIs for handling blog posts

Let's start by adding the API methods for handling blog posts.

Execute the following steps to create the API:

1. In the **WebAssembly.Server** project, add a new folder called `Endpoints`.
2. In the **Endpoints** folder, create a class called `BlogPostEndpoints.cs`. The idea is to create an extension method we can use later in `Program.cs`.

    Add these using statements at the top of the file:

    ```
    using Data.Models;
    using Data.Models.Interfaces;
    using Microsoft.AspNetCore.Authorization;
    using Microsoft.AspNetCore.Mvc;
    ```

3. Replace the class with the following code:

    ```
    public static class BlogPostEndpoints
    {
        public static void MapBlogPostApi(this WebApplication app)
    ```

```
    {
        app.MapGet("/api/BlogPosts",
            async (IBlogApi api, [FromQuery] int numberofposts,
    [FromQuery] int startindex) =>
            {
                return Results.Ok(await api.
    GetBlogPostsAsync(numberofposts, startindex));
            });
    }
}
```

We are creating an extension method, we must ensure the class is static. The MapBlogPostApi method uses the this keyword, which makes the method available on any WebApplication class.

We set up the Minimal API by using MapGet and a path, which means that the method will run if we access that path with the correct parameters using a *Get* verb.

The method takes a couple of parameters. The first is of the type IBlogApi, which will use dependency injection to get an instance of the class we need, in this case, BlogApiJsonDirectAccess, which will access the JSON files we have stored.

The other parameters will use the query string (since we are using the query attribute); in most cases, a Minimal API will figure these things out but it's never wrong to nudge it in the right direction.

We have created a method that returns the data directly from the database (the same API the Blazor Server project is using).

We also need to make sure to call it from Program.cs.

4. In Program.cs, add the following namespace:

    ```
    using BlazorWebAssembly.Server.Endpoints;
    ```

5. Also, add the following code just under app.UseRouting();:

    ```
    app.MapBlogPostApi();
    ```

6. Time to test the API; make sure to start the **BlazorWebAssembly.Server** project.

    Go to the following URL: https://localhost:5001/Api/BlogPosts?numberofposts=10 &startindex=0 (the port number might be something else). We will get some JSON back with a list of our blog posts.

We are off to a good start! Now we need to implement the rest of the API as well.

7. In the Endpoints/BlogPostEndpoint.cs file, let's add the code to get the blog post count:

   ```
   app.MapGet("/api/BlogPostCount",
   async (IBlogApi api) =>
   {
       return Results.Ok(await api.GetBlogPostCountAsync());
   });
   ```

   We use the *Get* verb but with another route.

8. We also need to be able to get one blog post. Add the following code:

   ```
   app.MapGet("/api/BlogPosts/{*id}",
   async (IBlogApi api, string id) =>
   {
       return Results.Ok(await api.GetBlogPostAsync(id));
   });
   ```

   In this case, we are using the *Get* verb but with another URL, containing the ID for *Post* that we want to get.

   We are using a string as an ID and some databases (like RavenDB, for example), uses an ID that looks like this: CollectionName/IdOfThePost; we also make sure to add a * to the parameter. This way, it will use anything that comes after as an ID otherwise it would interpret the slash as part of the routing and not find the endpoint.

   Next, we need an API that is protected, typically the one that updates or deletes things.

9. Let's add an API that saves a blog post. Add the following code under the code we just added:

   ```
   app.MapPut("/api/BlogPosts",
   async (IBlogApi api, [FromBody] BlogPost item) =>
   {
       return Results.Ok(await api.SaveBlogPostAsync(item));
   }).RequireAuthorization();
   ```

   As I mentioned earlier in this chapter, we will only add one API for creating and updating blog posts, and we will use the *Put* verb (replace) to do that. We have added the RequireAuthorization method at the end, which will ensure that the user needs to be authenticated to call the method.

10. Next up, we add a code for deleting blog posts. To do this, add the following code:

```
app.MapDelete("/api/BlogPosts/{*id}",
async (IBlogApi api, string id) =>
{
    await api.DeleteBlogPostAsync(id);
    return Results.Ok();
}).RequireAuthorization();
```

In this case, we use the *Delete* verb, and just as with saving, we add the RequireAuthorization method at the end.

Next, we need to do this for **Categories** and **Tags** as well.

Adding APIs for handling categories

Let's start with **Categories**. Follow these steps:

1. In the **Endpoints** folder, add a new class called CategoryEndpoints.cs. Replace the code with the following:

```
using Data.Models;
using Data.Models.Interfaces;
using Microsoft.AspNetCore.Mvc;

namespace BlazorWebAssembly.Server.Endpoints;
public static class CategoryEndpoints
{
    public static void MapCategoryApi(this WebApplication app)
    {
        app.MapGet("/api/Categories",
        async (IBlogApi api) =>
        {
            return Results.Ok(await api.GetCategoriesAsync());
        });

        app.MapGet("/api/Categories/{*id}",
        async (IBlogApi api, string id) =>
        {
            return Results.Ok(await api.GetCategoryAsync(id));
        });
```

```
            app.MapDelete("/api/Categories/{*id}",
            async (IBlogApi api, string id) =>
            {
                await api.DeleteCategoryAsync(id);
                return Results.Ok();
            }).RequireAuthorization();

            app.MapPut("/api/Categories",
            async (IBlogApi api, [FromBody] Category item) =>
            {
                return Results.Ok(await api.SaveCategoryAsync(item));
            }).RequireAuthorization();
        }
    }
```

2. In Program.cs, add the following code just under var: app=builder.Build();

    ```
    app.MapCategoryApi();
    ```

    These are all the methods needed to handle **Categories**.

Next, let's do the same thing with **Tags**.

Adding APIs for handling tags

Let's do the same things for tags by following these steps:

1. In the **Endpoints** folder, add a new class called TagEndpoints.cs. Add the following code:

    ```
    using Data.Models;
    using Data.Models.Interfaces;
    using Microsoft.AspNetCore.Mvc;

    namespace BlazorWebAssembly.Server.Endpoints;
    public static class TagEndpoints
    {
        public static void MapTagApi(this WebApplication app)
    ```

```csharp
        {
            app.MapGet("/api/Tags",
            async (IBlogApi api) =>
            {
                return Results.Ok(await api.GetTagsAsync());
            });

            app.MapGet("/api/Tags/{*id}",
            async (IBlogApi api, string id) =>
            {
                return Results.Ok(await api.GetTagAsync(id));
            });

            app.MapDelete("/api/Tags/{*id}",
            async (IBlogApi api, string id) =>
            {
                await api.DeleteTagAsync(id);
                return Results.Ok();
            }).RequireAuthorization();

            app.MapPut("/api/Tags",
            async (IBlogApi api, [FromBody] Tag item) =>
            {
                return Results.Ok(await api.SaveTagAsync(item));
            }).RequireAuthorization();
        }
    }
```

2. In Program.cs, add the following code just under var: app=builder.Build();

   ```csharp
   app.MapTagApi();
   ```

Great! We have an API! Now it's time to write the client that will access that API.

Creating the client

To access the API, we need to create a client. There are many ways of doing this, but we will do it the simplest way possible by writing the code ourselves.

The client will implement the same **IBlogApi** interface. This way, we have the same code regardless of which implementation we are using, and direct JSON access with **BlogApiJsonDirectAccess** or **BlogApiWebClient**, which we are going to create next:

1. Right-click on the **Dependencies** node under **BlazorWebAssembly.Client** and select **Manage NuGet Packages**.
2. Search for Microsoft.AspNetCore.Components.WebAssembly.Authentication and click **Install**.
3. Also, search for Microsoft.Extensions.Http and click **Install**.
4. In the **BlazorWebAssembly.Client** project, add a new class and name it BlogApiWebClient.cs.
5. Open the newly created file.
6. Add the following namespaces:

   ```
   using Data.Models;
   using Data.Models.Interfaces;
   using Microsoft.AspNetCore.Components.WebAssembly.Authentication;
   using System.Net.Http.Json;
   using System.Text.Json;
   ```

7. Add IBlogApi to the class and make it public like this:

   ```
   namespace BlazorWebAssembly.Client;

   public class BlogApiWebClient : IBlogApi
   {

   }
   ```

8. Some API calls will be public (do not require authentication), but HttpClient will be configured to require a token.

   So, we are going to need one authenticated HttpClient and one unauthenticated HttpClient, depending on what API we are calling.

   To be able to call the API, we need to inject HttpClient. Add the following code to the class:

   ```
   private readonly IHttpClientFactory _factory;
   public BlogApiWebClient(IHttpClientFactory factory)
   {
   ```

```
        _factory = factory;
    }
```

9. Now it's time to implement calls to the API. Let's begin with the *Get* calls for blog posts. Add the following code:

```
public async Task<BlogPost?> GetBlogPostAsync(string id)
    {
        var httpclient = _factory.CreateClient("Public");
        return await httpclient.GetFromJsonAsync<BlogPost>($"api/BlogPosts/{id}");
    }

    public async Task<int> GetBlogPostCountAsync()
    {
        var httpclient = _factory.CreateClient("Public");
        return await httpclient.GetFromJsonAsync<int>("/api/BlogPostCount");
    }

    public async Task<List<BlogPost>?> GetBlogPostsAsync(int numberofposts, int startindex)
    {
        var httpclient = _factory.CreateClient("Public");
        return await httpclient.GetFromJsonAsync<List<BlogPost>>($"/api/BlogPosts?numberofposts={numberofposts}&startindex={startindex}");
    }
```

We use the HttpClient we injected and then call GetFromJsonAsync, which will automatically download the JSON and convert it in to the class we supply to the generic method.

Now it gets a little trickier: we need to handle authentication. Luckily, this is built into HttpClient so we only need to handle AccessTokenNotAvailableException. If a token is missing, it will automatically try and renew it, but if there is a problem (for example, the user is not logged in), we can redirect to the login page.

We will come back to tokens and how authentication works in *Chapter 8, Authentication and Authorization*.

10. Next, we add the API calls that need authentication, such as saving or deleting a blog post.

    Add the following code under the code we just added:

    ```csharp
    public async Task<BlogPost?> SaveBlogPostAsync(BlogPost item)
    {
        try
        {
            var httpclient = _factory.CreateClient("Authenticated");
            var response = await httpclient.PutAsJsonAsync<BlogPost>
                ("api/BlogPosts", item);
            var json = await response.Content.ReadAsStringAsync();
            return JsonSerializer.Deserialize<BlogPost>(json);
        }
        catch (AccessTokenNotAvailableException exception)
        {
            exception.Redirect();
        }
        return null;
    }
    public async Task DeleteBlogPostAsync(string id)
    {
        try
        {
            var httpclient = _factory.CreateClient("Authenticated");
            await httpclient.DeleteAsync($"api/BlogPosts/{id}");
        }
        catch (AccessTokenNotAvailableException exception)
        {
            exception.Redirect();
        }
    }
    ```

    If the call throws AccessTokenNotAvailableException, that means HttpClient couldn't get or renew a token automatically, and the user needs to log in.

    This state should probably never happen because we will ensure that when the user navigates to that page, they will need to be logged in, but it's better to be safe than sorry.

We also use an HttpClient named Authenticated, which we need to configure, but we will return to that in *Chapter 8, Authentication and Authorization.*

11. Now we need to do the same for **Categories**. Add the following code to the BlogApiWebClient class:

```
public async Task<List<Category>?> GetCategoriesAsync()
{
    var httpclient = _factory.CreateClient("Public");
    return await httpclient.GetFromJsonAsync<List<Category>>($"api/Categories");
}
public async Task<Category?> GetCategoryAsync(string id)
{
    var httpclient = _factory.CreateClient("Public");
    return await httpclient.GetFromJsonAsync<Category>($"api/Categories/{id}");
}
public async Task DeleteCategoryAsync(string id)
{
    try
    {
        var httpclient = _factory.CreateClient("Authenticated");
        await httpclient.DeleteAsync($"api/Categories/{id}");
    }
    catch (AccessTokenNotAvailableException exception)
    {
        exception.Redirect();
    }
}
public async Task<Category?> SaveCategoryAsync(Category item)
{
    try
    {
        var httpclient = _factory.CreateClient("Authenticated");
        var response = await httpclient.PutAsJsonAsync<Category>("api/Categories", item);
        var json = await response.Content.ReadAsStringAsync();
```

```
            return JsonSerializer.Deserialize<Category>(json);
        }
        catch (AccessTokenNotAvailableException exception)
        {
            exception.Redirect();
        }
        return null;
    }
```

12. And next up, we will do the same for **Tags**. Add the following code just under the code we just added:

```
public async Task<Tag?> GetTagAsync(string id)
{
    var httpclient = _factory.CreateClient("Public");
    return await httpclient.GetFromJsonAsync<Tag>($"api/Tags/{id}");
}
public async Task<List<Tag>?> GetTagsAsync()
{
    var httpclient = _factory.CreateClient("Public");
    return await httpclient.GetFromJsonAsync<List<Tag>>($"api/Tags");
}
public async Task DeleteTagAsync(string id)
{
    try
    {
        var httpclient = _factory.CreateClient("Authenticated");
        await httpclient.DeleteAsync($"api/Tags/{id}");
    }
    catch (AccessTokenNotAvailableException exception)
    {
        exception.Redirect();
    }
}
```

```csharp
public async Task<Tag?> SaveTagAsync(Tag item)
{
    try
    {
        var httpclient = _factory.CreateClient("Authenticated");
        var response = await httpclient.PutAsJsonAsync<Tag>("api/Tags", item);
        var json = await response.Content.ReadAsStringAsync();
        return JsonSerializer.Deserialize<Tag>(json);
    }
    catch (AccessTokenNotAvailableException exception)
    {
        exception.Redirect();
    }
    return null;
}
public Task InvalidateCacheAsync()
{
    throw new NotImplementedException();
}
```

Great job! Our API client is now done!

Summary

In this chapter, we learned how to create an API using Minimal APIs and an API client, which is an important part of most applications. This way, we can get blog posts from our database and show them in our Blazor WebAssembly app.

In the next chapter, we will add login functionality to our sites and call our API for the first time.

Join our community on Discord

Join our community's Discord space for discussions with the author and other readers:

https://packt.link/WebDevBlazor2e

8
Authentication and Authorization

In this chapter, we will learn how to add **authentication** and **authorization** to our blog because we don't want just anyone to be able to create or edit blog posts.

Covering authentication and authorization could take a whole book, so we will keep things simple here. This chapter aims to get the built-in authentication and authorization functionalities working, building on the already existing functionality that's built into ASP.NET. That means that there is not a lot of Blazor magic involved here; many resources already exist that we can take advantage of.

Almost every system today has some way to log in, whether it is an admin interface (like ours) or a member login portal. There are many different login providers, such as Google, Twitter, and Microsoft. We can use all of these providers since we will just be building on existing architecture.

Some sites might already have a database for storing login credentials, but for our blog, we will use a service called Auth0 to manage our users. It is a very powerful way to add many different social providers (if we want to), and we don't have to manage the users ourselves.

We can check the option to add authentication when creating our project. The authentication works differently when it comes to Blazor Server and Blazor WebAssembly, which we will look at in more detail in this chapter.

We will cover the following topics in this chapter:

- Setting up authentication
- Securing Blazor Server

- Securing Blazor WebAssembly
- Securing the API
- Adding authorization

Technical requirements

Make sure you have followed the previous chapters or use the Chapter07 folder as a starting point.

You can find the source code for this chapter's end result at https://github.com/PacktPublishing/Web-Development-with-Blazor-Second-Edition/tree/main/Chapter08.

Setting up authentication

There are a lot of built-in functionalities when it comes to authentication. The easiest way to add authentication is to select an authentication option when creating a project.

We need to implement authentication separately for the Blazor Server project and the Blazor WebAssembly project because they work differently.

But there are still things we can share between these two projects. First, we need to set up Auth0.

Auth0 is a service that can help us with handling our users. There are many different services like this, but Auth0 is the one that seems to be a very good service to use. We can connect one or many social connectors, which will allow our users to log in with Facebook, Twitter, Twitch, or whatever we add to our site.

Even though all of this can be achieved by writing code ourselves, integration like this is a great way to add authentication fast and also get a very powerful solution. Auth0 is free for up to 7,000 users (which our blog probably won't reach, especially not the admin interface).

It also has great functionality to add data to our users that we have access to. We will do that later in the chapter when we add roles to our users. You'll need to take the following steps:

1. Head over to https://auth0.com and create an account.
2. Click the **Create Application** button.
3. Now it's time to name our application. Use MyBlog, for example. Then it's time to select what kind of application type we are using. Is it a native app? Is it a **Single-Page Web Application**, **Regular Web Application**, or **Machine to Machine Application**?

    This depends on what version of Blazor we are going to run.

But it won't limit the functionality, only what we need to configure when setting up our application.

We will start with Blazor server, which is a regular web application. But we want to be able to use the same authentication for both Blazor Server and Blazor WebAssembly, and we can do that by selecting **Single Page Application**.

And if we are only making a Blazor Server Application, we should use **Regular Web Application**, but since we are doing both, select **Single Page Web Application** since this will make it possible to run both.

Next, we will choose what technology we are using for our project. We have got Apache, .NET, Django, Go, and many other choices, but we don't have a choice for Blazor specifically, at least not at the time of writing.

Just skip this and click the **Setting** tab.

4. Now we will set up our application. There are a couple of values we need to save and use later. You need to make sure that you write down the **Domain, Client ID**, and **Client Secret**, as we will use those in a bit.

    If we scroll down, we can change the logo, but we will skip that.

5. We need to set up the **Application Login URI**, our application URL (`localhost` for now), and the port number.

    Starting with .NET 6, the port numbers are random, so make sure you add your application's port number:

    i. **Allowed Callback URLs**: `https://localhost:PORTNUMBER/callback`

    ii. **Allowed Logout URLs**: `https://localhost:PORTNUMBER/`

    Allowed Callback URLs are the URLs Auth0 will make a call to after the user authentication and Allowed Logout URLs are where the user should be redirected after logout.

    Now press **Save Changes** at the bottom of the page.

Configuring Blazor Server

We are done with configuring Auth0. Next, we will configure our Blazor application.

There are many ways to store secrets in .NET (a file that is not checked in, Azure Key Vault, etc.). You can use the one that you are most familiar with.

We will keep it very simple and store secrets in our appsettings.json. Make sure to remember to exclude the file when you check in. You don't check the secrets in source control.

To configure our Blazor Server project, follow these steps:

1. In the **BlazorServer** project, open appsettings.json and add the following code:

    ```
    {
      "Auth0": {
        "Authority": "Get this from the domain for your application at Auth0",
        "ClientId": "Get this from Auth0 setting"
      }
    }
    ```

    These are the values we made a note of in the previous section.

    Blazor server is an ASP.NET site with some added Blazor functionality, which means we can use a NuGet package to get some of the functionality out of the box.

2. In the **BlazorServer** project, add a reference to the NuGet package **Auth0.AspNetCore.Authentication**.

3. Open Program.cs and add the following code just before WebApplication app = builder.Build();:

    ```
    builder.Services
        .AddAuth0WebAppAuthentication(options =>
        {
            options.Domain = builder.Configuration["Auth0:Authority"]??"";;
            options.ClientId = builder.Configuration["Auth0:ClientId"]??"";;
        });
    ```

4. Also, add the following code just after app.UseRouting();. This code will allow us to secure our site:

    ```
    app.UseAuthentication();
    app.UseAuthorization();
    ```

5. Add the following using at the top of the file:

    ```
    using Auth0.AspNetCore.Authentication;
    ```

```
using Microsoft.AspNetCore.Authentication;
using Microsoft.AspNetCore.Authentication.Cookies;
```

6. Blazor Server communication is done over SignalR, and OpenID and OpenAuth rely on HTTP. This is the only thing I don't like about Blazor, because I sometimes need to build Razor pages instead of components.

    Minimal APIs are a great way to do this by adding two get methods. This way, we don't need to create a Razor page.

7. In Program.cs, add the following code just before app.Run():

    ```
    app.MapGet("authentication/login", async (string redirectUri,
    HttpContext context) =>
    {
        var authenticationProperties = new
    LoginAuthenticationPropertiesBuilder()
            .WithRedirectUri(redirectUri)
            .Build();

        await context.ChallengeAsync(Auth0Constants.
    AuthenticationScheme, authenticationProperties);
    });
    ```

    When our site redirects to "authentication/login", the minimal API endpoint will kick off the login functionality.

8. We need to add similar functionality for logout. Add the following code below the previous endpoint from step 7:

    ```
    app.MapGet("authentication/logout", async (HttpContext context) =>
    {
        var authenticationProperties = new
    LogoutAuthenticationPropertiesBuilder()
            .WithRedirectUri("/")
            .Build();

        await context.SignOutAsync(Auth0Constants.AuthenticationScheme,
    authenticationProperties);
        await context.SignOutAsync(CookieAuthenticationDefaults.
    AuthenticationScheme);
    });
    ```

The configuration is all set. Now, we need something to secure.

Securing Blazor Server

Blazor uses `App.razor` for routing. To enable securing Blazor, we need to add a couple of components in the app component.

We need to add a `CascadingAuthenticationState`, which will send the authentication state to all the components that are listening for it. We also need to change the route view to an `AuthorizeRouteView`, which can have different views depending on whether or not you are authenticated:

1. In the end, the `App.razor` component should look like this:

```
<CascadingAuthenticationState>
    <Router AppAssembly="@typeof(App).Assembly"
AdditionalAssemblies="new[] { typeof(Components.Pages.Index).
Assembly}">
        <Found Context="routeData">
            <AuthorizeRouteView RouteData="@routeData"
DefaultLayout="@typeof(MainLayout)">
                <Authorizing>
                    <p>Determining session state, please wait...</p>
                </Authorizing>
                <NotAuthorized>
                    <h1>Sorry</h1>
                    <p>You're not authorized to reach this page. You
need to log in.</p>
                </NotAuthorized>
            </AuthorizeRouteView>
            <FocusOnNavigate RouteData="@routeData" Selector="h1" />
        </Found>
        <NotFound>
            <PageTitle>Not found</PageTitle>
            <LayoutView Layout="@typeof(MainLayout)">
                <p role="alert">Sorry, there's nothing at this
address.</p>
            </LayoutView>
        </NotFound>
    </Router>
```

```
</CascadingAuthenticationState>
```

Now only two things remain, a page that we can secure and a login link display.

2. In the **Components** project, add the NuGet package:

   Microsoft.AspNetCore.Components.Authorization

3. Open _Imports.razor and add the namespaces:

   ```
   @using Microsoft.AspNetCore.Components.Authorization
   @using Components.RazorComponents
   ```

4. In the RazorComponents folder, add a new interface called ILoginStatus and replace the content with:

   ```
   namespace Components.RazorComponents;

   public interface ILoginStatus
   {
   }
   ```

5. In the RazorComponents folder, add a new razor component called LoginStatus.razor.

   Replace the content with:

   ```
   @implements ILoginStatus
   <AuthorizeView>
       <Authorized>
           <a href="authentication/logout">Log out</a>
       </Authorized>
       <NotAuthorized>
           <a href="authentication/login?redirectUri=/">Log in</a>
       </NotAuthorized>
   </AuthorizeView>
   ```

LoginStatus is a component that will show a login link if we are not authenticated and a logout link if we are authenticated.

The code above is the Blazor Server implementation of that control. For Blazor WebAssembly, we need to change the component just a bit, but since all the components, including the layout, are in a shared library, it's not entirely easy to do.

Here is where the `DynamicComponent` component can help us. It makes it possible to load a component using a type or a string. We will solve this by dependency-injecting the component type we want the `MainLayout` to use.

6. Open `Shared/MainLayout.razor` and add the following:

   ```
   @inject ILoginStatus status
   ```

   We are injecting a component of the type `LoginStatus`; another way would be to create an interface and use it instead, but to keep it simple, let's use the `LoginStatus` component for now.

7. Replace the about link with:

   ```
   <DynamicComponent Type="@status.GetType()"/>
   ```

   So, based on what type of component the dependency injection returns to us, it will render that component.

   In the next section, we will also create one for Blazor WebAssembly.

8. Add the `authorize` attribute to the component we wish to secure. The choices are:

   `Pages/Admin/BlogPostEdit.razor`

   `Pages/Admin/BlogPostList.razor`

   `Pages/Admin/CategoryList.razor`

   `Pages/Admin/TagList.razor`

   Add the following attribute to all of them:

   ```
   @attribute [Authorize]
   ```

9. In the **BlazorServer** project, in the file `Program.cs`, add the following line:

   ```
   builder.Services.AddTransient<ILoginStatus,LoginStatus>();
   ```

10. Add the following namespaces:

    ```
    using Components.RazorComponents;
    ```

    The dependency injection will return an instance of an `ILoginStatus` and we will get the `LoginStatus` class.

    This is all it takes, some configuration, and then we are all set.

Now set the `BlazorServer`-project as a startup project and see if you can access the /admin/blogposts page (spoiler: you shouldn't be able to); log in (create a user), and see if you can access the page now.

Our admin interface is secured.

In the next section, we will secure the Blazor WebAssembly version of our blog and the API.

Securing Blazor WebAssembly

The WebAssembly project has some of the same functionalities; it is a bit more complicated because it requires API authentication, but we will start with securing the client.

By default (if we choose to add authentication when we create the project), it will use `IdentityServer` to authenticate both the client and the API.

We will use Auth0 for this instead, the same application we created earlier in this chapter:

1. In the **BlazorWebAssembly.Client** project, in the `wwwroot` folder, add a new JSON file called `appsettings.json`.

    The `appsettings` file will automatically be picked up by Blazor.

2. Add the following JSON:

    ```
    {
        "Auth0": {
            "Authority": "Get this from the domain for your application from Auth0",
            "ClientId": "Get this from Auth0 setting"
        }
    }
    ```

    Replace the values with the same ones we did with the Blazor Server project – the values from the *Setting up Authentication* section.

    Make sure to add `https://` at the beginning of the `Authority` (this is not needed in the Blazor Server project).

3. Add the following NuGet packages:

    ```
    Microsoft.AspNetCore.Components.WebAssembly.Authentication
    Microsoft.Extensions.Http
    ```

4. For us to be able to access our API, we need to set up an HttpClient.

   In Program.cs, add the following lines:

   ```
   builder.Services.AddHttpClient("Public",
       client => client.BaseAddress = new Uri(builder.HostEnvironment.
   BaseAddress));
   builder.Services.AddHttpClient("Authenticated", client => client.
   BaseAddress = new Uri(builder.HostEnvironment.BaseAddress))
       .AddHttpMessageHandler<BaseAddressAuthorizationMessageHandler>();
   ```

   We will create one for getting requests (non-authenticated calls) called public, and one for authenticated calls called authenticated.

   These are the names we used in *Chapter 7, Creating an API*.

5. Add the following namespaces:

   ```
   using Microsoft.AspNetCore.Components.WebAssembly.Authentication;
   using Data;
   ```

6. We also need to set up dependency injection so that when we ask for an IBlogAPI, we will get the BlogApiWebClient that we created in *Chapter 7, Creating and API*.

   In Program.cs, add the following code:

   ```
   builder.Services.AddTransient<IBlogApi, BlogApiWebClient>();
   ```

7. Now it's time to configure the authentication. Add the following code:

   ```
   builder.Services.AddOidcAuthentication(options =>
   {
       builder.Configuration.Bind("Auth0", options.ProviderOptions);
       options.ProviderOptions.ResponseType = "code";
   });
   ```

   We are getting the configuration from our appsettings.json file. In this case, we are using built-in functionality in .NET instead of using a library that Auth0 has provided for us.

8. In wwwroot/index.html, we need to add a reference to JavaScript.

9. Just above the </body> tag, add this JavaScript:

   ```
   <script src="_content/Microsoft.AspNetCore.Components.WebAssembly.
   Authentication/AuthenticationService.js"></script>
   ```

Chapter 8 169

It will handle any authentication logic on the client.

Great, our app is configured. Next, let's secure it.

Now everything is prepared for us to secure our WebAssembly app.

This process is pretty much the same as for the Blazor server, but we need to implement it a bit differently.

We need to add a `CascadingAuthenticationState`, which will send the authentication state to all the components that are listening for it. We also need to change the route view to an `AuthorizeRouteView`, which can have different views depending on whether or not you are authenticated:

1. In the **BlazorWebAssembly.Client** project, in the end, the App.razor component should look like this:

```
@using Microsoft.AspNetCore.Components.Authorization
<CascadingAuthenticationState>
    <Router AppAssembly="@typeof(App).Assembly"
AdditionalAssemblies="new[] { typeof(Components.Pages.Index).
Assembly}">
        <Found Context="routeData">
            <AuthorizeRouteView RouteData="@routeData"
DefaultLayout="@typeof(MainLayout)">
                <Authorizing>
                    <p>Determining session state, please wait...</p>
                </Authorizing>
                <NotAuthorized>
                    <h1>Sorry</h1>
                    <p>You're not authorized to reach this page. You
need to log in.</p>
                </NotAuthorized>
            </AuthorizeRouteView>
            <FocusOnNavigate RouteData="@routeData" Selector="h1" />
        </Found>
        <NotFound>
            <PageTitle>Not found</PageTitle>
            <LayoutView Layout="@typeof(MainLayout)">
```

```
                <p role="alert">Sorry, there's nothing at this
address.</p>
            </LayoutView>
        </NotFound>
    </Router>
</CascadingAuthenticationState>
```

Now only two things remain, a page that we can secure and a login link display.

2. Add the NuGet package:

Microsoft.AspNetCore.Components.WebAssembly.Authentication

3. Open _Imports.razor and add the namespace:

```
@using Microsoft.AspNetCore.Components.Authorization
@using Microsoft.AspNetCore.Authorization
@using Components.RazorComponents;
@using Microsoft.AspNetCore.Components.WebAssembly.Authentication;
```

4. Add a new Razor component called LoginStatusWasm.razor. This is the same component we created in our shared library, but this one is specific for WebAssembly.

5. Replace the content with:

```
@implements ILoginStatus
@inject NavigationManager Navigation

<AuthorizeView>
    <Authorized>
        <a href="#" @onclick="BeginSignOut">Log out</a>
    </Authorized>
    <NotAuthorized>
        <a href="authentication/login">Log in</a>
    </NotAuthorized>
</AuthorizeView>

@code {
    private async Task BeginSignOut(MouseEventArgs args)
    {
        Navigation.NavigateToLogout("authentication/logout");
    }
}
```

6. The implementation uses an extension method, `NavigateToLogout`. `LoginStatusWasm` is a component that will show a login link if we are not authenticated and a logout link if we are authenticated.

We also have a route called authentication that we will implement in just a bit.

The `LoginStatusWasm` will be injected using dependency injection, just like we did with the Blazor Server implementation.

7. In the `Program.cs`, add the following line:

   ```
   builder.Services.AddTransient<ILoginStatus, LoginStatusWasm>();
   ```

When our `MainLayout` is rendered, it will get an instance of `LoginStatusWasm` and render that component.

Now it's time to implement the authentication route. Create a new Razor component called `Authentication.razor` and add the following code:

```
@page "/authentication/{action}"

@inject NavigationManager Navigation
@inject IConfiguration Configuration

<RemoteAuthenticatorView Action="@Action">
    <LogOut>
        @{
            var authority = Configuration["Auth0:Authority"]??string.Empty;
            var clientId = Configuration["Auth0:ClientId"]?? string.Empty;

            Navigation.NavigateTo($"{authority}/v2/logout?client_id={clientId}");
        }
    </LogOut>
</RemoteAuthenticatorView>

@code{
    [Parameter] public string Action { get; set; } = "";
}
```

It uses a built-in component called `RemoteAuthenticatorView`. It makes the necessary calls and also makes sure to protect us from cross-site calls.

The call to await `SignOutManager.SetSignOutState();` that we added in our `LoginStatusWasm` component will set a state that will be checked in the `RemoteAuthenticatorView`.

It will then make a call to Auth0 to log out the client.

We now have secured our WebAssembly project. We also need to secure the pages we want to protect, but since they are in the **Components** project, they are already secured since we did that in the *Securing Blazor Server* section.

Adjusting Auth0

We also need to update the Auth0 Allowed Logout URLs and Allowed Callback URLs as follows:

1. Log in to Auth0, click **Applications**, and select the application.

2. Add a new URL to **Allowed Callback URLs** add (with a comma separating the URLs):

   `https://localhost:PORTNUMBER/authentication/login-callback`

   Note: this port number is something else (not the same port we added earlier).

   In my case it looks like this:

   `https://localhost:7174/callback,https://localhost:7276/authentication/login-callback`

3. In the **Allowed Logout URLs** box, add the following to the beginning of the string (the WASM URL needs to go first):

   `https://localhost:PORTNUMBER`

   In my case, it looks like this: `https://localhost:7276/,https://localhost:7174/`

Set the **BlazorWebAssembly.Server** project as our startup project and run.

We should now be able to click **Login** in the top right corner, log in, and you will end up with a logout link in the top left corner.

If we navigate to /admin/blogposts, we will see a list of blog posts if we are authenticated; if we are not, we will see a message saying: **Sorry, You're not authorized to reach this page. You need to log in**.

Fantastic! Our pages are secure, but our API is still wide open. We need to secure the API using the same login mechanism used to secure the client.

Securing the API

When working with Blazor WebAssembly, we need a central place that handles authentication since we need to authenticate both the client and use the same authentication for the API.

Auth0 has support for APIs as well.

Configure Auth0

To secure our API, we need to let Auth0 know about the API:

1. Log in to Auth0, click **Applications**, then click **APIs**, and then click **Create API**.
2. Add a name, MyBlogAPI, and add an identifier, https://MyBlogApi. This is what we will later use as **Audience**; Auth0 will never call this URL.

   Leave **Signing Algorithm** as is.
3. Click **Create**.

Our authentication for our API is all done; next, we will limit access inside the API.

Configure the API

Now we need to configure the API:

1. In the **BlazorWebAssembly.Server** project, add the NuGet package:

   Microsoft.AspNetCore.Authentication.JwtBearer

2. Open Program.cs and add the using statement:

   ```
   using Microsoft.AspNetCore.Authentication.JwtBearer;
   ```

3. Add the following code just above var app=builder.Build;:

   ```
   builder.Services.AddAuthentication(JwtBearerDefaults.
   AuthenticationScheme)
       .AddJwtBearer(JwtBearerDefaults.AuthenticationScheme, c =>
       {
           c.Authority = builder.Configuration["Auth0:Authority"];
           c.TokenValidationParameters = new Microsoft.IdentityModel.
   Tokens.TokenValidationParameters
   ```

```
            {
                ValidAudience = builder.Configuration["Auth0:Audience"],
                ValidIssuer = builder.Configuration["Auth0:Authority"]
            };
        });
    builder.Services.AddAuthorization();
```

4. Just under app.UseRouting();, add:

   ```
   app.UseAuthentication();
   app.UseAuthorization();
   ```

5. Open appsettings.json and add:

   ```
   "Auth0": {
     "Authority": "Get this value from the Domain in Auth0 application settings",
     "Audience": "Get this value from the Identifier in Auth0 API settings"
   }
   ```

   Replace the placeholder with values from Auth0. Make sure to add https:// at the beginning of the Authority.

6. In the **BlazorWebAssembly.Client** project, we now need to add the audience. Open wwwroot/appsettings.json in the Auth0 JSON object, and add:

   ```
   "Audience": "Get this value from the Identifier in Auth0 API settings"
   ```

7. In Program.cs, inside the AddOidcAuthentication method call, add:

   ```
   options.ProviderOptions.AdditionalProviderParameters.Add("audience",
   builder.Configuration["Auth0:Audience"]);
   ```

   That should be all it takes to configure the API.

   Set **BlazorWebAssembly.Server** as the startup project and run the project. You should now be able to log in, add blog posts, and manage tags and categories.

But what if different users have different permissions?

That is where roles come in.

Adding roles

Blazor Server and Blazor WebAssembly handle roles a bit differently; it's nothing major but we need to do different implementations.

Configuring Auth0 by adding roles

Let's start by adding roles in Auth0:

1. Log in to Auth0, navigate to **User Management**, **Roles**, and click **Create Role**.
2. Enter the name `Administrator` and the description `Can do anything` and press **Create**.
3. Go to the **Users** tab, click **Add Users**, and search for your user and click **Assign**. You can also manage roles from the **Users** menu to the left.
4. By default, roles won't be sent to the client, so we need to enrich the data to include roles.

    We do that by adding an action.

5. Go to **Actions**, and then **Flows**.

    Flows are a way to execute code in a particular flow.

    We want Auth0 to add our roles when we log in.

6. Select **Login**, and there we will see the flow; in our case, we don't have anything yet.
7. On the right-hand side, click **Custom** and the plus sign. As a small pop-up menu appears, select **Build Custom**.
8. Name the action `Add Roles`, leave **Trigger** and **Runtime** as is, and press **Create**.

    We will see a window where we can write our action.

9. Replace all the code with the following:

    ```
    /**
     * @param {Event} event - Details about the user and the context in
     which they are logging in.
     * @param {PostLoginAPI} api - Interface whose methods can be used
     to change the behavior of the login.
     */
    exports.onExecutePostLogin = async (event, api) => {
      const claimName = 'http://schemas.microsoft.com/ws/2008/06/identity/claims/role'
      if (event.authorization) {
    ```

```
        api.idToken.setCustomClaim(claimName, event.authorization.
roles);
        api.accessToken.setCustomClaim(claimName, event.authorization.
roles);
    }
}
```

10. Click **Deploy** and then **Back to flow**.
11. Click **Custom** again, and we will see our newly created action.
12. Drag the **Add Roles** action to the arrow between **Start** and **Complete**.
13. Click **Apply**.

    Now we have an action that will add the roles to our login token.

Our user is now an administrator. It's worth noting that roles are a paid feature in Auth0 and will only be free during the trial.

Now let's set up Blazor Server to use this new role.

Adding roles to Blazor Server

Since we are using the Auth0 library the setup is almost done for Blazor Server.

Let's modify a component to show if the user is an administrator:

1. In the **Components** project, open Shared/NavMenu.razor:

   At the top of the component, add:

   ```
   <AuthorizeView Roles="Administrator">
       <Authorized>
           Hi admin!
       </Authorized>
       <NotAuthorized>
           You are not an admin =(
       </NotAuthorized>
   </AuthorizeView>
   ```

   Set BlazorServer as a startup project and run it.

   If we log in, we should be able to see text to the left saying, **Hi Admin!** in black text on top of dark blue, so it might not be very visible. We will take care of this in *Chapter 9, Sharing Code and Resources*.

Next, we will add the same roles to the BlazorWebAssembly project.

Adding roles to Blazor WebAssembly

Adding roles to Blazor WebAssembly is almost as easy. There is one challenge we need to fix first.

When we get the roles from Auth0, we get them as an array, but we need to split them up into separate objects, and to do that, we need to create a class that does that for us:

1. In the **BlazorWebAssembly.Client** project, create a new class called `ArrayClaimsPrincipalFactory.cs`.

2. Replace the code with the following:

   ```
   using Microsoft.AspNetCore.Components.WebAssembly.Authentication;
   using Microsoft.AspNetCore.Components.WebAssembly.Authentication.Internal;
   using System.Security.Claims;
   using System.Text.Json;

   namespace BlazorWebAssembly.Client;

   public class ArrayClaimsPrincipalFactory<TAccount> :
   AccountClaimsPrincipalFactory<TAccount> where TAccount :
   RemoteUserAccount
   {
       public ArrayClaimsPrincipalFactory(IAccessTokenProviderAccessor accessor)
           : base(accessor)
       { }

       public async override ValueTask<ClaimsPrincipal>
   CreateUserAsync(TAccount account, RemoteAuthenticationUserOptions options)
       {
           var user = await base.CreateUserAsync(account, options);
           var claimsIdentity = (ClaimsIdentity?)user.Identity;

           if (account != null)
           {
               foreach (var kvp in account.AdditionalProperties)
   ```

```
                    {
                        var name = kvp.Key;
                        var value = kvp.Value;
                        if (value != null && (value is JsonElement element
    && element.ValueKind == JsonValueKind.Array))
                        {
                            claimsIdentity?.RemoveClaim(claimsIdentity.
    FindFirst(kvp.Key));

                            var claims = element.EnumerateArray()
                                .Select(x => new Claim(kvp.Key,
    x.ToString()));

                            claimsIdentity?.AddClaims(claims);
                        }
                    }
                }

            return user;
        }
    }
```

The class checks if the roles we got back are in an array, and if so, splits them up into multiple entries.

In the Git repo, there is a page in the components project showing the roles if you would like to dig deeper (Pages/AuthTest.razor).

3. In Program.cs, add the following just after the call to AddOidcAuthentication:

    ```
    .AddAccountClaimsPrincipalFactory<ArrayClaimsPrincipalFactory
    <RemoteUserAccount>>();
    ```

In the end, it should look something like this:

```
builder.Services.AddOidcAuthentication(options =>
{
    //Removed for brevity
}).AddAccountClaimsPrincipalFactory<ArrayClaimsPrincipalFactory
<RemoteUserAccount>>();
```

Set **BlazorWebAssembly.Server** as a startup project and run it. If we log in, we should be able to see text to the left saying **Hi Admin!** in black text on top of dark blue, so it might not be very visible. We will take care of this in *Chapter 9, Sharing Code and Resources*.

Awesome! We have authentication and authorization working for both Blazor Server and Blazor WebAssembly and secured our API!

Summary

In this chapter, we learned how to add authentication to our existing site. It is easier to add authentication at the point of creating a project, but now we have a better understanding of what is going on under the hood and how to handle adding an external source for authentication.

Throughout the book, we have been sharing components between the two projects.

In the next chapter, we will look at sharing even more things like static files and CSS and try to make everything look nice.

9
Sharing Code and Resources

Throughout the book, we have been building Blazor Server and Blazor WebAssembly side by side. This is a great way to build our projects if we want to switch technologies further down the road or, as we do at work, share components between the customer portal and our internal CRM system.

Most of us will probably have one hosting model that we are working with, not usually two, but building it this way does have some perks.

Always think about if there might be a sharable part of the component we are building; that way, we can reuse it, and if we add something to the component, we get that benefit for all our components.

But it's not only about sharing components inside our own projects. What if we want to create a library that can be shared with other departments, or even an open-source project sharing components with the world?

In this chapter, we will look at some of the things we already use when sharing components, and also at sharing CSS and other static files.

In this chapter, we will cover the following topics:

- Adding static files
- CSS isolation

Technical requirements

Make sure you have followed the previous chapters or use the Chapter08 folder as a starting point.

You can find the source code for this chapter's result at https://github.com/PacktPublishing/Web-Development-with-Blazor-Second-Edition/tree/main/Chapter09.

If you are jumping into this chapter using the code from GitHub, make sure you have added Auth0 account information in the settings files. You can find the instructions in *Chapter 8*, *Authentication and Authorization*.

Adding static files

Blazor can use static files, such as images, CSS, and JavaScript. If we put our files in the wwwroot folder, they will automatically be exposed to the internet and be accessible from the root of our site. The nice thing about Blazor is that we can do the same with a library; it is super easy to distribute static files within a library.

At work, we share components between all of our Blazor projects, and the shared library can also depend on other libraries. By sharing components and building our own components (sometimes on top of other libraries), we ensure we have the same look and feel throughout a site. We also share static content like images and CSS, and this makes it simple and fast if we need to change something and we want all our sites to be affected.

To link to a resource in another library/assembly, we can use the _content folder.

Take a look at this example:

```
<link rel="stylesheet" href="_content/Components/MyBlogStyle.min.css" />
```

The HTML link tag, rel, and href are ordinary HTML tags and attributes, but adding the URL that starts with _content tells us that the content we want to access is in another library. The name of the library (assembly name), in our case Components, is followed by the file we want to access, which is stored in the wwwroot folder in our library.

Blazor is, in the end, just HTML, and HTML can be styled using CSS. As mentioned, the Blazor templates are using Bootstrap by default, and we will continue to use that as well.

There is an excellent site with easy-to-use Bootstrap themes ready to be downloaded, which can be found at https://bootswatch.com/.

I like the Darkly theme, so that's the one we'll use, but feel free to experiment with this later on.

Choosing between frameworks

I often get asked about how to style out Blazor apps, and the truth is you can use all the things you are used to. In the end, Blazor will output HTML. There are many languages and frameworks we can use to write our CSS.

We can use CSS, SASS, and LESS. As long as the output is CSS, we can use it.

In this chapter, we will stick with Bootstrap and continue using CSS. SASS and LESS are outside this book's scope.

Tailwind is a popular framework for Blazor, and it is absolutely possible to use it together with Blazor. Tailwind is very component-focused and needs a bit of configuration to start, but if it is something you have worked with and like, you can use it together with Blazor.

Adding a new style

Many templates use Bootstrap as a base, so if you are looking for a design for your website, using a Bootstrap-based template will be an easy implementation.

The problem with Bootstrap (and why some people don't like it) is that many sites use Bootstrap and "all" sites look the same. This can be good if we are building a **LOB (Line of Business)**, but it can be bad if we are trying to be innovative. Bootstrap is also quite large when it comes to downloading, so that is also an argument against it.

This chapter is about making our blog look a bit nicer, so we will stick with Bootstrap, but we should know that if we use something else to handle our CSS, it will work with Blazor.

One of these template sites is Bootswatch, which gives us some nice variations from the traditional Bootstrap themes:

1. Navigate to `https://bootswatch.com/darkly/`.
2. In the top menu called **Darkly**, there are some links. Download `bootstrap.min.css`.
3. In the **Components** project, in the `wwwroot` folder, add the `bootstrap.min.css` file.

We have all the prerequisites and CSS that we can add to our site.

Adding CSS to BlazorServer

Now it's time to add a new style to our sites. Let's start with **BlazorServer**:

1. In the **BlazorServer** project, open `Pages/_Host.cshtml`.
2. Replace this row:

   ```
   <link rel="stylesheet" href="css/bootstrap/bootstrap.min.css" />
   ```

   With:

   ```
   <link rel="stylesheet" href="_content/Components/bootstrap.min.css" />
   ```

3. Set **BlazorServer** as the startup project and run the project by pressing *Ctrl + F5*.

Great! Our Blazor Server project is now updated to use the new style. The main color should now be dark, but there is still some work to do.

Adding CSS to BlazorWebAssembly.Client

Now let's do the same with the Blazor WebAssembly project:

1. In the **BlazorWebAssembly.Client** project, open `wwwroot/index.html`.
2. Replace this line:

   ```
   <link href="css/bootstrap/bootstrap.min.css" rel="stylesheet" />
   ```

   With:

   ```
   <link rel="stylesheet" href="_content/Components/bootstrap.min.css" />
   ```

3. Set **BlazorWebAssembly.Server** as the startup project and run the project by pressing *Ctrl + F5*.

Now we have the same layout for both projects.

Making the admin interface more usable

Let's now clean it up some more. We have only started with the admin functionality, so let's make it more accessible. The menu on the left is no longer required, so let's change it so that it is only visible if you are an administrator:

Chapter 9 185

1. Open Components/Shared/MainLayout.razor and put AuthorizeView around the sidebar div like this:

```
<AuthorizeView Roles="Administrator">
    <div class="sidebar">
        <NavMenu />
    </div>
</AuthorizeView>
```

In this case, we are not specifying Authorized or NotAuthorized. The default behavior is Authorized, so if we are only looking for an authorized state, we don't need to specify it by name.

Since this is already a shared component, we are all set. Start one of the projects (**BlazorServer** or **BlazorWebAssembly.Server**) to see it in action. The menu should not be shown if we are not logged in.

Now we need to make the menu look better. Even though the counter is really fun to click on, it doesn't make much sense regarding our blog.

Since the nav menu is now shared, we can put it in one place, which will change for both Blazor Server and Blazor WebAssembly.

Making the menu more useful

We should replace the links with links to our admin pages instead:

1. In the **Components** project, open the Shared/Navmenu.razor file.

    Edit the code so that it looks like this (keep the code block as is):

```
<div class="top-row pl-4 navbar navbar-dark">
    <a class="navbar-brand" href="">MyBlog Admin</a>
    <button class="navbar-toggler" @onclick="ToggleNavMenu">
        <span class="navbar-toggler-icon"></span>
    </button>
</div>
<div class="@NavMenuCssClass" @onclick="ToggleNavMenu">
    <ul class="nav flex-column">
        <li class="nav-item px-3">
            <NavLink class="nav-link" href="" Match="NavLinkMatch.All">
```

```
                    <span class="oi oi-home" aria-hidden="true"></span>
Home
                </NavLink>
            </li>
            <li class="nav-item px-3">
                <NavLink class="nav-link" href="Admin/Blogposts">
                    <span class="oi oi-signpost" aria-hidden="true"></span> Blog posts
                </NavLink>
            </li>
            <li class="nav-item px-3">
                <NavLink class="nav-link" href="Admin/Tags">
                    <span class="oi oi-tags" aria-hidden="true"></span>
Tags
                </NavLink>
            </li>
            <li class="nav-item px-3">
                <NavLink class="nav-link" href="Admin/Categories">
                    <span class="oi oi-tags" aria-hidden="true"></span>
Categories
                </NavLink>
            </li>
        </ul>
    </div>
```

2. Also, remove the AuthorizeView we added; we don't need that anymore.

Great! Our blog is looking more like a blog, but we can do more!

Making the blog look like a blog

The admin interface is done (at least, for now), and we should focus on the front page of our blog. The front page should have the title of the blog post and some descriptions.

1. In the **Components** project, open the Pages/Index.razor file.
2. Add a using statement for Markdig at the top of the file:

    ```
    @using Markdig;
    ```

3. Add an OnInitializedAsync method to handle the instantiation of the Markdig pipeline (this is the same code we have in the Post.razor file):

```
MarkdownPipeline pipeline;
protected override Task OnInitializedAsync()
{
    pipeline = new MarkdownPipelineBuilder()
                .UseEmojiAndSmiley()
                .Build();
    return base.OnInitializedAsync();
}
```

4. Inside the Virtualize component, change the content (RenderFragment) to the following:

```
<Virtualize ItemsProvider="LoadPosts" Context="p">
    <article>
        <h2>@p.Title</h2>
        @((MarkupString)Markdig.Markdown.ToHtml(new string(p.Text.Take(100).ToArray()), pipeline))
        <a href="/Post/@p.Id">Read more</a>
    </article>
</Virtualize>
```

5. Also, remove the `<ul>` tags.

Now, run the project using *Ctrl + F5* and look at our new front page. Our blog is starting to take form, but we still have work to do.

CSS isolation

In .NET 5, Microsoft added something called isolated CSS. This is something that many other frameworks have as well. The idea is to write CSS specifically for one component. The upsides, of course, are that the CSS that we create won't impact any of the other components.

The template for Blazor uses isolated CSS for Components/Shared/MainLayout.razor and NavMenu.Razor. If we expand MainLayout.razor, we'll see a file called MainLayout.razor.css.

We can also use SASS here by adding a file called MainLayout.razor.scss. The important thing is that the file we add should generate a file called MainLayout.razor.css for the compiler to pick up.

This naming convention will make sure to rewrite CSS and the HTML output.

CSS has the following naming convention:

```
main {
    flex: 1;
}
```

It will be rewritten as follows:

```
main[b-bf15h5967n] {
    flex: 1;
}
```

This means the elements need to have an attribute called `b-bf15h5967n` (in this case) for the style to be applied.

The `div` tag that has the CSS tag within the `MainLayout` component will be outputted like this:

```
<main b-bf15h5967n>
```

For all of this to happen, we also need to have a link to the CSS (which is provided by the template), and it looks like this:

```
<link href="{Assemblyname}.styles.css" rel="stylesheet">
```

This becomes useful for component libraries. We have components that have isolated CSS in our shared library (`NavMenu` and `MainLayout`), and the CSS for the `NavMenu` component is included in the `{Assemblyname}.styles.css` file.

We don't have to do anything extra for our shared CSS to be included. If we are creating a library for anyone to use, we should think about using the isolated CSS approach if our components need some CSS to work correctly.

If we are starting our Blazor project from an empty template, we need to add a link to the isolated CSS.

This way, our users won't have to add a reference to our CSS, and there is no risk of our CSS breaking something in the user's app (since it's isolated). The important thing is that we use the right approach when it makes sense.

Suppose we are creating a component that has very specific styles, which only that component will use. In that case, isolated CSS is a great way to go, it is easier to find (right by the component), and we can use CSS variables for colors and such.

We should be careful when styling similar things inside of the isolated CSS, so we don't end up having a bunch of different CSS files styling a button, for example.

As mentioned, the isolated CSS only affects the HTML tags inside the component, but what if we have a component inside our component?

If we open `Component/Shared/NavMenu.css`, we can see that for the `.nav-item` styles, some of them are using the keyword `::deep`; this is to say that even child components should also be affected by this style.

Take a look at this code:

```
.nav-item ::deep a {…}
```

It is targeting the `<a>` tag, but the Razor code looks like this:

```
<li class="nav-item px-3">
    <NavLink class="nav-link" href="Admin/Blogposts">
        <span class="oi oi-signpost" aria-hidden="true"></span> Blog posts
    </NavLink>
</li>
```

It is the `NavLink` component that renders the `<a>` tag; by adding `::deep`, we are saying we want to apply this style to all elements with the class `.nav-item` and all the `<a>` tags inside that element.

There is one more thing we need to know about – `::deep`; it makes sure to share the ID of the attribute (b-bf15h5967n, for example), and it needs an HTML tag to do so. So if we have a component that consists of other components (not adding any HTML tags at all), we need to add an HTML tag around the content to make `::deep` work.

Before we summarize this chapter, let us do one more thing.

Let's fix the background color of the menu:

1. Open `Components/Shared/MainLayout.razor.css`.
2. Look for the `.sidebar` style and replace it with:

    ```
    .sidebar {
        background-image: linear-gradient(180deg, var(--bs-body-bg) 0%, var(--bs-gray-800) 70%);
    }
    ```

3. Replace the `.top-row` style with:

   ```
   .top-row {
       background-color: var(--bs-primary);
       justify-content: flex-end;
       height: 3.5rem;
       display: flex;
       align-items: center;
   }
   ```

   We replaced the background color and removed a border.

4. In the `.top-row ::deep a, .top-row ::deep .btn-link` style, add:

   ```
   color:white;
   ```

Now we are able to see the login/logout link a bit better.

We now have a working admin interface and a good-looking site.

Summary

In this chapter, we have moved components into a shared library and used that library with both our Blazor Server and Blazor WebAssembly projects.

Using shared libraries like this is the way to create shared libraries (for others to use), and it is also a great way to structure our in-house projects (so that it is easy to change from Blazor Server to Blazor WebAssembly, or the other way around). If you have a site already, you can build your Blazor components in a shared library, which we have done throughout the book.

Using components as part of your site (using Blazor Server), you can get started with Blazor bit by bit until you have converted the whole thing. When that is done, you can decide whether or not to keep using Blazor Server (as I mentioned, we use Blazor Server at work) or move to Blazor WebAssembly.

We talked about how we can use SASS and CSS in our site, both *regular* CSS and *isolated* CSS.

In the next chapter, we will learn about the one thing we are trying to avoid (at least I am) as Blazor developers – JavaScript.

10
JavaScript Interop

In this chapter, we will take a look at JavaScript. In specific scenarios, we still need to use JavaScript, or we will want to use an existing library that relies on JavaScript. Blazor uses JavaScript to update the **Document Object Model (DOM)**, download files, and access local storage on the client.

So, there are, and always will be, cases when we need to communicate with JavaScript or have JavaScript communicate with us. Don't worry. The Blazor community is an amazing one, so chances are someone has already built the interop we need.

In this chapter, we will cover the following topics:

- Why do we need JavaScript?
- .NET to JavaScript
- JavaScript to .NET
- Implementing an existing JavaScript library
- JavaScript interop in WebAssembly

Technical requirements

Ensure you have followed the previous chapters or use the Chapter09 folder as a starting point.

You can find the source code for this chapter's result at https://github.com/PacktPublishing/Web-Development-with-Blazor-Second-Edition/tree/main/Chapter10.

> If you are jumping into this chapter using the code from GitHub, make sure you have added Auth0 account information in the settings files. You can find the instructions in *Chapter 8, Authentication and Authorization*.

Why do we need JavaScript?

Many say Blazor is the JavaScript killer, but the truth is that Blazor needs JavaScript to work. Some events only get triggered in JavaScript, and if we want to use those events, we need to make an interop.

I jokingly say that I have never written so much JavaScript as when I started developing with Blazor. Calm down... it's not that bad.

I have written a couple of libraries that require JavaScript to work. They are called **Blazm.Components** and **Blazm.Bluetooth**.

The first one is a grid component that uses JavaScript interop to trigger C# code (JavaScript to .NET) when the window is resized, to remove columns if they can't fit inside the window.

When that is triggered, the C# code calls JavaScript to get the size of the columns based on the client width, which only the web browser knows, and based on that answer, it removes columns if needed.

The second one, **Blazm.Bluetooth**, makes it possible to interact with Bluetooth devices using Web Bluetooth, which is a web standard accessible through, you guessed it, JavaScript.

It uses two-way communication; Bluetooth events can trigger C# code, and C# code can iterate over devices and send data to them. They are both open source, so if you are interested in looking at a real-world project, you can check them out on my GitHub: https://github.com/EngstromJimmy.

In most cases, I would argue that we won't need to write JavaScript ourselves. The Blazor community is very big, so chances are that someone has already written what we need. But we don't need to be afraid of using JavaScript, either. Next, we will look at different ways to add JavaScript calls to our Blazor project.

.NET to JavaScript

Calling JavaScript from .NET is pretty simple. There are two ways of doing that:

- Global JavaScript
- JavaScript Isolation

We will go through both ways to see what the difference is.

Global JavaScript (the old way)

To access the JavaScript method, we need to make it accessible. One way is to define it globally through the JavaScript window object. This is a bad practice since it is accessible by all scripts and could replace the functionality in other scripts (if we accidentally use the same names).

What we can do is, for example, use scopes, create an object in the global space, and put our variables and methods on that object so that we lower the risk a bit at least.

Using a scope could look something like this:

```
window.myscope = {};
window.myscope.methodName = () => { ... }
```

We create an object with the name `myscope`. Then we declare a method on that object called `methodName`. In this example, there is no code in the method; this only demonstrates how it could be done.

Then, to call the method from C#, we would call it using `JSRuntime` like this:

```
@inject IJSRuntime jsRuntime
await jsRuntime.InvokeVoidAsync("myscope.methodName");
```

There are two different methods we can use to call JavaScript:

- `InvokeVoidAsync`, which calls JavaScript, but doesn't expect a return value
- `InvokeAsync<T>`, which calls JavaScript and expects a return value of type T

We can also send in parameters to our JavaScript method if we want. We also need to refer to JavaScript, and JavaScript must be stored in the wwwroot folder.

The other way is **JavaScript Isolation**, which uses the methods described here, but with modules.

JavaScript Isolation

In .NET 5, we got a new way to add JavaScript using JavaScript Isolation, which is a much nicer way to call JavaScript. It doesn't use global methods, and it doesn't require us to refer to the JavaScript file.

This is awesome for component vendors and end users because JavaScript will be loaded when needed. It will only be loaded once (Blazor handles that for us), and we don't need to add a reference to the JavaScript file, which makes it easier to start and use a library.

So, let's implement that instead.

Isolated JavaScript can be stored in the wwwroot folder, but since an update in .NET 6, we can add them in the same way we add isolated CSS. Add them to your component's folder and name it js at the end (mycomponent.razor.js).

Let's do just that!

In our project, we can delete categories and components. Let's implement a simple JavaScript call to reveal a prompt to make sure that the user wants to delete the category or tag:

1. In the **Components** project, select the RazorComponents/ItemList.razor file, create a new JavaScript file, and name the file ItemList.razor.js.

2. Open the new file and add the following code:

    ```
    export function showConfirm(message) {
        return confirm(message);
    }
    ```

    JavaScript Isolation uses the standard ES modules and can be loaded on demand. The methods it exposes are only accessible through that object and not globally, as with the *old* way.

3. Open ItemList.razor and inject IJSRuntime at the top of the file:

    ```
    @inject IJSRuntime jsRuntime
    ```

4. In the code section, let's add a method that will call JavaScript:

    ```
    IJSObjectReference jsmodule;
    private async Task<bool> ShouldDelete()
    {
        jsmodule = await jsRuntime.InvokeAsync<IJSObjectReference>("import", "/_content/Components/RazorComponents/ItemList.razor.js");
        return await jsmodule.InvokeAsync<bool> ("showConfirm", "Are you sure?");
    }
    ```

    IJSObjectReference is a reference to the specific script that we will import further down. It has access to the exported methods in our JavaScript, and nothing else.

We run the Import command and send the filename as a parameter. This will run the JavaScript command let mymodule = import("/_content/Components/RazorComponents/ItemList.razor.js") and return the module.

Now we can use that module to access our `showConfirm` method and send in the argument `"Are you sure?"`.

5. Change the `Delete` button we have in the component to the following:

   ```
   <td><button class="btn btn-danger" @onclick="@(async ()=>{ if (await ShouldDelete()) { await DeleteEvent.InvokeAsync(item); } })">Delete</button></td>
   ```

   Instead of just calling our `Delete` event callback, we first call our new method. Let JavaScript confirm that you really want to delete it, and if so, then run the `Delete` event callback.

This is a simple implementation of JavaScript.

JavaScript to .NET

What about the other way around? I would argue that calling .NET code from JavaScript isn't a very common scenario, and if we find ourselves in that scenario, we might want to think about what we are doing.

As Blazor developers, we should avoid using JavaScript as much as possible.

I am not bashing JavaScript in any way, but I see this often happen where developers use what they used before and kind of shoehorn it into their Blazor project.

They are solving things with JavaScript that are easy to do with an `if` statement in Blazor. So that's why I think it's essential to think about when to use JavaScript and when not to use JavaScript.

There are, of course, times when JavaScript is the only option, and as I mentioned earlier, Blazm uses communication both ways.

There are three ways of doing a callback from JavaScript to .NET code:

- A static .NET method call
- An instance method call
- A component instance method call

Let's take a closer look at them.

Static .NET method call

To call a .NET function from JavaScript, we can make the function static, and we also need to add the `JSInvokable` attribute to the method.

We can add a function such as this in the code section of a Razor component, or inside a class:

```
[JSInvokable]
public static Task<int[]> ReturnArrayAsync()
{
    return Task.FromResult(new int[] { 1, 2, 3 });
}
```

In the JavaScript file, we can call that function using the following code:

```
DotNet.invokeMethodAsync('BlazorWebAssemblySample', 'ReturnArrayAsync')
    .then(data => {
      data.push(4);
        console.log(data);
    });
```

The `DotNet` object comes from the `Blazor.js` or `blazor.server.js` file.

`BlazorWebAssemblySample` is the name of the assembly, and `ReturnArrayAsync` is the name of the static .NET function.

It is also possible to specify the name of the function in the `JSInvokeable` attribute if we don't want it to be the same as the method name like this:

```
[JSInvokable("DifferentMethodName")]
```

In this sample, JavaScript calls back to .NET code, which returns an `int` array.

It is returned as a promise in the JavaScript file that we are waiting for, and then (using the then operator) we continue with the execution, adding a 4 to the array and then outputting the values in the console.

Instance method call

This method is a bit tricky; we need to pass an instance of the .NET object to call it (this is the method that `Blazm.Bluetooth` is using).

First, we need a class that will handle the method call:

```
using Microsoft.JSInterop;
public class HelloHelper
{
    public HelloHelper(string name)
```

```
    {
        Name = name;
    }
    public string Name { get; set; }
    [JSInvokable]
    public string SayHello() => $"Hello, {Name}!";
}
```

This class takes a string (a name) in the constructor and a method called SayHello that returns a string containing "Hello,", and the name we supplied when we created the instance.

So, we need to create an instance of that class, supply a name, and create DotNetObjectReference<T>, which will give JavaScript access to the instance.

But first, we need JavaScript that can call the .NET function:

```
export function sayHello (hellohelperref) {
    return hellohelperref.invokeMethodAsync('SayHello').then(r => console.log(r));
}
```

In this case, we are using the export syntax, and we export a function called sayHello, which takes an instance of DotNetObjectReference called dotnetHelper.

In that instance, we invoke the SayHello method, which is the SayHello method on the .NET object. In this case, it will reference an instance of the HelloHelper class.

We also need to call the JavaScript method, and we can do that from a class or, in this case, from a component:

```
@page "/interop"
@inject IJSRuntime jsRuntime
@implements IDisposable
<button type="button" class="btn btn-primary" @onclick="async ()=> {
await TriggerNetInstanceMethod(); }">    Trigger .NET instance method
HelloHelper.SayHello </button>
@code {
    private DotNetObjectReference<HelloHelper> objRef;

    IJSObjectReference jsmodule;
    public async ValueTask<string>
```

```
    TriggerNetInstanceMethod()
{
    objRef = DotNetObjectReference.Create(new HelloHelper("Bruce
Wayne"));
    jsmodule = await jsRuntime.
InvokeAsync<IJSObjectReference>("import", "/_content/MyBlog.Shared/
Interop.razor.js");
    return await jsmodule.InvokeAsync<string>("sayHello", objRef);
}
public void Dispose()
{
    objRef?.Dispose();
}
}
```

Let's go through the class. We inject `IJSRuntime` because we need one to call the JavaScript function. To avoid any memory leaks, we also have to make sure to implement `IDiposable`, and toward the bottom of the file, we make sure to dispose of the `DotNetObjectReference` instance.

We create a private variable of the `DotNetObjectReference<HelloHelper>` type, which is going to contain our reference to our `HelloHelper` instance. We create `IJSObjectReference` so that we can load our JavaScript function.

Then we create an instance of `DotNetObjectReference.Create(new HelloHelper("Bruce Wayne"))` of our reference to a new instance of the `HelloHelper` class, which we supply with the name `"Bruce Wayne"`.

Now we have `objRef`, which we will send to the JavaScript method, but first, we load the JavaScript module, and then we call `JavaScriptMethod` and pass in the reference to our `HelloHelper` instance. Now, the JavaScript sayHello method will run `hellohelperref.invokeMethodAsync('SayHello')`, which will make a call to `SayHelloHelper` and get back a string with `"Hello, Bruce Wayne"`.

There are two more ways that we can use to call .NET functions from JavaScript. We can call a method on a component instance where we can trigger an action, and it is not a recommended approach for Blazor Server. We can also call a method on a component instance by using a `helper` class.

Since calling .NET from JavaScript is rare, we won't go into the two examples. Instead, we'll dive into things to think about when implementing an existing JavaScript library.

Implementing an existing JavaScript library

The best approach, in my opinion, is to avoid porting JavaScript libraries. Blazor needs to keep the DOM and the render tree in sync, and having JavaScript manipulate the DOM can jeopardize that.

Most component vendors, such as Telerik, Synfusion, Radzen, and, of course, Blazm, have native components. They don't just wrap a JavaScript but are explicitly written for Blazor in C#. Even though the components use JavaScript in some capacity, the goal is to keep that to a minimum.

So, if you are a library maintainer, my recommendation would be to write a native Blazor version of the library, keep JavaScript to a minimum, and, most importantly, not force Blazor developers to write JavaScript to use your components.

Some components will be unable to use JavaScript implementations since they need to manipulate the DOM.

Blazor is pretty smart when syncing the DOM and render tree, but try to avoid manipulating the DOM. If we need to use JavaScript for something, make sure to put a tag outside the manipulation area, and Blazor will then keep track of that tag and not think about what is inside the tag.

Since we started with Blazor at my workplace very early, many vendors had not yet completed their Blazor components. We needed a graph component fast. On our previous website (before Blazor), we used a component called **Highcharts**.

Highcharts is not a free component but is free to use for non-commercial projects. When building our wrapper, we had a couple of things we wanted to ensure. We wanted the component to work in a similar way to the existing one, and we wanted it to be as simple to use as possible.

Let's walk through what we did.

First, we added a reference to the `Highcharts` JavaScript:

```
<script src="https://code.highcharts.com/highcharts.js"></script>
```

And then we added a JavaScript file as follows:

```
export function loadHighchart(id, json) {
var obj = looseJsonParse(json);
    Highcharts.chart(id, obj);
};
export function looseJsonParse(obj) {
    return Function('"use strict";return (' + obj + ')')();
}
```

The `loadHighchart` method takes `id` of the `div` tag, which should be converted to a chart and the JSON for configuration.

There is also a method that converts the JSON to a JSON object so that it can be passed into the chart method.

The Highchart Razor component looks like this:

```
@inject Microsoft.JSInterop.IJSRuntime jsruntime
<div>
    <div id="@id.ToString()"></div>
</div>
@code
{
    [Parameter] public string Json { get; set; }
    private string id { get; set; } = "Highchart" + Guid.NewGuid().ToString();
    protected override void OnParametersSet()
    {
        StateHasChanged();
        base.OnParametersSet();
    }
    IJSObjectReference jsmodule;
    protected async override Task OnAfterRenderAsync(bool firstRender)
    {
        if (!string.IsNullOrEmpty(Json))
        {
            jsmodule = await jsruntime.InvokeAsync<IJSObjectReference>("import", "/_content/Components/RazorComponents/HighChart.razor.js");
            await jsmodule.InvokeAsync<string>("loadHighchart", new object[] { id, Json });
        }
        await base.OnAfterRenderAsync(firstRender);
    }
}
```

The important thing to notice here is that we have two nested `div` tags: one on the outside that we want Blazor to track and one on the inside that Highchart will add things to.

We pass a JSON parameter in the JSON for the configuration and then call our JavaScript function. We run our JavaScript interop in the `OnAfterRenderAsync` method because otherwise, it would throw an exception, as you may recall from *Chapter 4, Understanding Basic Blazor Components*.

Now, the only thing left to do is to use the component, and that looks like this:

```
@page "/HighChartTest"
<HighChart Json="@chartjson">
</HighChart>
@code {
    string chartjson = @" {
    chart: { type: 'pie'},
    series: [{
        data: [{
            name: 'Does not look like Pacman',
            color:'black',
            y: 20,
        }, {
            name: 'Looks like Pacman',
            color:'yellow',
            y: 80
        }]
    }]
}";
}
```

This test code will show a pie chart that looks like *Figure 10.1*:

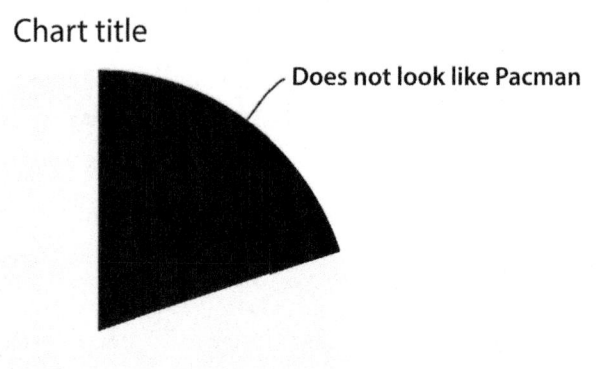

Figure 10.1: Chart example

We have now gone through how we got a JavaScript library to work with Blazor, so this is an option if there is something we need.

As mentioned, the component vendors are investing in Blazor, so chances are that they have what we need, so we might not need to invest time in creating our own component library.

JavaScript interop in WebAssembly

All the things mentioned so far in this chapter will work great for Blazor Server and Blazor WebAssembly.

But with Blazor WebAssembly we have direct access to the JSRuntime (since all the code is running inside the browser. Direct access will give us a really big performance boost. For most applications, we are doing one or two JavaScript calls. Performance is not really going to be a problem. Some applications are more JavaScript-heavy though and would benefit from using the JSRuntime directly.

We have had direct access to the JSRuntime using the `IJSInProcessRuntime` and `IJSUnmarshalledRuntime`. But with .NET 7, both are now obsolete, and we have gotten a nicer syntax.

In the GitHub repo, I have added a couple of files to the **BlazorWebAssembly.Client** project if you want to try the code.

We will start by looking at calling JavaScript from .NET.

To be able to use these features, we need to enable them in the project file by enabling `AllowUnsafeBlocks`.

```
<PropertyGroup>
  <AllowUnsafeBlocks>true</AllowUnsafeBlocks>
</PropertyGroup>
```

.NET to JavaScript

To show the difference, the sample below is the same `ShowAlert` function as earlier in the chapter.

The Razor file looks like this:

```
@page "/nettojswasm"
@using System.Runtime.InteropServices.JavaScript

<h3>This is a demo how to call JavaScript from .NET</h3>

<button @onclick="ShowAlert">Show Alert</button>
@code {
    protected async void ShowAlert()
    {
        ShowAlert("Hello from .NET");
    }

    protected override async Task OnInitializedAsync()
    {
        await JSHost.ImportAsync("nettojs", "../JSInteropSamples/NetToJS.razor.js");
    }
}
```

We are using JSHost to import the JavaScript and give it the name `"nettojs"`. A Source Generator generates the implementation for calling the JavaScript, and to be sure that it can pick up what it should do, we need to add some code in a code-behind.

The code-behind it looks like this:

```
using System.Runtime.InteropServices.JavaScript;
namespace BlazorWebAssembly.Client.JSInteropSamples;
public partial class NetToJS
{
    [JSImport("showAlert", "nettojs")]
    internal static partial string ShowAlert(string message);
}
```

The JavaScript file looks like this:

```
export function showAlert(message) {
    return alert(message);
}
```

We add a JSImport attribute to a method, which will automatically be mapped to the JavaScript call.

This is a much nicer implementation, I think, and a lot faster.

Next, we will look at calling .NET from JavaScript.

JavaScript to .NET

When calling a .NET method from JavaScript, a new attribute makes that possible called JSExport.

The Razor file implementation looks like this:

```
@page "/jstostaticnetwasm"
@using System.Runtime.InteropServices.JavaScript

<h3>This is a demo how to call .NET from JavaScript</h3>

<button @onclick="ShowMessage">Show alert with message</button>

@code {
    protected override async Task OnInitializedAsync()
    {
        await JSHost.ImportAsync("jstonet", "../JSInteropSamples/JSToStaticNET.razor.js");
    }
}
```

Chapter 10

Calling JSHost.ImportAsync is not necessary for the JSExport part of the demo, but we need it to call JavaScript so that we can make the .NET call from JavaScript.

Similarly, here we need to have the methods in a code behind class that looks like this:

```
using System.Runtime.InteropServices.JavaScript;
using System.Runtime.Versioning;
namespace BlazorWebAssembly.Client.JSInteropSamples;

[SupportedOSPlatform("browser")]
public partial class JSToStaticNET
{
    [JSExport]
    internal static string GetAMessageFromNET()
    {
        return "This is a message from .NET";
    }

    [JSImport("showMessage", "jstonet")]
    internal static partial void ShowMessage();
}
```

Here we are using the SupportedOSPlatform attribute to ensure that this code can only run on a browser.

The JavaScript portion of this demo looks like this:

```
export async function setMessage() {
    const { getAssemblyExports } = await globalThis.getDotnetRuntime(0);
    var exports = await getAssemblyExports("BlazorWebAssembly.Client.dll");
    alert(exports.BlazorWebAssembly.Client.JSInteropSamples.JSToStaticNET.GetAMessageFromNET());
}

export async function showMessage() {
    await setMessage();
}
```

We call the `showMessage` JavaScript function from .NET, and it will then call the `setMessage` function.

The `setMessage` function uses the `globalThis` object to access the .NET runtime and get access to the `getAssemblyExports` method.

It will retrieve all the exports for our assembly and then run the method. The .NET method will return the string `"This is a message from .NET"` and show the string in an alert box.

Even though I prefer not to make any JavaScript calls in my Blazor applications, I love having the power to bridge between .NET code and JavaScript code with ease.

Summary

This chapter taught us about calling JavaScript from .NET and calling .NET from JavaScript. In most cases, we won't need to do JavaScript calls, and chances are that the Blazor community or component vendors have solved the problem for us.

We also looked at how we can port an existing library if needed.

In the next chapter, we will continue to look at state management.

Join our community on Discord

Join our community's Discord space for discussions with the author and other readers:

`https://packt.link/WebDevBlazor2e`

11
Managing State – Part 2

In this chapter, we continue to look at managing state. Most applications manage state in some form.

A state is simply information that is persisted in some way. It can be data stored in a database, session states, or even something stored in a URL.

The user state is stored in memory either in the web browser or on the server. It contains the component hierarchy and the most recently rendered UI (render tree). It also contains the values or fields and properties in the component instances as well as the data stored in service instances in dependency injection.

If we make JavaScript calls, the values we set are also stored in memory. Blazor Server relies on the circuit (SignalR connection) to hold the user state, and Blazor WebAssembly relies on the browser's memory. If we reload the page, the circuit and the memory will be lost. Managing state is not about handling connections or connection issues but rather how we can keep the data even if we reload the web browser.

Saving state between page navigations or sessions improves the user experience and could be the difference between a sale and not. Imagine reloading the page, and all your items in the shopping cart are gone; chances are you won't shop there again.

Now imagine returning to a page a week or month later, and all those things are still there.

In this chapter, we will cover the following topics:

- Storing data on the server side
- Storing data in the URL

- Implementing browser storage
- Using an in-memory state container service

Some of these things we have already talked about and even implemented. Let's take this opportunity to recap the things we have already talked about, as well as introduce some new techniques.

Technical requirements

Make sure you have followed the previous chapters or use the Chapter10 folder as a starting point.

You can find the source code for this chapter's end result at https://github.com/PacktPublishing/Web-Development-with-Blazor-Second-Edition/tree/main/Chapter11.

> If you are jumping into this chapter using the code from GitHub, make sure you have added Auth0 account information in the settings files. You can find the instructions in *Chapter 8, Authentication and Authorization*.

Storing data on the server side

There are many different ways in which to store data on the server side. The only thing to remember is that Blazor WebAssembly will always need an API. Blazor Server doesn't need an API since we can access the server-side resources directly.

I have had discussions with many developers regarding APIs or direct access, which all boils down to what you intend to do with the application. If you are building a Blazor Server application and have no interest in moving to Blazor WebAssembly, I would probably go for direct access, as we have done in the **MyBlog** project.

I would not do direct database queries in the components, though. I would keep it in an API, just not a Web API. As we have seen, exposing those API functions in an API, as we did in *Chapter 7, Creating an API*, does not require a lot of steps. We can always start with direct server access and move to an API if we want to.

When it comes to storing data, we can save it in blob storage, key-value storage, a relational database, a document database, table storage, etc.

There is no end to the possibilities. If .NET can communicate with the technology, we will be able to use it.

Storing data in the URL

At first glance, this option might sound horrific, but it's not. Data, in this case, can be the blog post ID or the page number if we use paging. Typically, the things you want to save in the URL are things you want to be able to link to later on, such as blog posts, in our case.

To read a parameter from the URL, we use the following syntax:

```
@page "/post/{BlogPostId:int}"
```

The URL is post followed by Id of the post.

To find that particular route, `BlogPostId` must be an integer; otherwise, the route won't be found.

We also need a `public` parameter with the same name:

```
[Parameter]
public int BlogPostId{ get; set; }
```

If we store data in the URL, we need to make sure to use the `OnParametersSet` or `OnParametersSetAsync` method;, otherwise, the data won't get reloaded if we change the parameter. If the parameter changes, Blazor won't run `OnInitializedAsync` again.

This is why our `post.razor` component loads the things that change based on the parameter in the URL in `OnParametersSet`, and load the things that are not affected by the parameter in `OnInitializedAsync`.

We can use optional parameters by specifying them as nullable like this:

```
@page "/post/{BlogPostId:int?}"
```

Route constraints

When we specify what type the parameter should be, this is called a **route constraint**. We add a constraint so the match will only happen if the parameter value can be converted into the type we specified.

The following constraints are available:

- bool
- datetime
- decimal
- float

- guid
- int
- long

The URL elements will be converted to a **C#** object. Therefore, it's important to use an invariant culture when adding them to a URL.

Using a query string

So far, we have only talked about routes that are specified in the page directive, but we can also read data from the query string.

`NavigationManager` gives us access to the URI, so by using this code, we can access the query string parameters:

```
@inject NavigationManager Navigation
@code{
var query = new Uri(Navigation.Uri).Query;
}
```

We won't dig deeper into this, but now we know that it is possible to access query string parameters if we need to.

We can also access the query parameter using an attribute like this:

```
[Parameter, SupplyParameterFromQuery(Name = "parameterName")] public string ParameterFromQuery { get; set; }
```

This syntax is a bit nicer to work with.

Scenarios that are not that common

Some scenarios might not be as common, but I didn't want to leave them out of the book completely since I have used them in some of my implementations. I want to mention them in case you might run into the same requirements as I did.

By default, Blazor will assume that a URL that contains a dot is a file and will try and serve the user a file (and will probably not find one if we are trying to match a route).

By adding the following in `Startup.cs` to the Blazor WebAssembly server project (a server-hosted WebAssembly project), the server will redirect the request to the `index.html` file:

```
app.MapFallbackToFile("/example/{param?}", "index.html");
```

If the URL is example/some.thing, it will redirect the request to the Blazor WebAssembly entry point, and the Blazor routes will take care of it. Without it, the server would say **file not found**.

The routing, including a dot in the URL, will work, and to do the same, we would need to add the following to Startup.cs in our Blazor Server project:

```
app.MapFallbackToPage("/example/{param?}", "/_Host");
```

We are doing the same thing here, but instead of redirecting to index.html, we are redirecting to _Host, which is the entry point for Blazor Server.

The other scenario that is not that common is handling routes that catch everything. Simply put, we are catching a URL that has multiple folder boundaries, but we are catching them as one parameter:

```
@page "/catch-all/{*pageRoute}"
@code {
    [Parameter]
    public string PageRoute{ get; set; }
}
```

The preceding code will catch "/catch-all/OMG/Racoons/are/awesome" and the pageRoute parameter will contain "OMG/Racoons/are/awesome". This is what we are using for our MyBlog project, because if we change the implementation to use RavenDB, for example, the default behavior is that the Id is collectionname/Id. This would be interpreted as a path, not a value, and would not hit our route unless we use the * in the route.

I used both techniques when I created my own blog in order to be able to keep the old URLs and make them work even though everything else (including the URLs) had been rewritten.

Having data in the URL is not really storing the data. If we navigate to another page, we need to make sure to include the new URL; otherwise, it would be lost. We can use the browser storage instead if we want to store data that we don't need to include every time in the URL.

Implementing browser storage

The browser has a bunch of different ways of storing data in the web browser. They are handled differently depending on what type we use. **Local storage** is scoped to the user's browser window. The data will still be saved if the user reloads the page or even closes the web browser.

The data is also shared across tabs. **Session storage** is scoped to the **Browser** tab; if you reload the tab, the data will be saved, but if you close the tab, the data will be lost. `SessionsStorage` is, in a way, safer to use because we avoid risks with bugs that may occur due to multiple tabs manipulating the same values in storage.

To be able to access the browser storage, we need to use JavaScript. Luckily, we won't need to write the code ourselves.

In .NET 5, Microsoft introduced **Protected Browser Storage**, which uses data protection in ASP.NET Core and is not available in WebAssembly. We can, however, use an open-source library called `Blazored.LocalStorage`, which can be used by both Blazor Server and Blazor WebAssembly.

But we are here to learn new things, right?

So, let's implement an interface so that we can use both versions in our app, depending on which hosting model we are using.

Creating an interface

First, we need an interface that can read and write to storage:

1. In the **Components** project, create a new folder called `Interfaces`.
2. In the new folder, create a new class called `IBrowserStorage.cs`.
3. Replace the content in the file with the following code:

   ```
   namespace Components.Interfaces;

   public interface IBrowserStorage
   {
       Task<T?> GetAsync<T>(string key);
       Task SetAsync(string key, object value);
       Task DeleteAsync(string key);
   }
   ```

Now we have an interface containing get, set, and `delete` methods.

Implementing Blazor Server

For Blazor Server, we will use protected browser storage:

1. In the **BlazorServer** project, add a new folder called `Services`.
2. In the new folder create a new class called `BlogProtectedBrowserStorage.cs`.

(I realize the naming is overkill, but it will be easier to tell the Blazor Server and the Blazor WebAssembly implementation apart because we will soon create another one.)

3. Open the new file and add the following using statements:

    ```
    using Microsoft.AspNetCore.Components.Server.
    ProtectedBrowserStorage;
    using Components.Interfaces;
    ```

4. Replace the class with this one:

    ```
    public class BlogProtectedBrowserStorage : IBrowserStorage
    {
        ProtectedSessionStorage Storage { get; set; }
        public BlogProtectedBrowserStorage(ProtectedSessionStorage storage)
        {
            Storage = storage;
        }
        public async Task DeleteAsync(string key)
        {
            await Storage.DeleteAsync(key);
        }
        public async Task<T?> GetAsync<T>(string key)
        {
            var value = await Storage.GetAsync<T>(key);
            if (value.Success)
            {
                return value.Value;
            }
            else
            {
                return default(T);
            }
        }
        public async Task SetAsync(string key, object value)
        {
            await Storage.SetAsync(key, value);
        }
    }
    ```

The `BlogProtectedBrowserStorage` class implements the `IBrowserStorage` interface for protected browser storage. We inject a `ProtectedSessionStorage` instance and implement the `set`, `get`, and `delete` methods.

5. In `Program.cs`, add the following namespaces:

    ```
    using Components.Interfaces;
    using BlazorServer.Services;
    ```

6. Add the following:

    ```
    builder.Services.
    AddScoped<IBrowserStorage,BlogProtectedBrowserStorage>();
    ```

We are configuring Blazor to return an instance of `BlogProtectedBrowserStorage` when we inject `IBrowserStorage`.

This is the same as we did with the API. We inject different implementations depending on the platform.

Implementing WebAssembly

For Blazor WebAssembly, we will use `Blazored.SessionStorage`:

1. In the **BlazorWebAssembly.Client**, add a NuGet reference to `Blazored.SessionStorage`.
2. Add a new folder called `Services`.
3. In the new folder, create a new class called `BlogBrowserStorage.cs`.
4. Open the new file and replace the content with the following code:

    ```
    using Blazored.SessionStorage;
    using Components.Interfaces;

    namespace BlazorWebAssembly.Client.Services;

    public class BlogBrowserStorage : IBrowserStorage
    {
        ISessionStorageService Storage { get; set; }
        public BlogBrowserStorage(ISessionStorageService storage)
        {
            Storage = storage;
        }
    ```

```csharp
        public async Task DeleteAsync(string key)
        {
            await Storage.RemoveItemAsync(key);
        }
        public async Task<T?> GetAsync<T>(string key)
        {
            return await Storage.GetItemAsync<T>(key);
        }
        public async Task SetAsync(string key, object value)
        {
            await Storage.SetItemAsync(key, value);
        }
}
```

The implementations of ProtectedBrowserStorage and Blazored.SessionStorage are pretty similar to one another. The names of the methods are different, but the parameters are the same.

5. In the Program.cs file, add the following namespaces:

    ```csharp
    using Blazored.SessionStorage;
    using Components.Interfaces;
    using BlazorWebAssembly.Client.Services;
    ```

6. Add the following code just above await builder.Build().RunAsync();:

    ```csharp
    builder.Services.AddBlazoredSessionStorage();
    builder.Services.AddScoped<IBrowserStorage, BlogBrowserStorage>();
    ```

The AddBlazoredSessionStorage extension method hooks up everything so that we can start using the browser session storage.

Then we add our configuration for IBrowserStorage, just as we did with the server, but in this case, we return BlogBrowserStorage when we ask the dependency injection for IBrowserStorage.

Implementing the shared code

We also need to implement some code that calls the services we just created:

1. In the **Components** project, open Pages/Admin/BlogPostEdit.razor. We are going to make a couple of changes to the file.

2. Inject IBrowserStorage:

   ```
   @inject Components.Interfaces.IBrowserStorage _storage
   ```

3. Since we can only run JavaScript calls when doing an action (like a click) or in the OnAfterRender method, let's create an OnAfterRenderMethod:

   ```
   override protected async Task OnAfterRenderAsync(bool firstRender)
   {
       if (firstRender && string.IsNullOrEmpty(Id))
       {
           var saved = await _storage.GetAsync<BlogPost>("EditCurrentPost");
           if (saved != null)
           {
               Post = saved;
       StateHasChanged();
           }
       }
       await base.OnAfterRenderAsync(firstRender);
   }
   ```

   When we load the component and Id is null, this means we are editing a new file and then we can check whether we have a file saved in browser storage.

   This implementation can only have one file in the drafts and only saves new posts. If we were to edit an existing post, it would not save those changes.

   Here is more information on handling protected browser storage with prerender: https://docs.microsoft.com/en-us/aspnet/core/blazor/state-management?view=aspnetcore-7.0&pivots=server.

4. We need our UpdateHTML method to become async. Change the method to look like this:

   ```
   protected async Task UpdateHTMLAsync()
   {
       if (Post.Text != null)
       {
           markDownAsHTML = Markdig.Markdown.ToHtml(Post.Text, pipeline);
           if (string.IsNullOrEmpty(Post.Id))
   ```

```
            {
                await _storage.SetAsync("EditCurrentPost", Post);
            }
        }
    }
```

If Id on the blog post is null, we will store the post in the browser storage. Make sure to change all the references from UpdateHTML to UpdateHTMLAsync.

Make sure to await the call as well in the OnParametersSetAsync method like this:

```
await UpdateHTMLAsync();
```

We are done. Now it's time to test the implementation:

1. Set the **BlazorServer** project as **Startup Project**, and run the project by pressing *Ctrl + F5*.
2. Log in to the site (so we can access the admin tools).
3. Click **Blog posts** followed by **New blog post**.
4. Type anything in the boxes, and as soon as we type something in the text area, it will save the post to storage.
5. Click **Blog posts** (so we navigate away from our blog post).
6. Click **New blog post** and all the information will still be there.
7. Press *F12* to see the browser developer tools. Click **Application | Session storage | https://localhost:portnumber**.

You should see one post with the key EditCurrentPost, and the value of that post should be an encrypted string, as seen in *Figure 11.1*:

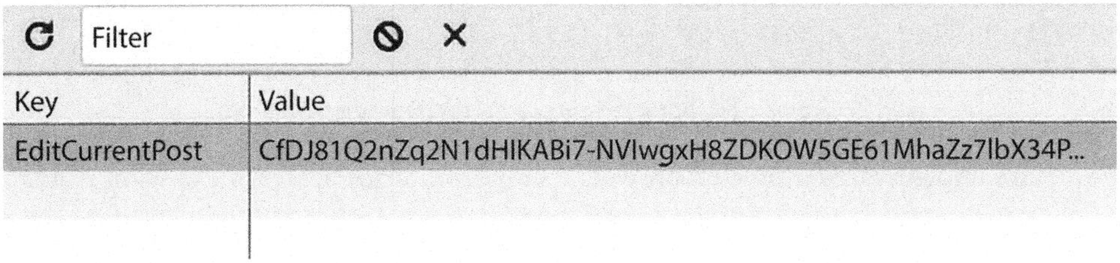

Key	Value
EditCurrentPost	CfDJ81Q2nZq2N1dHIKABi7-NVIwgxH8ZDKOW5GE61MhaZz7lbX34P...

Figure 11.1: The encrypted protected browser storage

Let's test Blazor WebAssembly next:

1. Set the **BlazorWebAssembly.Server** project as **Startup Project** and run the project by pressing *Ctrl + F5*.

2. Log in to the site (so we can access the admin tools).
3. Click **Blog posts** and then **New blog post**.
4. Type anything in the boxes, and as soon as we type something in the text area, it will save the post to storage.
5. Click **Blog posts** (so we navigate away from our blog post).
6. Click **New blog post** and all the information should still be there.
7. Press *F12* to see the browser developer tools. Click **Application** | **Session storage** | **https://localhost:portnumber**.

You should see one post with the key `EditCurrentPost`, and the value of that post should be a JSON string, as seen in *Figure 11.2*.

If we were to change the data in the storage, it would also change in the application, so keep in mind that this is plain text, and the end user can manipulate the data:

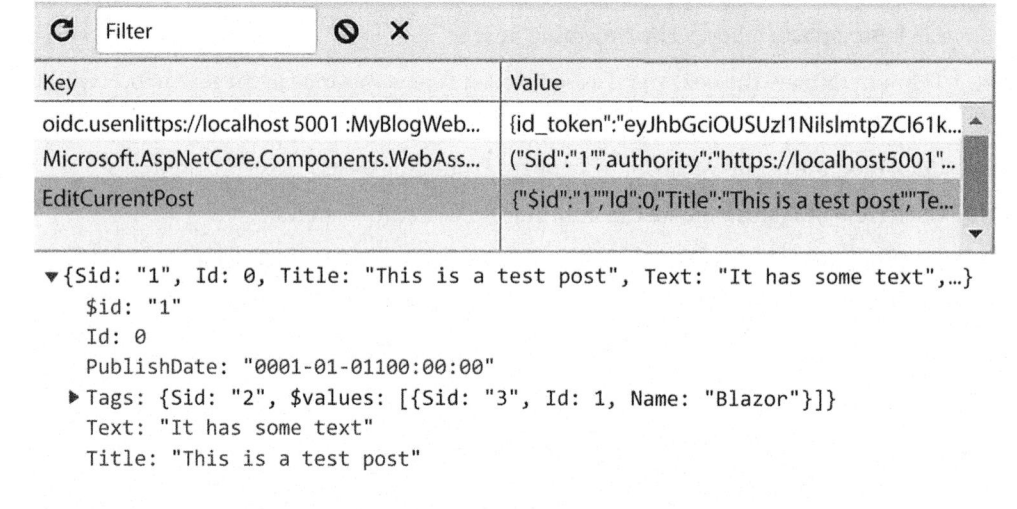

Key	Value
oidc.usenlittps://localhost 5001 :MyBlogWeb...	{id_token":"eyJhbGciOUSUzl1NilsImtpZCl61k...
Microsoft.AspNetCore.Components.WebAss...	("Sid":"1","authority":"https://localhost5001"...
EditCurrentPost	{"$id":"1","Id":0,"Title":"This is a test post","Te...

```
▼{Sid: "1", Id: 0, Title: "This is a test post", Text: "It has some text",…}
    $id: "1"
    Id: 0
    PublishDate: "0001-01-01T00:00:00"
  ▶ Tags: {Sid: "2", $values: [{Sid: "3", Id: 1, Name: "Blazor"}]}
    Text: "It has some text"
    Title: "This is a test post"
```

Figure 11.2: Browser storage that is unprotected

Now we have implemented protected browser storage for Blazor Server and session storage for Blazor WebAssembly.

We only have one way left to go through, so let's make it the most fun.

Using an in-memory state container service

When it comes to in-memory state containers, we simply use dependency injection to keep the instance of the service in memory for the predetermined time (scoped, singleton, transient).

In *Chapter 4*, *Understanding Basic Blazor Components*, we discussed how the scope of dependency injections differs from Blazor Server and Blazor WebAssembly. The big difference for us in this section is the fact that Blazor WebAssembly runs inside the web browser and doesn't have a connection to the server or other users.

To show how the in-memory state works, we will do something that might seem a bit overkill for a blog, but it will be cool to see. When we edit our blog post, we will update all the web browsers connected to our blog in real time (I did say overkill).

We will have to implement that a bit differently, depending on the host. Let's start with Blazor Server.

Implementing real-time updates on Blazor Server

The implementation for Blazor Server can also be used for Blazor WebAssembly. Since WebAssembly is running in our browser, it would only notify the users connected to the site, which would be just you. But it might be good to know that the same way works in Blazor Server as well as Blazor WebAssembly:

1. In the **Components** project, in the **Interfaces** folder, create an interface called `IBlogNotificationService.cs`.

2. Add the following code:

   ```
   using Data.Models;
   namespace Components.Interfaces;

   public interface IBlogNotificationService
   {
       event Action<BlogPost>? BlogPostChanged;
       Task SendNotification(BlogPost post);
   }
   ```

   We have an action that we can subscribe to when the blog post is updated and a method we can call when we update a post.

3. In the **BlazorServer** project, in the **Services** folder, add a new class called `BlazorServerBlogNotificationService.cs`.

   It might seem unnecessary to give the class a name that includes `BlazorServer`, but it makes sure we can easily tell the classes apart.

Replace the content with the following code:

```
using Components.Interfaces;
using Data.Models;

namespace BlazorServer.Services;

public class BlazorServerBlogNotificationService :
IBlogNotificationService
{
    public event Action<BlogPost>? BlogPostChanged;

    public Task SendNotification(BlogPost post)
    {
        BlogPostChanged?.Invoke(post);
        return Task.CompletedTask;
    }
}
```

The code is pretty simple here. If we call `SendNotification`, it will check whether anyone is listening for the `BlogPostChanged` action and whether to trigger the action.

4. In `Program.cs`, add the dependency injection:

```
builder.Services.AddSingleton<IBlogNotificationService,
BlazorServerBlogNotificationService>();
```

Whenever we ask for an instance of the type `IBlogNotificationService`, we will get back an instance of `BlazorServerBlogNotificationService`.

We add this dependency injection as a `Singleton`. I can't stress this enough. When using Blazor Server, this will be the same instance for *ALL* users, so we must be careful when we use `Singleton`.

In this case, we want the service to notify all the visitors of our blog that the blog post has changed.

5. In the **Components** project, open `Post.razor`.
6. Add the following code at the top (or close to the top) of the page:

```
@using Components.Interfaces
@inject IBlogNotificationService notificationService
```

```
@implements IDisposable
```

We add dependency injection for `IBlogNotificationService` and we also need to implement `IDisposable` to avoid any memory leaks.

At the top of the `OnInitializedAsync` method, add the following:

```
notificationService.BlogPostChanged += PostChanged;
```

We added a listener to the event so we know when we should update the information.

7. We also need the `PostChanged` method, so add this code:

    ```
    private async void PostChanged(BlogPost post)
    {
        if (BlogPost?.Id == post.Id)
        {
            BlogPost = post;
            await InvokeAsync(()=>this.StateHasChanged());
        }
    }
    ```

    If the parameter has the same ID as the post we are currently viewing, then replace the content with the post in the event and call `StateHasChanged`.

    Since this is happening on another thread, we need to call `StateHasChanged` using `InvokeAsync` so that it runs on the UI thread.

    The last thing in this component is to stop listening to the updates by implementing the `Dispose` method. Add the following:

    ```
    void IDisposable.Dispose()
    {
    notificationService.BlogPostChanged -= PostChanged;
    }
    ```

    We remove the event listener to avoid any memory leaks.

8. Open the `Pages/Admin/BlogPostEdit.Razor` file.

9. When we make changes to our blog post, we need to send a notification as well. At the top of the file, add the following:

    ```
    @using Components.Interfaces
    ```

```
@inject IBlogNotificationService notificationService
```

We add a namespace and inject our notification service.

10. In the `UpdateHTMLAsync` method, add the following just under the `Post.Text!=null` if statement:

```
await notificationService.SendNotification(Post);
```

Every time we change something, it will now send a notification that the blog post changed. I do realize that it would make more sense to do this when we save a post, but it makes for a much cooler demo.

11. Set the **BlazorServer** project as **Startup Project** and run the project by pressing *Ctrl + F5*.
12. Copy the URL and open another web browser. We should now have two web browser windows open showing us the blog.

In the first window, open a blog post (doesn't matter which one), and in the second window, log in and edit the same blog post.

When we change the text of the blog post in the second window, the change should be reflected in real time in the first window.

I am constantly amazed how a feature that would be a bit tricky to implement without using Blazor only requires 10 steps (not counting the test), and if we didn't prepare for the next step, it would take even fewer steps.

Next, we will implement the same feature for Blazor WebAssembly, but Blazor WebAssembly runs inside the user's web browser. There is no real-time communication built in, as with Blazor Server.

Implementing real-time updates on Blazor WebAssembly

We already have a lot of things in place. We only need to add a real-time messaging system. Since SignalR is both easy to implement and awesome, let's use that.

The first time I used SignalR, my first thought was, wait, it can't be that easy. I must have forgotten something, or something must be missing. Hopefully, we will have the same experience now.

Let's see whether that still holds true today:

1. In the **BlazorWebAssembly.Server** project, add a new folder called `Hubs`.
2. In the new folder create a class called `BlogNotificationHub.cs`.

3. Replace the code with the following:

```
using Data.Models;
using Microsoft.AspNetCore.SignalR;

namespace BlazorWebAssembly.Server.Hubs;

public class BlogNotificationHub : Hub
{
    public async Task SendNotification(BlogPost post)
    {
        await Clients.All.SendAsync("BlogPostChanged", post);
    }
}
```

The class inherits from the Hub class. There is a method called SendNotification. Keep that name in mind; we will come back to that.

We call Clients.All.SendAsync, which means we will send a message called BlogPostChanged with the content of a blog post.

The name BlogPostChanged is also important, so keep that in mind as well.

4. In the Program.cs file add the following:

```
builder.Services.AddSignalR();
```

This adds SignalR.

5. Add the following namespace:

```
using BlazorWebAssembly.Server.Hubs;
```

6. Just above app.MapFallbackToFile("index.html"), add:

```
app.MapHub<BlogNotificationHub>("/BlogNotificationHub");
```

Here, we configure what URL BlogNotificationHub should use. In this case, we are using the same URL as the name of the hub.

The URL here is also important. We will use that in just a bit.

7. In the BlazorWebAssembly.Client add a reference to the NuGet package Microsoft.AspNetCore.SignalR.Client.

8. In the **Services** folder, create a class called `BlazorWebAssemblyBlogNotificationService.cs`.

   In this file, we will implement the SignalR communication.

9. Add the following namespaces:

   ```
   using Microsoft.AspNetCore.Components;
   using Microsoft.AspNetCore.SignalR.Client;
   using Data.Models;
   using Components.Interfaces;
   ```

10. Add this class:

    ```
    public class BlazorWebAssemblyBlogNotificationService :
    IBlogNotificationService, IAsyncDisposable
    {

        public
    BlazorWebAssemblyBlogNotificationService(NavigationManager
    navigationManager)
        {
            _hubConnection = new HubConnectionBuilder()
            .WithUrl(navigationManager.ToAbsoluteUri("/
    BlogNotificationHub"))
            .Build();
            _hubConnection.On<BlogPost>("BlogPostChanged", (post) =>
            {
                BlogPostChanged?.Invoke(post);
            });
            _hubConnection.StartAsync();
        }

        private readonly HubConnection _hubConnection;
        public event Action<BlogPost>? BlogPostChanged;

        public async Task SendNotification(BlogPost post)
        {
    ```

```
            await _hubConnection.SendAsync("SendNotification", post);
        }
        public async ValueTask DisposeAsync()
        {
            await _hubConnection.DisposeAsync();
        }
    }
```

A lot is happening here. The class is implementing IBlogNotificationService and IAsyncDisposable.

In the constructor, we use dependency injection to get NavigationManager, so we can figure out the URL to the server.

Then we configure the connection to the hub. Then we specify the URL to the hub; this should be the same as we specified in *step 7*.

Now we can configure the hub connection to listen for events. In this case, we listen for the BlogPostChanged event, the same name we specified in *step 3*. When someone sends the event, the method we specify will run.

The method, in this case, triggers the event we have in IBlogNotificationService. Then we start the connection. Since the constructor can't be async, we won't await the StartAsync method.

IBlogNotificationService also implements the SendNotification method, and we trigger the event with the same name on the hub, which will result in the hub sending the BlogPostChanged event to all connected clients.

The last thing we do is make sure that we dispose of the hub connection.

11. In the Program.cs file, we need to configure dependency injection. Just above await builder.Build().RunAsync();, add the following:

    ```
    builder.Services.AddSingleton<IBlogNotificationService,
    BlazorWebAssemblyBlogNotificationService>();
    ```

12. Now, it's time to carry out testing, and we do that the same way as for the Blazor Server project.

    Set the **BlazorWebAssembly.Server** project as **Startup Project** and run the project by pressing *Ctrl + F5*.

13. Copy the URL and open another web browser. We should now have two web browser windows open showing us the blog.

    In the first window, open a blog post (it doesn't matter which one), and in the second window, log in and edit the same blog post.

    When we change the text of the blog post in the second window, the change should be reflected in real time in the first window.

In 11 steps (not counting testing), we have implemented real-time communication between the server and client, a Blazor WebAssembly client with .NET code running inside the web browser.

And no JavaScript!

Summary

In this chapter, we learned how we can handle state in our application and how we can use local storage to store data, both encrypted and not. We looked at different ways of doing that, and we also made sure to include SignalR to be able to use real-time communication with the server.

Almost all applications need to save data in some form. Perhaps it can be settings or preferences. The things we covered in the chapter are the most common ones, but we should also know that there are many open-source projects we can use to persist state. We could save the information using IndexedDB.

In the next chapter, we will take a look at debugging. Hopefully, you won't have needed to know how to debug yet!

12
Debugging the Code

In this chapter, we will take a look at debugging. The debugging experience of Blazor is a good one; hopefully, you haven't gotten stuck earlier on in the book and had to jump to this chapter.

Debugging code is an excellent way to solve bugs, understand the workflow, or look at specific values. Blazor has three different ways to debug code, and we will look at each one.

In this chapter, we will cover the following:

- Making things break
- Debugging Blazor Server
- Debugging Blazor WebAssembly
- Debugging Blazor WebAssembly in the browser
- Hot Reload

To debug something, we should first make something break!

Technical requirements

Make sure you have followed the previous chapters or use the Chapter11 folder as a starting point.

You can find the source code for this chapter's end result at https://github.com/PacktPublishing/Web-Development-with-Blazor-Second-Edition/tree/main/Chapter12.

> If you are jumping into this chapter using the code from GitHub, make sure you have added Auth0 account information in the settings files. You can find the instructions in *Chapter 8, Authentication and Authorization*.

Making things break

Edsger W. Dijkstra once said,

"If debugging is the process of removing software bugs, then programming must be the process of putting them in."

This is definitely true in this section because we will add a page that will throw an exception:

1. In the **Components** project, in the `Pages` folder, create a new Razor component called `ThrowException.razor`.

2. Replace the contents of the file with the following code block:

    ```
    @page "/ThrowException"
    <button @onclick="@(()=> {throw new Exception("Something is broken"); })">Throw an exception</button>
    ```

    This page shows a button, and when you press it, it throws an exception.

    Great! We have our application's Ivan Drago (he wants to break you, but we might just beat him with some fancy debugging).

The next step is to take a look at Blazor Server debugging.

Debugging Blazor Server

If you have debugged any .NET application in the past, you will feel right at home. Don't worry; we will go through it if you haven't. Debugging Blazor Server is just as we might expect and is the best debugging experience of the three different types we will cover.

I usually keep my Razor pages in a shared library, and while building my project, I use Blazor Server for two reasons. First, running the project is a bit faster, and second, the debugging experience is better.

Let's give it a try!

1. Set **BlazorServer** as a startup project.
2. Press *F5* to start the project (this time with debugging).
3. Using the web browser, navigate to `https://localhost:portnumber/throwexception` (the port number may vary).
4. Press *F12* to show the web browser developer tools.
5. In the developer tools, click **Console**.

6. Click the **Throw exception** button on our page.

    At this point, Visual Studio should request focus and it should show the exception as shown in *Figure 12.1*:

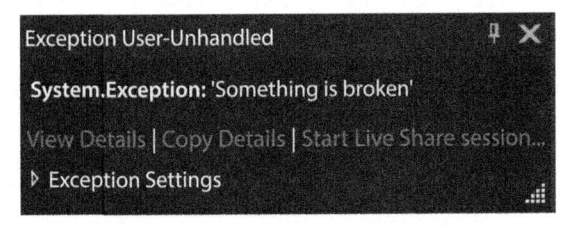

    Figure 12.1: Exception in Visual Studio

7. Press *F5* to continue and switch back to the web browser. We should now be able to see the exception message in the developer tools as shown in *Figure 12.2*:

    ```
    [2021-02-20T19:53:28.737Z] Error: System.Exception: Something is broken   Blazor.server.js:19
        at MyBlog.Shared.Pages.ThrowException.<>c.<BuildRenderTree>b__0_0() in
    C:\Code\B16009\Ch12\MyBlog\MyBlog.Shared\Pages\ThrowException.razor:line 3
        at Microsoft.AspNetCore.Components.EventCallbackWorkItem.InvokeAsync[T](MulticastDelegate
    delegate, T arg)
        at
    Microsoft.AspNetCore.Components.ComponentBase.Microsoft.AspNetCore.Components.IHandleEvent.Ha
    ndleEventAsync(EventCallbackWorkItem callback, Object arg)
        at Microsoft.AspNetCore.Components.RenderTree.Renderer.DispatchEventAsync(UInt64
    eventHandlerId, EventFieldInfo fieldInfo, EventArgs eventArgs)
    ```

    Figure 12.2: Exception in the web browser

As we can see in *Figure 12.1* and *Figure 12.2*, we get the exception both in Visual Studio while debugging and also in the developer tools.

This makes it quite easy to find the problem if there is an exception in an app in production (perish the thought) – that feature has saved us many times.

Now let's try a breakpoint:

1. In Visual Studio, open `Components/Pages/Index.razor`.
2. Anywhere in the `LoadPosts` method, set a breakpoint by clicking the leftmost border (making a red dot appear). We can also add a breakpoint by pressing *F9*.
3. Go back to the web browser and navigate to `https://localhost:portnumber/` (the port number may vary).

Visual Studio should now hit the breakpoint, and by hovering over variables, we should be able to see the current values.

Both breakpoints and exception debugging work as we might expect. Next, we will take a look at debugging Blazor WebAssembly.

Debugging Blazor WebAssembly

Blazor WebAssembly can, of course, be debugged as well, but there are some things we need to think about. Since we have our exception page in our shared library, we can go straight into debugging.

But let's start with breakpoints:

1. Set **BlazorWebAssembly.Server** as the startup project.
2. Press *F5* to debug the project.

Here we can notice the first difference – assuming we still have the breakpoint we set in the *Debugging Blazor Server* section (in the `LoadPosts` method), the breakpoint did not get hit.

Breakpoints won't get hit on the initial page load in Blazor WebAssembly. We need to navigate to another page and back to the index page again for it to hit.

We can't just change the URL, as we could in Blazor Server, simply because that will reload the app again and not trigger the breakpoint because it was an *initial page load*.

Debugging Blazor WebAssembly is made possible by the following line of code in the `launchSettings.json` file:

```
"inspectUri": "{wsProtocol}://{url.hostname}:{url.port}/_framework/debug/
ws-proxy?browser={browserInspectUri}"
```

But it is supplied for us when we create the project, so we don't need to add that manually.

We can also put breakpoints in our `BlazorWebAssembly.Server` server project if we want to, and they will get hit just as we would expect.

Now let's see what happens with our exception:

1. In the web browser, navigate to `https://localhost:portnumber/throwexception`.
2. Click the **Throw exception** button.
3. The unhandled exception won't get hit in Visual Studio. We get the exception in the developer tools in the web browser, as shown in *Figure 12.3*:

```
⊗ ▶ crit:                                    blazor.webassembly.js:1
  Microsoft.AspNetCore.Components.WebAssembly.Rendering.WebAssemblyRende
  rer[100]
       Unhandled exception rendering component: Something is broken
  System.Exception: Something is broken
    at MyBlog.Shared.Pages.ThrowException.<>c.<BuildRenderTree>b__0_0()
  in
  C:\Code\B16009\Ch12\MyBlog\MyBlog.Shared\Pages\ThrowException.razor:li
  ne 3
    at
  Microsoft.AspNetCore.Components.EventCallbackWorkItem.InvokeAsync[Obje
  ct](MulticastDelegate delegate, Object arg)
    at
  Microsoft.AspNetCore.Components.EventCallbackWorkItem.InvokeAsync[Obje
  ct arg)
    at
  Microsoft.AspNetCore.Components.ComponentBase.Microsoft.AspNetCore.Com
  ponents.IHandleEvent.HandleEventAsync(EventCallbackWorkItem callback,
  Object arg)
    at Microsoft.AspNetCore.Components.EventCallback.InvokeAsync(Object
  arg)
    at
  Microsoft.AspNetCore.Components.RenderTree.Renderer.DispatchEventAsync
  (UInt64 eventHandlerId, EventFieldInfo fieldInfo, EventArgs eventArgs)
```

Figure 12.3: WebAssembly error

The debugging experience in Blazor WebAssembly is not as polished as with Blazor Server but it is polished enough to get the job done.

We have one method left to explore – debugging in the web browser.

Debugging Blazor WebAssembly in the web browser

The first debugging experience for Blazor WebAssembly was the ability to debug right in the web browser:

1. In Visual Studio, start the project by pressing *Ctrl + F5* (run without debugging).
2. In the web browser, press *Shift + Alt + D*.

   We will get an error message with instructions on how to start the web browser in debug mode.

I am running Edge, so the way to start Edge would be something like this:

```
msedge --remote-debugging-port=9222 --user-data-dir="C:\Users\
Jimmy\AppData\Local\Temp\blazor-edge-debug" --no-first-run https://
localhost:5001/
```

The `port` and `user-data-dir` values will differ from the example above. Copy the command from your web browser.

3. Press *Win* + *R* and paste the command.
4. A new instance of Chrome or Edge will open. In this new instance, press *Shift* + *Alt* + *D*.
5. We should now see a source tab containing C# code from our project. From here, we can put breakpoints that will be hit and hover over variables.

The debug UI can be seen in *Figure 12.4*:

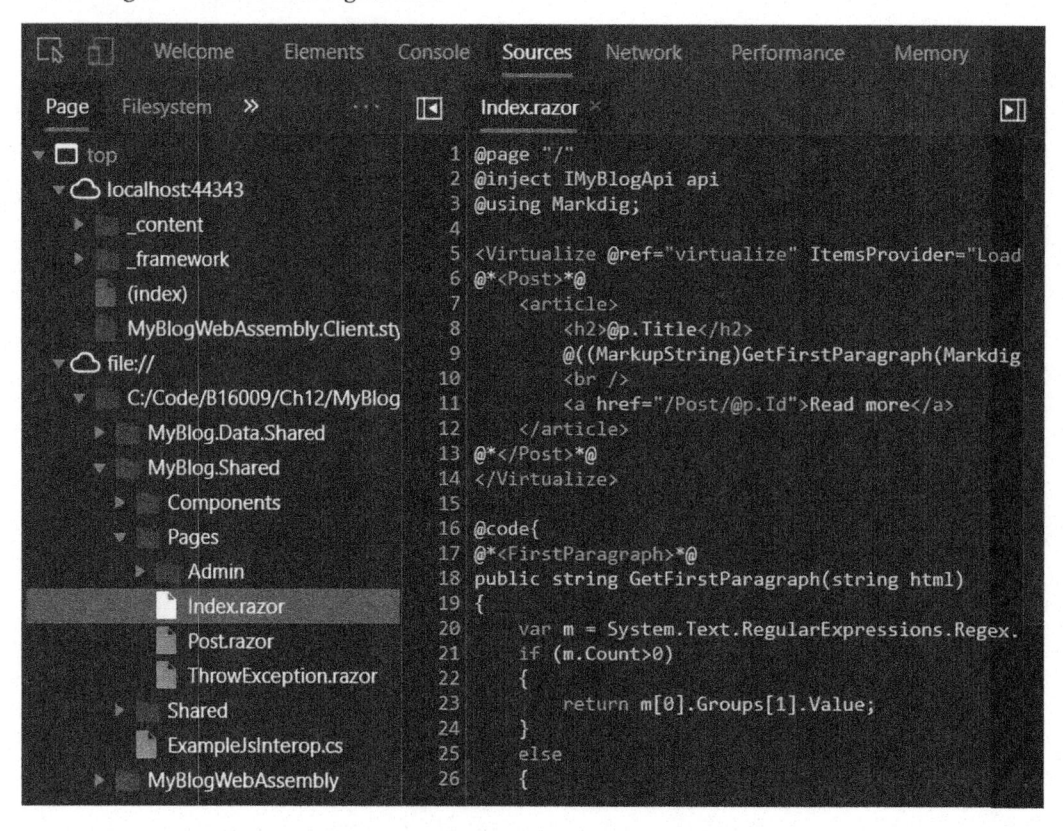

Figure 12.4: Screenshot of the in-browser debug

Debugging C# code in the browser is pretty amazing, but since we have been directly debugging in Visual Studio, I don't see much use for this kind of debugging.

Next, we will look at something that might not fall under debugging but is useful while developing Blazor apps.

Hot Reload

In Visual Studio and the **dotnet CLI**, we can enable **Hot Reload**. This means that as soon as we make changes in our application, our Blazor app will automatically get reloaded, and we will (in most cases) not lose the state.

To set this up, do the following:

1. In Visual Studio, there is a small fire icon. We can use this button to trigger hot reload manually.

    It is only clickable when the application is running (with or without debugging).

    We can also click on the small arrow just to the right of the fire icon and select **Hot Reload on File Save**.

2. Select the **Hot Reload on File Save** option.
3. Start the project by pressing *Ctrl + F5*.
4. In the web browser, bring up the counter page by adding /counter to the URL.
5. Make a change to the Components/Pages/Counter.razor file and click **Save**.

    Our web browser should now reload, and the change will be shown.

At the time of writing, Hot Reload does save time and is pretty amazing. However, there are some cases where our site will behave oddly, and then we need to rebuild. Therefore, you need to keep in mind that if there is an unexplainable issue, you will need to build the project again.

This also works from the command line by running the following command:

```
dotnet watch
```

There are a couple of limitations to this method, though:

- It doesn't work with Blazor WebAssembly running an ASP.NET server backend (as we have in our project). For this to work, we need to reload the browser manually.
- The state of the application will restart.
- Changes in a shared project won't be reflected.

So, for our setup, this feature isn't very beneficial, but it is really good if our project doesn't fall into any of the previously mentioned limitations.

Summary

This chapter looked at different ways to debug our Blazor application. There will always be moments when we need to step through the code to find a bug or see what is happening. When these moments are upon us, Visual Studio delivers world-class functionality to help us achieve our goals.

The nice thing is that debugging Blazor applications, whether it's Blazor Server or Blazor WebAssembly, will work as expected from a Microsoft product. We get C# errors that are (in most cases) easy to understand and solve.

In the next chapter, we will look at testing our Blazor components.

13
Testing

In this chapter, we will take a look at testing. Writing tests for our projects will help us develop things rapidly.

We can run the tests to ensure we haven't broken anything with the latest change, and also, we don't have to invest our time in testing the components manually since it is all done by the tests. Testing will improve the quality of the product since we'll know that things that worked earlier still function as they should.

But writing tests for UI elements isn't always easy; the most common way is to spin up the site, use tools that click on buttons, and then read the output to determine whether things work. The upside of this method is that we can test our site on different browsers and devices. The downside is that it usually takes a lot of time to do these tests. We need to spin up the website, start a web browser, verify the test, close the web browser, and repeat for the next test.

We can use this method in Blazor as well (as with any ASP.NET site), but with Blazor, we have other opportunities when it comes to testing.

Steve Sanderson created an embryo of a test framework for Blazor that Microsoft MVP Egil Hansen picked up and continued the development of.

Egil's framework is called **bUnit** and has become an industry standard in the Blazor community for testing Blazor components.

This chapter covers the following topics:

- What is bUnit?
- Setting up a test project

- Mocking the API
- Writing tests

Technical requirements

Make sure you have read the previous chapters or use the Chapter12 folder as a starting point.

You can find the source code for this chapter's result at https://github.com/PacktPublishing/Web-Development-with-Blazor-Second-Edition/tree/main/Chapter13.

> If you are jumping into this chapter using the code from GitHub, make sure you have added Auth0 account information in the settings files. You can find the instructions in *Chapter 8, Authentication and Authorization*.

What is bUnit?

As mentioned in the introduction, some tests spin up web browsers to test pages/components, but bUnit takes another approach.

bUnit is made specifically for Blazor. It can define and set up tests using C# or Razor syntax. It can mock JavaScript interop as well as Blazor's authentication and authorization. To make our components more testable, sometimes we need to think about these things from the beginning or make minor changes to our code.

bUnit doesn't rely on a web browser but renders the output internally and exposes it to us so that we can test against predefined outputs.

It's time for us to get our hands dirty, so let's create a test project.

Setting up a test project

To be able to run tests, we need a test project:

1. To install the bUnit templates, open PowerShell and run the following command:

    ```
    dotnet new install bunit.template
    ```

2. Check which is the latest version of the templates on the bUnit web page: https://bunit.dev/.

3. In Visual Studio, right-click **MyBlog** solution and choose **Add | New Project**.

Chapter 13   237

4. Search for **bUnit**, select **bUnit Test Project** in the results, and then click **Next**. Sometimes it takes time to find a template, and we can also change the **Project Type** dropdown to **bUnit** to find the template. We might need to reboot Visual Studio to find it.

5. Name the project MyBlog.Tests, leave the location as is, and click **Next**.

6. Select **xUnit** as the unit test framework and click **Create**.

7. At the time of writing, we also need to upgrade the test project to .NET7. Click on the MyBlog.Test project to open the project file.

    Change:

    ```
    <TargetFramework>net6.0</TargetFramework>
    ```

    To:

    ```
    <TargetFramework>net7.0</TargetFramework>
    ```

Great! We now have a test project.

Before we mock the API, let's look at the different methods available to us so we can get a feel for how bUnit works.

In MyBlog.Tests, we should have the following four files:

- _Imports.razor contains the namespaces that we want all of our Razor files to have access to.
- Counter.razor is a copy of the same Counter components we get by default in the Blazor template.
- CounterCSharpTest.cs contains tests written in C#.
- CounterRazorTest.razor contains tests written in Razor.

Let's start with the CounterCSharpTest.cs file, which contains two tests: one that checks that the counter starts at 0 and one that clicks the button and verifies the counter is now 1. These two simple tests make sense for testing the Counter component.

The CounterStartsAtZero test looks like this:

```
[Fact]
public void CounterStartsAtZero()
{
    // Arrange
    var cut = RenderComponent<Counter>();
```

```
        // Assert that content of the paragraph shows counter
        // at zero
        cut.Find("p").MarkupMatches("<p>Current count: 0</p>");
}
```

Let's break this down. The Fact attribute tells the test runner that this is a *normal* test with no parameters. We can also use the Theory attribute to tell the test runner that the test method needs parameter values, but we don't need parameters for this use case.

First, we arrange the test. Simply put, we set up everything we need to do the test. Egil uses cut as the component's name, which stands for **component under testing**.

We run the RenderComponent method and pass in the component type, which is the Counter component in this case. Next, we assert whether the component outputs the correct thing or not. We use the Find method to find the first paragraph tag and then verify that the HTML looks like <p>Current count: 0</p>.

The second test is a bit more advanced, and it looks like this:

```
[Fact]
public void ClickingButtonIncrementsCounter()
{
    // Arrange
    var cut = RenderComponent<Counter>();
    // Act - click button to increment counter
    cut.Find("button").Click();
    // Assert that the counter was incremented
    cut.Find("p").MarkupMatches("<p>Current count: 1</p>");
}
```

As with the previous test, we start arranging by rendering our Counter component. The next step is acting, where we click the button. We look for the button and then click the button in our Counter component. There is only one button, so in this case, it's safe to look for the button this way.

Then it's time to assert again, and we check the markup in the same way as the previous test, but we look for 1 instead of 0.

There is also another alternative where we can write out tests with Razor syntax. If we look at the CounterRazorTests.razor files, we can see the exact same tests but with different syntax:

```
        [Fact]
```

```
    public void CounterStartsAtZero()
    {
        // Arrange
        var cut = Render(@<Counter />);

        // Assert that content of the paragraph shows counter at zero
        cut.Find("p").MarkupMatches(@<p>Current count: 0</p>);
    }
```

This does the same thing and is only a matter of preference. I prefer using the Razor version; it is easier to read, and it's also easier to add parameters to our component while testing.

Now let's run the tests and see whether they pass:

1. In Visual Studio, bring up **Test Explorer** by searching for it using *Ctrl* + *Q*. We can also find it in **View | Test Explorer**.
2. Click **Run All Test** in the view. Test Explorer should look like *Figure 13.1*:

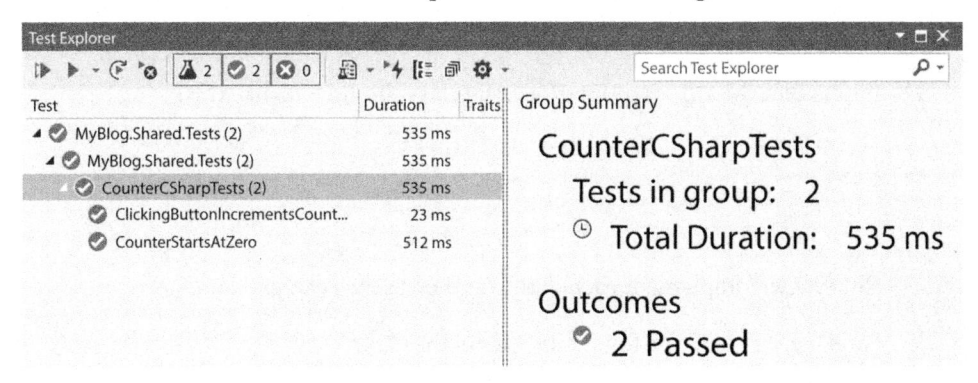

Figure 13.1: Visual Studio Test Explorer

Wonderful! Now our first test is running and hopefully passing.

Next, we will take a look at mocking the API.

Mocking the API

There are different ways to test our application. Testing the API is outside the scope of this book, but we still need to test the components, which are dependent on the API. We could spin up the API and test against the API, but in this case, we are only interested in testing the Blazor component.

We can then mock the API or create a fake copy of the API that doesn't read from the database but reads from a predefined dataset. This way, we always know what the output should be.

Luckily, the interface we created for our API is just what we need to create a mock API.

We won't implement 100% of the tests for the project, so we don't have to mock all the methods. Please feel free to implement tests for all methods as an exercise at the end of the chapter.

There are two ways we can implement the mock API. We could spin up an in-memory database, but to keep things simple, we will choose the other option and generate posts when we ask for them:

1. In the `MyBlog.Tests` project, add a project reference to the **Components** project.
2. Create a new class called `BlogApiMock.cs`.
3. Add the following namespaces:

    ```
    using Data.Models;
    using Data.Models.Interfaces;
    using System.Collections.Generic;
    using System.Threading.Tasks;
    ```

4. Implement the `IBlogApi` interface; the class should look like this:

    ```
    internal class BlogApiMock : IBlogApi
    {
    }
    ```

    Now we will implement each of the methods so we can get data.

5. For `BlogPost`, add the following code in the class:

    ```csharp
    public async Task<BlogPost?> GetBlogPostAsync(string id)
    {
        BlogPost post = new()
        {
            Id = id,
            Text = $"This is a blog post no {id}",
            Title = $"Blogpost {id}",
            PublishDate = DateTime.Now,
            Category = await GetCategoryAsync("1"),
        };
        post.Tags.Add(await GetTagAsync("1"));
        post.Tags.Add(await GetTagAsync("2"));
    ```

```
        return post;
}
public Task<int> GetBlogPostCountAsync()
{
    return Task.FromResult(10);
}
public async Task<List<BlogPost>?> GetBlogPostsAsync(int
numberofposts, int startindex)
    {
        List<BlogPost> list = new();
        for (int a = 0; a < numberofposts; a++)
        {
            list.Add(await GetBlogPostAsync($"{startindex + a}"));
        }
        return list;
    }
```

When we get a blog post, we create a blog post and fill it with predefined information we can use later in our tests. The same thing goes for getting a list of blog posts.

We also say that we have a total of 10 blog posts in the database.

For categories, add the following code:

```
    public async Task<List<Category>?> GetCategoriesAsync()
    {
        List<Category> list = new();
        for (int a = 0; a < 10; a++)
        {
            list.Add(await GetCategoryAsync($"{a}"));
        }
        return list;
}
    public Task<Category?> GetCategoryAsync(string id)
    {
        return Task.FromResult(new Category() { Id = id, Name =
$"Category {id}" });
    }
```

Here, we do the same thing: we create categories named Category followed by a number.

6. The same thing goes for tags; add the following code:

```
public Task<Tag?> GetTagAsync(string id)
{
    return Task.FromResult(new Tag() { Id = id, Name = $"Tag {id}" });
}
public async Task<List<Tag>?> GetTagsAsync()
{
    List<Tag> list = new();
    for (int a = 0; a < 10; a++)
    {
        list.Add(await GetTagAsync($"{a}"));
    }
    return list;
}
```

We will not add tests for other methods in the API. We do need to add them to the mock class to fulfill the interface.

7. Add the following methods:

```
public Task InvalidateCacheAsync()
{
    return Task.CompletedTask;
}

public Task<BlogPost?> SaveBlogPostAsync(BlogPost item)
{
    return Task.FromResult(item);
}

public Task<Category?> SaveCategoryAsync(Category item)
{
    return Task.FromResult(item);
}

public Task<Tag?> SaveTagAsync(Tag item)
```

```
        {
            return Task.FromResult(item);
        }

        public Task DeleteBlogPostAsync(string id)
        {
            return Task.CompletedTask;
        }

        public Task DeleteCategoryAsync(string id)
        {
            return Task.CompletedTask;
        }

        public Task DeleteTagAsync(string id)
        {
            return Task.CompletedTask;
        }
```

We now have a mock API that does the same thing repeatedly so we can make reliable tests.

Writing tests

Time to write some tests. As I mentioned earlier in the chapter, we won't create tests for the entire site; we will leave that to you to finish later if you want to. This is to get a feel for how to write tests:

1. In the MyBlog.Tests project, create a new folder called Pages. This is just so we can keep a bit of a structure (the same folder structure as the project we are testing).

2. Select the Pages folder and create a new Razor component called IndexTest.razor.

3. In the _Imports file, add the following namespaces:

   ```
   @using Components.Pages
   @using Data.Models.Interfaces
   @using Components.RazorComponents
   ```

4. In the IndexTest.razor file, inherit from TestContext by adding the following code:

   ```
   @inherits TestContext
   ```

5. Now we will add the test. Add the following code:

```csharp
[Fact(DisplayName ="Checks that the Index component shows 10 posts")]
    public void Shows10Blogposts()
    {
        // Act
        var cut = Render(@<Index />);

        // Assert that the content has 10 article tags (each representing a blogpost)
        Assert.Equal(10,cut.FindAll("article").Count());
    }
```

We give our test a display name so we understand what it does. The test is pretty simplistic; we know we have 10 blog posts from the mock API. We also know that each blog post is rendered within an `article` tag. We find all `article` tags and make sure we have 10 in total.

Since we are using injection, we need to configure the dependency injection, which we can do in the constructor.

6. We need to add the `IndexTest` method:

```csharp
public IndexTest()
{
    Services.AddScoped<IBlogApi, BlogApiMock>();
}
```

This method will run when the class is created, and here, we declare that if the components ask for an instance of `BlogApi`, it will return an instance of our mock API.

This works the same way as with Blazor Server, where we return an API that talks directly to the database, and with Blazor WebAssembly, where we return an instance of the API that talks to a web API.

In this case, it will return our mock API that returns data that is easy to test. Now we need to run the actual test.

7. Delete the default tests:

`Counter.razor`

CounterCSharpTests.cs

CounterRazorTests.cs

8. In Visual Studio, bring up Test Explorer by searching for it using *Ctrl* + *Q*. We can also find it in **View** | **Test Explorer**.

Run our tests to see whether we get a green light, as shown in *Figure 13.2*:

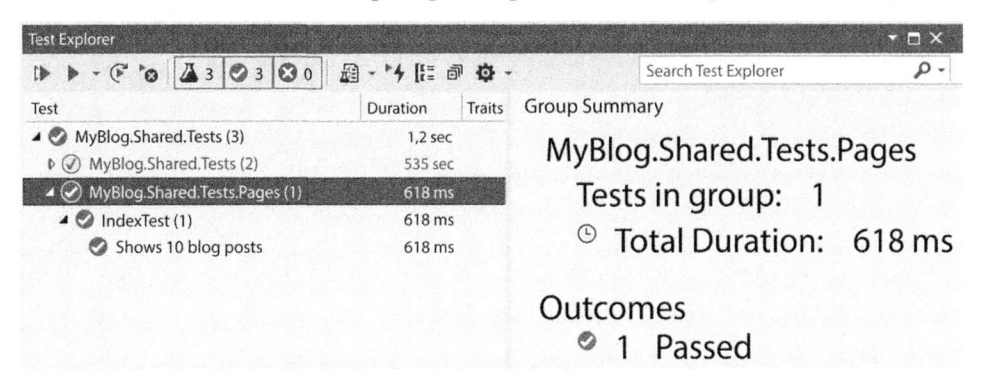

Figure 13.2: Test Explorer with IndexTest

Now we have a test that checks that 10 posts are rendered.

bUnit is an excellent framework for testing, and the fact that it is explicitly written for Blazor so that it takes advantage of Blazor's power makes it amazing to work with.

Now we have a simplistic test testing our blog, but bUnit has support for more advanced features, such as authentication.

Authentication

Using bUnit, we can test authentication and authorization.

It is, however, not the components themselves that are doing the authentication. We added AuthorizeRouteView to App.razor in *Chapter 8, Authentication and Authorization*, so testing that in individual components won't make a difference.

But we can use AuthorizeView, for example, and we do have it in our blog in the LoginStatus component, which displays a login link when we are not authorized and a logout link when we are authorized. Please feel free to add these tests as we did in the previous section, or use them as a reference.

We can use the `AddTestAuthorization` method to authorize our tests like this:

```
[Fact(DisplayName ="Checks if log in is showed")]
public void ShouldShowLogin()
{
    // Arrange
    this.AddTestAuthorization();
    // Act
    var cut = Render(@<LoginStatus />);

    // Assert that there is a link with the text Log in
    Assert.Equal("Log in",cut.Find("a").InnerHtml);
}
```

This method adds `TestAuthorization` but is not authorized. The page will then display a link with the text "Log in". To test when the user is authorized, we just set the user as authorized:

```
[Fact(DisplayName ="Checks if logout is showed")]
public void ShouldShowLogout()
{
    // Arrange
    var authContext = this.AddTestAuthorization();
    authContext.SetAuthorized("Testuser", AuthorizationState.Authorized);

    // Act
    var cut = Render(@<LoginStatus />);

    // Assert that there is a link with the text Log out
    Assert.Equal("Log out",cut.Find("a").InnerHtml);
}
```

We can add claims, roles, and much more. The user we utilize for testing does not correlate with the users or roles in the database; the authorization is mocked by bUnit.

Authentication and authorization could be tricky to test, but using bUnit is really simple. Testing JavaScript is a bit harder to do, but bUnit has great support for that.

Testing JavaScript

Testing JavaScript is not supported by bUnit, which is understandable. We can, however, test the interop ourselves.

In this book, we have used the .NET 5 syntax for our JavaScript. In our Components\RazorComponent\ItemList.razor component, we make a JavaScript interop to confirm the deletion of an item.

The JavaScript call looks like this:

```
jsmodule = await jsRuntime.InvokeAsync<IJSObjectReference>("import", "/_content/Components/RazorComponents/ItemList.razor.js");
return await jsmodule.InvokeAsync<bool> ("showConfirm", "Are you sure?");
```

We make sure that we load the JavaScript module and then execute the showConfirm method.

JavaScript testing in bUnit can be done in two modes – strict and loose. The default value is strict, so we need to specify every module and every method.

If we choose loose, all methods will just return the default value. For a Boolean, it would return false, for example.

To test the preceding JavaScript call, we can do that by adding something like this:

```
var moduleInterop = this.JSInterop.SetupModule("/_content/Components/RazorComponents/ItemList.razor.js");
    var showconfirm = moduleInterop.Setup<bool>("showConfirm", "Are you sure?").SetResult(true);
```

We set up a module with the same path to JavaScript as before. Then we specify the method and any parameters.

Lastly, we specify what the result should be. In this case, we return true, which would return from JavaScript if we want to delete the item. We could also verify if the JavaScript method is being called. A complete example for testing this in the ItemList component would look like this:

```
@using Data.Models;
@inherits TestContext

@code {
    [Fact(DisplayName = "Test if js method 'showConfirm' is called upon using JS interop")]
```

```csharp
    public void ShouldShowConfirm()
    {
        // Arrange
        var moduleInterop = this.JSInterop.SetupModule("/_content/Components/RazorComponents/ItemList.razor.js");
        moduleInterop.Setup<bool>("showConfirm", "Are you sure?").SetResult(true);

        var cut = RenderComponent<ItemList<BlogPost>>(parameters => parameters
            .Add(_ => _.Items, new() { new BlogPost() { Title = "Title" } })
            .Add(_ => _.ItemTemplate, blogpost => $"<span>{blogpost.Title}</span>"));

        // Act
        var buttons = cut.FindAll("button");
        buttons.First(_ => _.ClassList.Contains("btn-danger")).Click();

        // Assert
        JSInterop.VerifyInvoke("showConfirm");
    }
}
```

Great job! We now have tests in our project. Even though we aren't covering all the components, we should have all the building blocks to complete the tests.

If you want to learn more about bUnit, check out:

https://bunit.dev/docs/getting-started/index.html.

Their documentation is fantastic.

Summary

In this chapter, we looked at testing our application. We looked at how we can mock an API to make reliable tests. We also covered how to test JavaScript interop as well as authentication.

Tests can speed up our development and, most importantly, build quality. With bUnit combined with dependency injection, it is easy to build tests that can help us test our components.

Since we can test every component by itself, we don't have to log in, navigate to a specific place on our site, and then test the entire page as many other testing frameworks would have us do.

Now our site contains reusable components, authentication, APIs, Blazor Server, Blazor WebAssembly, authentication, shared code, JavaScript interop, state management, and tests. We only have one more thing to do: ship it!

In the next chapter, *Chapter 14, Deploy to Production*, it's time to ship.

Join our community on Discord

Join our community's Discord space for discussions with the author and other readers:

`https://packt.link/WebDevBlazor2e`

14
Deploy to Production

In this chapter, we will take a look at the different options we have when deploying our Blazor application to production. Since there are many different options, going through them all would be a book all by itself.

We won't go into detail, but rather cover the different things we need to think about so that we can deploy to any provider.

In the end, deploying is what we need to do to make use of what we build.

In this chapter, we will cover the following:

- Continuous delivery options
- Hosting options

Technical requirements
This chapter is about general deployment, so we won't need any code.

Continuous delivery options
When deploying anything to production, we should think about making sure to remove uncertain factors. For example, if we are deploying from our own machine, how do we know it's the latest version? How do we know that our teammates didn't recently solve a problem and we don't have the fix in our branch? To be honest, how do we even know that the version in source control is the same in production, or if the version in production even exists in source control?

This is where **Continuous Integration** and **Continuous Delivery/Deployment (CI/CD)** come into the picture. We make sure that something else makes the deployment to production. Entire books could be written on deployment, so we won't go that deep into the subject.

GitHub Actions and Azure DevOps (or Azure Pipelines) are two products from Microsoft for CI/CD. There are many more, such as Jenkins, TeamCity, and GitLab – the list is long. If the CI/CD system we are currently using supports deploying ASP.NET, it will be able to handle Blazor because, in the end, Blazor is just an ASP.NET site.

If we have tests (which we should have), we should also make sure to set up tests as part of our CI/CD pipeline. The nice thing is that we don't need to add any specific hardware to test our components; it will work if our CI/CD pipeline can run unit tests.

In our setup at work, we build and run all tests when we do a pull request. If the build and tests pass, someone else in the team does a code review and approves the change. If the team member approves the change, it will then trigger a release, and the release deploys the site to our test environment. Our testers run through the test protocols and approve the changes.

When the sprint is over, the tester will run through the complete test protocol and approve the site. We then trigger another release that will deploy the site to production.

Since Blazor is ASP.NET, nothing is stopping us from going even further with the automated testing of our site.

There is also something called **wasm-tools**, which we will take a look at in *Chapter 16, Going Deeper into WebAssembly*.

Hosting options

When it comes to hosting Blazor, there are many options. Any cloud service that can host ASP.NET Core sites should be able to run Blazor without any problems.

We need to think about some things, so let's go through the options one by one.

Hosting Blazor Server

If the cloud provider can enable/disable WebSockets, we want to enable them since that's the protocol used by SignalR. Depending on the load, we might want to use a service such as Azure SignalR Service, which will take care of all the connections and enable our application to handle more users.

Sometimes, the cloud provider may support .NET Core 3.x but not support .NET 7 out of the box. But don't worry; by making sure to publish our application with the deployment mode as self-contained, we make sure the deployment also adds any files necessary to run the project (this might not be true for all hosting providers).

This is also a good thing to do to make sure that we are running on the exact framework version we expect.

Hosting Blazor WebAssembly

If we are using a .NET Core backend (like we do for the blog), we are hosting a .NET Core website, so the same rules apply as with hosting Blazor Server. For our blog, we also added SignalR, so we need WebSockets enabled as well.

There are some other considerations when it comes to hosting Blazor WebAssembly, such as these:

- We may need a .NET Core backend.
- The data we are getting may be static or hosted somewhere else.

In either of these cases, we can host our application in Azure Static Web Apps or even GitHub Pages.

Hosting on IIS

We can also host our application on **Internet Information Server (IIS)**. Install the hosting bundle, and it will also make sure to include the ASP.NET Core IIS module if installed on a machine with IIS.

You need to make sure to enable the WebSocket protocol on the server.

We currently run our sites on IIS and use Azure DevOps to deploy our sites. Since we are using Blazor Server, the downtime is very evident. As soon as the web loses the SignalR connection, the site will show a reconnect message.

For the sites we are using, there is about 8 to 10 seconds of downtime when deploying a new version, which is pretty quick.

Summary

In this chapter, we talked about why we should use CI/CD since it makes a huge difference in ensuring the quality of the application. We looked at some of the things we need to do to run our Blazor app on any cloud provider supporting .NET 7.

Deploying is perhaps the most important step when it comes to an application. Without deploying our application, it's just code. With the things we mentioned in this chapter, such as CI/CD, hosting, and deployment, we are now ready to deploy the code.

In the next chapter, we will dig deeper into how we can port a current site, use Blazor with other technologies, or use other technologies with Blazor.

15

Moving from, or Combining, an Existing Site

In this chapter, we will take a look at how we can combine different technologies and frameworks with Blazor.

What if we already have a site?

There are different options when it comes to moving from an existing site; the first question is, do we want to move from it, or do we want to combine it with the new technology?

Microsoft has a history of making it possible for technology to co-exist, and this is what this chapter is all about.

How can we use Angular and React in our Blazor site, or how can we introduce Blazor into an existing Angular and React site?

In this chapter, we will cover the following:

- Introducing Web Components
- Exploring Custom Elements
- Exploring the Blazor Component
- Adding Blazor to an Angular site
- Adding Blazor to a React site
- Adding Blazor to MVC/Razor Pages

- Adding Web Components to a Blazor site
- Migrating from Web Forms

Combining technologies can be very useful, either because we can't convert a whole site in one go or because other technologies are a better fit for what we are trying to accomplish.

Having said that, I prefer using one technology on my site, not mixing Blazor with Angular or React. But during a migration period or if our team is mixed, there are benefits to mixing.

There is a cost to mixing technologies, which we will look at throughout the chapter.

While writing this chapter, revisiting Angular and React, I must take the opportunity to say how much I love the Razor syntax. React is JavaScript with an HTML tags inside, and Angular has templates, which I find pretty nice and reminds me of what the Razor syntax looks like.

However, there are a lot of things involved, almost 300 MB node modules, npm, TypeScript, and WebPack. Well, the list is long.

I love working with Blazor because I don't need to work with everything I just mentioned. In my opinion, Blazor has the best syntax out of the three options.

Technical requirements

This chapter is a reference chapter and is not connected in any way with the other chapters of the book.

You can find the source code for this chapter's end result at `https://github.com/PacktPublishing/Web-Development-with-Blazor-Second-Edition/tree/main/Chapter15`.

Introducing Web Components

To work with JavaScript, whether it's bringing JavaScript to Blazor or bringing Blazor into JavaScript, we can use a technology called Web Components.

Web Components are a set of web platform APIs that allow us to create new, custom, reusable HTML tags. They are packaged in an encapsulated way, and we can use them very similarly to how we use components in Blazor.

The really nice thing is that we can use them in any JavaScript library or framework that supports HTML.

Web Components are built on top of existing web standards like shadow DOM, ES modules, HTML templates, and custom elements.

Chapter 15 257

We will also recognize some of these technologies or variations of them in Blazor. Shadow DOM is the same as Blazor's Render tree, and ES Modules are the type of JavaScript modules we did in *Chapter 10, JavaScript Interop*.

The technology we are going to take a look at in this chapter is **Custom Elements**.

Exploring Custom Elements

To bring Blazor into an existing Angular or React site, we use a feature called `CustomElements`. It was introduced as an experimental feature in .NET 6 and is now part of the framework in .NET 7.

The idea is to create parts of your site in Blazor without having to migrate fully over to Blazor.

For this feature to work, we need to have an ASP.NET backend or manually make sure the _framework files are available. This is so that we can serve the Blazor framework files.

There are two ways of running **CustomElements**; we can run it as Blazor WebAssembly or as the Blazor Server. Since we are adding Blazor to a client framework like React or Angular, the most relevant method is to run it as Blazor WebAssembly. Therefore, the samples in these first sections will be for Blazor WebAssembly.

In the GitHub repo, there is a folder called `CustomElements` in which you will find the code for the projects, from which we will see sample code in this chapter.

It is worth mentioning that since the components are being served and used on the client, there is nothing that hinders us (or people who mean us harm) from decompiling the code (if we are using WebAssembly). This is something client-side developers face all the time, but it is worth mentioning again.

Exploring the Blazor Component

The first thing we need to try out is a Blazor Component. I have created a counter component inside a Blazor WebAssembly project named `BlazorCustomElements`.

The default template comes with a lot of things, and the repo project is stripped to the bare minimum, so it is easy to understand.

The component is nothing new from what we have seen in the book previously; it's a counter component with a parameter that sets how much the counter should count up. It looks like this:

```
<h1>Blazor counter</h1>

<p role="status">Current count: @currentCount</p>
```

```
<p>Increment amount: @IncrementAmount</p>

<button class="btn btn-primary" @onclick="IncrementCount">Click me</button>

@code {
    private int currentCount = 0;

    [Parameter] public int IncrementAmount { get; set; } = 1;

    private void IncrementCount()
    {
        currentCount += IncrementAmount;
    }
}
```

The project also needs a reference to the `NuGet` package:

Microsoft.AspNetCore.Components.CustomElements.

In the `Program.cs`, we need to register the Component/Custom Element like this:

```
builder.RootComponents.RegisterCustomElement<Counter>("my-blazor-counter");
```

That's it for the Blazor project.

Now it's time to use our custom element.

Adding Blazor to an Angular site

Let's look at how we can add Blazor to an existing Angular site. This demo is based on the ASP.NET Core with Angular template in Visual Studio.

The project is called `AngularProject`.

First, we need a reference to our Blazor library. I added the `BlazorCustomElement` project as a reference.

We need a reference to the **Microsoft.AspNetCore.Components.WebAssembly.Server** NuGet package; this is to be able to serve the framework files.

To make our site serve the framework files, we need to add the following to the `Program.cs`:

```
app.UseBlazorFrameworkFiles();
```

By default, Angular will be upset when we add our custom element because it does not recognize the tag. To fix this, we need to tell Angular that we are using custom elements. In the `ClientApp/src/app/app.module.ts`, add the following things:

```
import { CUSTOM_ELEMENTS_SCHEMA, NgModule } from '@angular/core';
```

Make sure to replace the row that already has an import for `NgModule`.

A bit further down in the same file, add:

```
schemas: [
  CUSTOM_ELEMENTS_SCHEMA // Tells Angular we will have custom tags in
our templates
]
```

Now Angular is okay with having custom elements.

Next, it's time to add our component. In the `ClientApp/src/app/Home/Home.component.html` we add our custom tag:

```
<my-blazor-counter [attr.increment-amount]="10"></my-blazor-counter>
```

In this case, we set the `increment-amount` parameter to 10, which will increase the counter by 10 every time we click it.

To make this all work, we need to load a couple of JavaScript scripts. In the `ClientApp/src/index.html`, we need to add:

```
    <script src="_content/Microsoft.AspNetCore.Components.CustomElements/
BlazorCustomElements.js"></script>
    <script src="_framework/blazor.webassembly.js"></script>
```

We have one last thing we need to fix. When running the Angular project, it spins up a developer server. Actually, it spins up two: one for the ASP.NET backend and one for the Angular frontend. We need to make the Angular server send all the framework requests to the ASP.NET backend.

In the default project template, this is already done for the `/weatherforecast` path. Add the following code to the `ClientApp/proxy.conf.js` file:

```
context: [
"/weatherforecast",
```

```
    "/_framework",
    "/_content",
],
```

We tell the developer server that if there is a request going to weatherforcast, _framework, or _content, we want to redirect that request to the ASP.NET backend.

We now have a working Angular/Blazor WebAssembly hybrid. I was honestly amazed at how easy and straightforward this was the first time I tried it. It makes it so easy to include some Blazor components on your Angular site, so you can convert it in to Blazor step by step, component by component.

Next, we will do the same using a React site.

Adding Blazor to a React site

Adding Blazor to a React site is very similar to Angular. This demo is based on the ASP.NET Core with React template in Visual Studio. The project is called ReactProject.

First, we need a reference to our Blazor library, and I added the BlazorCustomElement project as a reference.

We need a reference to the **Microsoft.AspNetCore.Components.WebAssembly.Server** NuGet package; this is to be able to serve the framework files.

To make our site serve the framework files, we need to add the following to the Program.cs:

```
app.UseBlazorFrameworkFiles();
```

Next, it's time to add our component. In the ClientApp/src/components/Home.js, we add our custom tag:

```
<my-blazor-counter increment-amount="10"></my-blazor-counter>
```

In this case, we set the increment-amount parameter to 10, which will increase the counter by 10 every time we click it.

To make this all work, we need to load a couple of JavaScript. In the ClientApp/public/index.html, we need to add:

```
    <script src="_content/Microsoft.AspNetCore.Components.CustomElements/BlazorCustomElements.js"></script>
    <script src="_framework/blazor.webassembly.js"></script>
```

These scripts will make sure our components load.

We have one last thing we need to fix. When running the React project, it spins up a developer server. Actually, it spins up two: one for the ASP.NET backend and one for the React frontend.

We need to make the React server send all the framework requests to the ASP.NET backend. In the default project template, this is already done for the /weatherforecast path.

Add the following code to the `ClientApp/src/setupProxy.js` file:

```
const context = [
    "/weatherforecast",
    "/_framework",
    "/_content",
];
```

We tell the developer server that if a request goes to weatherforcast, _framework, or _content, we want to redirect that request to the ASP.NET backend.

We now have a working React/Blazor WebAssembly hybrid. I was amazed at how easy and straightforward this was the first time I tried it. It makes it so easy to include some Blazor components on your React site, so you can convert it to Blazor step by step, component by component.

Next, we will do the same using a Razor Pages site.

Adding Blazor to MVC/Razor Pages

When I started with Blazor, this was exactly the scenario we wanted to address. We had an MVC/Razor Pages mix, and it was time for an upgrade.

We solved it by implementing Razor Pages that referred to Razor components. Looking back at it now, it was not a pretty solution, at least not for a while, until we got to the point where most of the code was rewritten in Blazor.

The challenge is that if we navigate to a page that has a Blazor component (a Razor component), that page is connected to the server and establishes a WebSocket. If we navigate away from a Blazor page to an MVC page, for example, we reload the entire page, and the script gets reloaded as well. A new connection was established, leaving the old one on the server for 3 minutes.

We don't have many users, and for us, that technique works long enough for us to finish the migration and launch a new Blazor version of the site.

But I have some good news!

We can also use the same custom elements to run on a Razor Pages site.

Let's take a look!

The project is called `RazorPagesProject`.

In the previous examples with Angular and React, those technologies are client-side; therefore, we used WebAssembly. Razor Pages are server-side, and even though we could use WebAssembly here as well, this is an excellent opportunity to take a look at making the **custom component** use Blazor Server.

First, we need a reference to our Blazor library. I added the `BlazorCustomElement` project as a reference.

Then we need to enable Blazor Server in our Razor Pages by adding the following code to `Program.cs`:

```
builder.Services.AddServerSideBlazor(options =>
{
    options.RootComponents.RegisterCustomElement<Counter>("my-blazor-counter");
});
```

And also:

```
app.MapBlazorHub();
```

In the `Pages/Shared/_Layout.cshtml`, we need to add the JavaScript:

```
<script src="_content/Microsoft.AspNetCore.Components.CustomElements/BlazorCustomElements.js"></script>
<script src="_framework/blazor.server.js"></script>
```

In this case, we add the script for Blazor Server.

Last but not least, we need to add our component. In the `Pages/Index.cshtml`, we add:

```
<my-blazor-counter increment-amount="10"></my-blazor-counter>
```

And we are done; the custom component is now running inside our Razor Pages site (which, of course, is an ASP.NET site with Razor Pages turned on).

The downside, as we touched on at the beginning of this section, is that when we switch pages, the connection to the server will be severed and take up memory on the server for the next 3 minutes. So, if we have a lot of page navigation, we might want to rethink this.

The cool part is that with only a few changes, we can switch this implementation to run WebAssembly instead of Blazor Server for the Blazor components.

The sample code is prepared with comments for both WebAssembly and Blazor Server.

I am again super impressed by this; it makes it so simple to migrate existing sites to Blazor.

Next, we will look at how we can use Angular or React controls on our Blazor website.

Adding Web components to a Blazor site

We have looked at adding Blazor to an existing Angular, React, and even MVC/Razor Pages site.

But sometimes, that perfect library you love to use might not have a Blazor counterpart. We know that we can make a JavaScript interop and build it ourselves, but can we also use Angular and React libraries from Blazor?

We have two options here; either we can convert our site in to an Angular/React site and use those examples, or we can convert the JavaScript library in to a Web Component and use that from Blazor.

Until now, we haven't used npm or anything like that because, in most cases, we don't need it. But now we are mixing technologies, and for that, NPM is the easiest way. NPM is outside the scope of this book, so I will not go into any details about it.

How to convert Angular/React or anything else into a Web Component is also outside the scope of this book.

The project is called `BlazorProject`.

We can browse some of the Web Components on this site: https://www.webcomponents.org/.

I found a Markdown editor from GitHub. Even though we are not implementing it on our blog, feel free to go back and do so if you want to.

We can read about the editor here:

https://www.webcomponents.org/element/@github/markdown-toolbar-element

To get the required JavaScript files, we need to set up NPM. In the project folder, run the following commands:

```
npm init
npm install -save @github/markdown-toolbar-element
```

This will bring down the JavaScript we need.

Next, copy the `BlazorProject\node_modules\@github\markdown-toolbar-element\` folder to the `wwwroot` folder and include it in the project.

Now the JavaScript will be accessible from our project.

In the `index.html`, we need to add a reference to the JavaScript, and we put it below the Blazor JavaScript:

```
<script type="module" src="markdown-toolbar-element/dist/index.js"></script>
```

This component is an ES6 module, so we set the type to `"module"`.

Now, all that is remaining is to add our component. In the demo project, I added it to the `index` component.

First, the component:

```
<markdown-toolbar for="textarea" role="toolbar">
    <md-bold class="btn btn-sm" tabindex="0">bold</md-bold>
    <md-header class="btn btn-sm" tabindex="-1">header</md-header>
    <md-italic class="btn btn-sm" tabindex="-1">italic</md-italic>
    <md-quote class="btn btn-sm" tabindex="-1">quote</md-quote>
    <md-code class="btn btn-sm" tabindex="-1">code</md-code>
    <md-link class="btn btn-sm" tabindex="-1">link</md-link>
    <md-image class="btn btn-sm" tabindex="-1">image</md-image>
    <md-unordered-list class="btn btn-sm" tabindex="-1">unordered-list</md-unordered-list>
    <md-ordered-list class="btn btn-sm" tabindex="-1">ordered-list</md-ordered-list>
    <md-task-list class="btn btn-sm" tabindex="-1">task-list</md-task-list>
    <md-mention class="btn btn-sm" tabindex="-1">mention</md-mention>
    <md-ref class="btn btn-sm" tabindex="-1">ref</md-ref>
    <md-strikethrough class="btn btn-sm" tabindex="-1">strikethrough</md-strikethrough>
</markdown-toolbar>
```

Then the text area with binding to a C# variable `markdown`.

```
<textarea @bind="markdown" @bind:event="oninput" rows="6" class="mt-3 d-block width-full" id="textarea" contenteditable="false" spellcheck="false"></textarea>
```

```
@markdown

@code
{
    private string markdown = "Hello, **world**!";
}
```

The C# variable changes as soon as we edit the textbox, either by using the toolbar or typing some text.

We have integrated a Web Component into our Blazor project, which binds to a C# variable.

This is super powerful and gives us new possibilities to add existing functionality to our Blazor site.

Now we know how to handle SPA frameworks like React and Angular. But what about server frameworks like Web Forms? This is what we will look at next.

Migrating from Web Forms

Last but not least, we have **Web Forms**.

There is honestly not any good upgrade path for Web Forms; there was a project that aimed for code reuse when migrating to Blazor, but it is not being actively worked on.

The first thing we should know is that Blazor is in many ways very similar to Web Forms, so the learning curve to get to Blazor is almost nonexistent since we have state management in Web Forms as well as Blazor.

There are some migration strategies where you would use **Yet Another Reverse Proxy (YARP)**. Still, my recommendation would be to migrate a part of the website to Blazor and have two sites running, until we reach the point where it is feature-complete. Moving to Blazor is fairly quick to do, and in the end, I believe it will save you time.

When we moved our site from MVC to Blazor, we realized that, in some cases, it was faster to rewrite the component to Blazor than trying to solve it in MVC.

Web Forms should be even faster to convert since the backend code is more similar to Blazor than MVC.

So what should we do? Should we upgrade or keep using Web Forms? Upgrade – you will not be disappointed!

Summary

We discussed adding Blazor to other technologies like Angular, React, and Razor Pages using Web Components in this chapter. We looked at how to add Web Components to a Blazor project and leverage JavaScript libraries in our Blazor app.

Upgrading a current site to Blazor can be a lot of work. At work, we made this journey 3 years ago. In our case, we wanted to update our MVC site to be more interactive. We went for Blazor, and I would argue it saved our project and made us more productive, resulting in a more interactive user experience.

In the next chapter, we will delve deeper into Blazor WebAssembly.

16

Going Deeper into WebAssembly

In this chapter, we will go deeper into technologies that are only relevant for Blazor **WebAssembly**.

Most things in Blazor can be applied to Blazor Server and Blazor WebAssembly. Still, since Blazor WebAssembly is running inside the web browser, we can do some things to optimize the code and use other libraries that we can't use server-side.

We will also look at some common problems and how to solve them.

In this chapter, we will cover the following:

- .NET WebAssembly build tools
- AOT compilation
- WebAssembly **Single Instruction, Multiple Data (SIMD)**
- Trimming
- Lazy loading
- PWA
- Native dependencies
- Common problems

The idea for this chapter is not that you have to follow along but rather for reference so that you can implement the features discussed in this chapter on your own.

Technical requirements

This chapter is a reference chapter and is not connected with the book's other chapters. You can find the source code for this chapter's result at https://github.com/PacktPublishing/Web-Development-with-Blazor-Second-Edition/tree/main/Chapter16.

.NET WebAssembly build tools

When it comes to the more "advanced" scenarios, we need additional tooling installed. There are two ways of installing the tools. We can select the **.NET WebAssembly Build Tools** option when installing Visual Studio (or add them using the Visual Studio installer) or by running the following command in a command prompt (as administrator):

```
dotnet workload install wasm-tools
```

The .NET WebAssembly build tools are based on **Emscripten**, a compiler toolchain for the web platform.

AOT compilation

By default, the only thing that is running as WebAssembly in a Blazor WebAssembly app is the runtime. Everything else is ordinary .NET assemblies running on the browser using a .NET **Intermediate Language** (**IL**) interpreter implemented in WebAssembly.

I was not too fond of that when I started playing around with Blazor; it felt wasteful to run everything using IL instead of something the browser would understand natively. Then I thought the browser was running the same code as I would on the server. The same code! In the browser. That is pretty amazing!

However, we have the option to compile directly to WebAssembly; this is called **AOT** (**ahead-of-time**) compilation. It has a downside: the app download size will increase but run and load faster.

An AOT-compiled app is generally twice the size of an IL-compiled app. AOT will take the .NET code and compile that directly into WebAssembly.

AOT does not trim managed assemblies, and more code is needed to represent high-level .NET IL instructions when using native WebAssembly. That is why the size is much larger, and it is also less compressible over HTTP.

AOT is not for everyone; most apps running without AOT will work fine. For CPU-intensive apps, there is a lot to gain by using AOT.

My ZX Spectrum emulator is one of those apps; it runs many iterations per second, and the performance gain by running AOT for these scenarios is remarkable.

To compile our Blazor WebAssembly project using AOT, we add the following property in the csproj file:

```
<PropertyGroup>
  <RunAOTCompilation>true</RunAOTCompilation>
</PropertyGroup>
```

AOT compilation is only performed when the app is published. It can take a long time to compile (7 minutes for the ZX Spectrum emulator), so it is pretty nice that we don't have to wait for that every time we compile our application.

However, running in release mode may be a problem, so if you want to do a quick test in release mode, temporarily disable the setting above.

Don't forget to enable it again; I have some experience in that area.

WebAssembly Single Instruction, Multiple Data (SIMD)

One of the new features in .NET7 is SIMD, a type of parallel processing recently added to WebAssembly.

SIMD stands for Single Instruction, Multiple Data. It is a type of computer architecture that allows a **central processing unit (CPU)** to perform the same operation on multiple data points simultaneously, improving the performance of certain kinds of tasks. SIMD instructions are often used to perform vector arithmetic, in which a single instruction is applied to multiple elements of a vector simultaneously. SIMD can be beneficial for tasks such as image and video processing, where large amounts of data need to be processed quickly.

To enable SIMD, we need to enable it in the project file like this:

```
<PropertyGroup>
  <WasmEnableSIMD>true</WasmEnableSIMD>
  <RunAOTCompilation>true</RunAOTCompilation>
</PropertyGroup>
```

We need to use AOT compilation for SIMD to work.

This is outside of the scope of this book, but I wanted to mention it in case this is what you need for your project.

Trimming

By default, when publishing a Blazor WebAssembly app, trimming will be performed. It will remove unnecessary things and, by doing so, reduce the size of the app.

If our application uses reflection, the trimmer may have problems identifying what can and cannot be removed.

For most applications, the trimming is automatic and will work. To read more about trimming options, you can look here: https://learn.microsoft.com/en-us/dotnet/core/deploying/trimming/trimming-options?pivots=dotnet-7-0.

Lazy loading

When working with Blazor WebAssembly, one of the challenges is download size. Even though it's not a big problem, in my opinion, we can do some things to handle the download and loading time. We will get back to this in the *Common problems* section later in this chapter.

When navigating to a Blazor WebAssembly application, all the DLLs for our application and the DLLs from the .NET Framework are downloaded. It takes a bit of time to get everything started up. We can load some DLLs when needed by using **lazy loading** to solve this.

Let's say that our application is massive where there is a reporting part of the application. Reporting is perhaps not used every day and not used by everyone, and it would make sense to remove that part from the initial download and only load it when we need to.

To make that happen, the part we want to lazy load must be in a separate project/DLL. In the `csproj` file of the Blazor WebAssembly client project, add a reference to the DLL by adding the following code:

```
<ItemGroup>
  <BlazorWebAssemblyLazyLoad Include="{ASSEMBLY NAME}.dll" />
</ItemGroup>
```

The snippet will make sure the file is not downloaded from the start. To load the DLL when we need it, we will use a built-in service called `LazyAssemblyLoader`.

The `LazyAssemblyLoader` service will make a JS Interop call to download the assembly and load it into the runtime.

We make sure to download the necessary assemblies/DLLs in the router (so we make sure they are downloaded before we navigate to the component that is using them:

```
@using Microsoft.AspNetCore.Components.Routing
@using Microsoft.AspNetCore.Components.WebAssembly.Services
@using Microsoft.Extensions.Logging
@inject LazyAssemblyLoader AssemblyLoader
@inject ILogger<App> Logger

<Router AppAssembly="@typeof(App).Assembly"
    OnNavigateAsync="@OnNavigateAsync">
    ...
</Router>

@code {
    private async Task OnNavigateAsync(NavigationContext args)
    {
        try
        {
            if (args.Path == "{PATH}")
            {
                var assemblies = await AssemblyLoader.LoadAssembliesAsync(
                    new[] { {LIST OF ASSEMBLIES} });
            }
        }
        catch (Exception ex)
        {
            Logger.LogError("Error: {Message}", ex.Message);
        }
    }
}
```

We need to inject `LazyAssemblyLoader`; it is registered as a singleton by default in a Blazor WebAssembly project.

Set up an event `OnNavigateAsync`, and in that method, check the path and make sure to load the assemblies we need.

This can also be used for routable components by doing something similar to this:

```
@using System.Reflection
@using Microsoft.AspNetCore.Components.Routing
@using Microsoft.AspNetCore.Components.WebAssembly.Services
@using Microsoft.Extensions.Logging
@inject LazyAssemblyLoader AssemblyLoader
@inject ILogger<App> Logger

<Router AppAssembly="@typeof(App).Assembly"
    AdditionalAssemblies="@lazyLoadedAssemblies"
    OnNavigateAsync="@OnNavigateAsync">
    ...
</Router>

@code {
    private List<Assembly> lazyLoadedAssemblies = new();

    private async Task OnNavigateAsync(NavigationContext args)
    {
        try
        {
            if (args.Path == "{PATH}")
            {
                var assemblies = await AssemblyLoader.LoadAssembliesAsync(
                    new[] { {LIST OF ASSEMBLIES} });
                lazyLoadedAssemblies.AddRange(assemblies);
            }
        }
        catch (Exception ex)
        {
            Logger.LogError("Error: {Message}", ex.Message);
        }
    }
}
```

We need to replace the {PATH} in the snippet above with the path where we want to load the assemblies, something like this: "/fetchdata". The {LIST OF ASSEMBLIES}, which contains a list of assemblies we wish to load, can be: "sample.dll".

This makes it possible not to load the Admin interface for the users that don't have access to it, for example.

PWA

Both Blazor Server and Blazor WebAssembly can create **PWA (Progressive Web Apps)**. But it is much more common for Blazor WebAssembly. PWA makes it possible to download the web as an app to your phone or computer. It will make it possible to add nice-looking icons and launch in a web browser without a URL input field, it will feel more like an app.

When creating our project, we select **Progressive Web App**. By doing that, we will get some configuration and JavaScript to set everything up.

PWA is outside the scope of this book, but there are great resources to get us started. You can find more information here: https://learn.microsoft.com/en-us/aspnet/core/blazor/progressive-web-app?view=aspnetcore-7.0&tabs=visual-studio.

Native dependencies

Since we are running WebAssembly, we can use WebAssembly assemblies written in other languages in our project. This means that we can use any native dependencies right inside our project.

One way is to add C files right into our project. In the Chapter16 folder in the repo, you will find an example.

I have added a file called Test.c with the following content:

```
int fact(int n)
{
    if (n == 0) return 1;
    return n * fact(n - 1);
}
```

In the project file, I have added a reference to that file:

```
<ItemGroup>
    <NativeFileReference Include="Test.c" />
</ItemGroup>
```

In Index.razor, I have added the following code:

```
@page "/"
@using System.Runtime.InteropServices
<PageTitle>Native C</PageTitle>
<h1>Native C Test</h1>
<p>
    @@fact(3) result: @fact(3)
</p>

@code {
    [DllImport("Test")]
    static extern int fact(int n);
}
```

In our C# project, we now have a C file that we can call from our Blazor project. We can take this even further by using a library that is using a C++ library. Skia is an open-source graphics engine written in C++.

Read more here: https://github.com/mono/SkiaSharp. We can add that library to a Blazor WebAssembly app by adding the NuGet package SkiaSharp.Views.Blazor.

In the Chapter16 folder in the repo, you can explore a project called SkiaSharpDemo.

In the Index.razor file, I have added the following code:

```
<SKCanvasView OnPaintSurface="@OnPaintSurface" />

@code {
    private void OnPaintSurface(SKPaintSurfaceEventArgs e)
    {
        var canvas = e.Surface.Canvas;

        canvas.Clear(SKColors.White);

        using var paint = new SKPaint
        {
            Color = SKColors.Black,
            IsAntialias = true,
            TextSize = 24
```

```
            };

            canvas.DrawText("Raccoons are awesome!", 0, 24, paint);
    }
}
```

The page will draw "Raccoons are awesome" on the canvas.

In this case, we are using a C# library that is using a C++ library.

We can even refer to libraries that have already been built with Emscripten directly by adding **Object files** (.o), **Archive files** (.a), **Bitcode** (.bc), and **Standalone WebAssembly modules** (.wasm). If we find a library written in another language, we could compile that to WebAssembly and then use it from our Blazor application. This opens up so many doors!

Next, we will look at some common problems I have encountered.

Common problems

Let's dive into this one right from the start.

The most common comments regarding Blazor WebAssembly are download size and load time. A small project is around 1 MB in size, but I believe the problem is loading time and not download size/time since everything is cached and in most parts of the world, we have access to high-speed internet.

There are a couple of solutions to this problem.

Progress indicators

When it comes to **UX** (**User Experience**), we can give the users a perceived sense of speed.

The default Blazor WebAssembly template has a loading progress indicator that gives the users something to look at instead of a blank page. It is built so that it is easy to customize using CSS variables. We can use the variables `--blazor-load-percentage` and `--blazor-load-percentage-text` to customize and create our progress bar.

It doesn't even have to indicate what is happening; Dragons Mania Legends has comments like "Sewing mini Vikings," which is obviously not what is going on. So depending on the application we are building, showing something is more important than showing nothing.

Prerendering on the server

We have seen that Blazor Server and Blazor WebAssembly work separately, but there is a way to combine the two. Adding a few lines of code to the app can prerender the app on the server and then serve the prerendered HTML to the browser.

When Blazor WebAssembly is loaded, it will take its place once it's loaded. The downside of this approach is that it requires an ASP.NET backend.

The project is in the `WasmServerPrerendered` folder.

We will get three different projects when we create a new Blazor WebAssembly project with an ASP.NET Core backend: Client, Server, and Shared.

They are named `TheNameOfOurProject.Server`, for example. For this, we need to create a Razor page that will hook everything up. To keep the same naming conventions as with a Blazor Server project, we can name the page `_host.cshtml`.

Next, we need to copy the HTML located in the `index.html` file and make some changes.

We need to add a tag helper and a namespace:

```
@addTagHelper *, Microsoft.AspNetCore.Mvc.TagHelpers
@using WasmServerPrerendered.Client
```

This will give us access to the component-tag helper.

We need to add the following to the page (where we want our components to render):

```
<component type="typeof(App)" render-mode="WebAssemblyPrerendered" />
```

The secret here is the render mode, `WebAssemblyPrerendered`. It means render on the server and then replace with the WebAssembly version.

In `Program.cs`, we also need to change this line:

```
app.MapFallbackToFile("index.html");
```

to:

```
app.MapFallbackToPage("/_Host");
```

We say that instead of redirecting to `index.html`, we want Blazor to redirect to the Razor page we just created.

In the client project, we also need to remove a couple of lines, by default, it hooks up the WebAssembly, but that is already taken care of by the component helper tag.

In `Program.cs`, remove these two lines:

```
builder.RootComponents.Add<App>("#app");
builder.RootComponents.Add<HeadOutlet>("head::after");
```

That's it, we now have prerendered components on the server that gets replaced by WebAssembly.

This is a great and simple way to add SEO to our site.

There is one problem: it will load data when rendering on the server, and then again when the WebAssembly loads.

There is a way to work around that, which we will take a look at next.

Preloading and persisting the state

We don't want our component to call the database twice if we can avoid it.

If you run the `WasmServerPrerendered` example and go to the **Fetch data** page, you should be able to see it load twice since the data is random and generated every time we request it.

This goes for Blazor Prerender, which is the same functionality on the server: it first renders the page before sending the response to the web browser, hooks up SignalR, and then renders the component again.

We can solve that by adding another component called `persist-component-state`.

The source for this example is the `WasmServerPrerenderedWPersist` project.

The sample is the same setup as the `WasmServerPrerendered` example but with some added state persistence. In the server project in the file `_Host.cshtml`, we add a component:

```
<persist-component-state />
```

This component will render the saved state of the component. When WebAssembly is finished, it will load the data from that field instead of making an HTTP request to retrieve data again.

In the Client project and in the component where we want to have the persistence (`FetchData.razor` in the sample), we inject a `PersistanceComponentState` and also make the component implement `Idisposable`:

```
@inject PersistentComponentState ApplicationState
```

```
@implements IDisposable
```

We add a `PersistingComponentStateSubscription` component that saves the data to the application state:

```
private PersistingComponentStateSubscription _subscription;
```

In `OnInitializedAsync`, we register to listen to run code when the component wants to persist the data:

```
_subscription = ApplicationState.RegisterOnPersisting(PersistState);
```

When we load the data, we make sure first to check the application state. If the data is not available, we can continue and make an HTTP request:

```
if (ApplicationState.TryTakeFromJson<WeatherForecast[]>("weatherdata", out var stored))
    {
        forecasts = stored;
    }
    else
    {
        forecasts = await Http.GetFromJsonAsync<WeatherForecast[]>("WeatherForecast");
    }
```

It refers to a method that will persist the data in the application state:

```
private Task PersistState()
{
    ApplicationState.PersistAsJson("weatherdata", forecasts);
    return Task.CompletedTask;
}

public void Dispose()
{
    _subscription.Dispose();
}
```

The server will first render the content, and when the server is done, it will respond with the whole page, including a `Base64`-encoded JSON string with data that looks something like this:

```
<!–Blazor:{"prerenderId":"20e8ba483175467fbc45be3a822c2d58"}(–!--Blazor-
Component-State:eyJ3ZWF0aGVyZGF0YSI6IlczczlaR0YwWlNJNklqSXdNakl0TVRF
dE...-->
```

Since everything we put into the application state is stored as JSON, it is important not to include any sensitive data that we were not thinking of displaying. This is, of course, true for all calls since we are sending data with JSON.

We can also use `PersistentComponentState` on Blazor Server (in the same way we just did). These components work in both Blazor Server and Blazor WebAssembly.

Now we know a couple of common problems and how to solve them.

Summary

In this chapter, we looked at some of the Blazor WebAssembly-specific things in Blazor. For the most part, we can reuse components in both Blazor Server and Blazor WebAssembly. But we can speed up WebAssembly by using what we learned in this chapter.

We also looked at native dependencies opening up possibilities to reuse other libraries and mixing languages. If our application doesn't need to support both scenarios, we can use WebAssembly to the fullest.

In the next chapter, we will examine *source generators*.

Join our community on Discord

Join our community's Discord space for discussions with the author and other readers:

`https://packt.link/WebDevBlazor2e`

17
Examining Source Generators

In this chapter, we will look at writing code that generates code. Even though this chapter isn't directly related to Blazor development, it still has a connection to Blazor, as we'll discover.

The subject of source generators is a book on its own, but I wanted to introduce this since it is used by Blazor and, honestly, is one of my favorite features.

I am the kind of person that spends a day writing source code that saves me 10 minutes, if I know I will need to repeat those 10 minutes over and over again. Repetitive tasks have never been a favorite of mine.

In this chapter, we will cover the following:

- What a source generator is
- How to get started with source generators
- Community projects

The idea for this chapter is for you to use it as a reference so that you can implement a new project on your own.

Technical requirements

This chapter is a reference chapter and is not connected in any way with the book's other chapters.

You can find the source code for this chapter's result at https://github.com/PacktPublishing/Web-Development-with-Blazor-Second-Edition/tree/main/Chapter17.

What a source generator is

In many cases, we find ourselves writing the same kind of code over and over again. In the past, I have used T4 templates to generate code and even written **stored procedures** and applications that can help me generate code. **Source generators** are part of the .NET compiler platform (Roslyn) SDK.

A generator gives us access to a compilation object representing all the user code currently being compiled. From there, the object can be inspected, and we can, based on that, write additional code.

Okay, this sounds complicated, and I would be lying if I said it was easy to write a source generator, but it instantly saves us a lot of time. So let's break it down a bit.

When we compile our code, the compiler does the following steps:

1. The compilation runs.
2. Source generators analyze code.
3. The source generators generate new code.
4. The compilation continues.

Steps 2 and 3 are what source generators do.

In Blazor, source generators are used all the time; it is a source generator that takes the `.razor` files and converts them to C# code.

We can look at what Blazor is generating by adding the following to our `csproj` file:

```
<EmitCompilerGeneratedFiles>true</EmitCompilerGeneratedFiles>
```

Adding this code will emit generated files into the `obj` folder for the `razor` component.

We can find them here: `\obj\Debug\net7.0\generated\Microsoft.NET.Sdk.Razor.SourceGenerators\Microsoft.NET.Sdk.Razor.SourceGenerators.RazorSourceGenerator`

We can choose where to emit the files by using:

```
<CompilerGeneratedFilesOutputPath>THEPATH</CompilerGeneratedFilesOutputPath>
```

You can replace `THEPATH` with a path you would like to have the files emitted to.

In that folder, we can find a file called `Pages_Counter_razor.g.cs`, which is the C# representation of the counter component.

The `Microsoft.NET.Sdk.Razor.SourceGenerators`-generator is, of course, a very advanced source generator.

Let's think of a scenario: at work, we create services and interfaces for those services. The only use of this interface is for testing purposes, the same way we have built our repositories throughout the book.

In this case, adding a method to a service means we need to add the method to the class and the interface. We tried simplifying the process by putting the interface and the class in the same file. However, we still forgot about the interface, pushed the code, and didn't notice the mistake until everything was built and a NuGet package was generated.

We found a source generator called **InterfaceGenerator**; adding an attribute to our class will generate the interface for us.

Let's take a look at this example:

```
public class SampleService
{
    public double Multiply(double x, double y)
    {
        return x * y;
    }

    public int NiceNumber => 42;
}
```

This is a simple service class (taken from the InterfaceGenerator GitHub page). Adding an attribute to the code will automatically generate an interface, and we can add a reference to that interface:

```
[GenerateAutoInterface]
public class SampleService: ISampleService
...
```

The generated interface will always be up to date. This sample is an excellent example of when source code generators will save time and remove pain points.

Source generators are powerful; we get access to a syntax tree that we can query. We can iterate over all classes and find the ones with a specific attribute or that implement an interface, for example, and based on that, generate code.

There are some limitations. There is no way to know in what order the source generators will run, so we can't generate code based on generated code. We can only add code, not modify code.

The following section will look at how we can build our source generators.

How to get started with source generators

It's time to look at how we can build our source code generators. The Chapter17 folder is a finished example of what we discuss here. The instructions will not be a step-by-step guide.

To create a source code generator, we need a class library targeting *.NET Standard 2.0*. We also need to add a reference to the NuGet packages **Microsoft.CodeAnalysis.CSharp** and **Microsoft.CodeAnalysis.Analyzers** in that library.

To create a source generator, we need to create a class that has two things:

- It needs to have the [Generator] attribute.
- It needs to implement ISourceGenerator.

The template code should look something like this:

```
using Microsoft.CodeAnalysis;
namespace SourceGenerator;
[Generator]
public class HelloSourceGenerator : ISourceGenerator
{
    public void Execute(GeneratorExecutionContext context)
    {
        // Code generation goes here
    }

    public void Initialize(GeneratorInitializationContext context)
    {
        // No initialization required for this one
    }
}
```

In the Initialize method, we add any initialization that may be needed; and in the Execute method, we write the generated code.

The generator we are building now is, of course, a silly example, but it also shows some of the power of source generators.

In the Execute method, we add the following code:

```
        // Build up the source code
        string source = """
```

```
namespace BlazorWebAssemblyApp;
public class GeneratedService
    {
        public string GetHello()
        {
            return "Hello from generated code";
        }
    }
""";
        // Add the source code to the compilation
        context.AddSource($"GeneratedService.g.cs", source);
```

It will take the code in the source variable and save it as GeneratedService.g.cs. We also use raw string literals in this file – the feature in .NET7 I have been the most excited about. By adding three double quotes, we don't need to escape the string; we are free to add more double quotes inside of the string. If you want to escape more than three double quotes, you can add more at the start and end.

To add a source generator to our project, we can add the project like this:

```
<ItemGroup>
  <ProjectReference
      Include="..\SourceGenerator\SourceGenerator.csproj"
      OutputItemType="Analyzer"
      ReferenceOutputAssembly="false"/>
</ItemGroup>
```

When we compile our project, the GeneratedService will be generated, and we can use the code.

Now we can inject the service and use it inside of our components:

```
@page "/"
@inject GeneratedService service
<h1>@service.GetHello()</h1>
```

Don't forget to add it to Program.cs as well:

```
builder.Services.AddScoped<GeneratedService>();
```

The sample above isn't really how you would use it in a real-world scenario, but I wanted to show that it is not that tricky to get started.

Sometimes the Visual Studio editor won't pick up these generated files, and we will see some red squiggles in the code editor. This is because the order of the source generators (there is no guaranteed order) will result in these problems, especially when combining source generators with other classes that are also generated, like razor files.

In the next section, we will look at some of the source generators we can use in our projects.

Community projects

Source generators have been around since .NET5/6, and there are a lot of community/open-source projects we can use in our projects. Let's explore them in the following sections.

InterfaceGenerator

We have already talked about InterfaceGenerator. Generating interfaces without having to write the same thing twice will save time and help you avoid problems, especially if you use interfaces only for testing.

We can find it here:

https://github.com/daver32/InterfaceGenerator

Blazorators

David Pine, with many contributors, has built Blazorators that can take a TypeScript definition file and generate JavaScript interop, ready to be used in any Blazor project. Blazorators take away a lot of the pain points when writing JavaScript interop.

Check out his project here:

https://github.com/IEvangelist/blazorators

C# source generators

Amadeusz Sadowski, with many contributors, has made an impressive list of where to find more information on source generators and some outstanding ones. You can find this fantastic resource here:

https://github.com/amis92/csharp-source-generators

Roslyn SDK samples

Microsoft has added some samples to their Roslyn SDK repository. It's a great start to dig a bit deeper into source generators. You can find the samples here:

https://github.com/dotnet/roslyn-sdk/tree/main/samples/CSharp/SourceGenerators

Microsoft Learn

Microsoft Learn is an excellent source for learning anything C# related, and source generators are no exception.

If you think, just like me, that source generators sound like the best thing since sliced bread, I recommend that you dive into the documentation found at Microsoft Learn:

https://learn.microsoft.com/en-us/dotnet/csharp/roslyn-sdk/source-generators-overview

Summary

In this chapter, we looked at code that writes code to save time and reduce repetitive tasks.

Blazor uses source generators to convert the razor code into C# code, so, indirectly, we are using them all the time.

In the next chapter, we will look at Blazor Hybrid by visiting .NET MAUI.

18

Visiting .NET MAUI

So far, we have talked about Blazor WebAssembly and Blazor Server, but what about the third option?

In this chapter, we will visit **.NET MAUI**, Microsoft's new cross-platform development platform.

This chapter will not be a deep dive into .NET MAUI, since that can be a book all in itself.

In this chapter, we will cover the following:

- What is .NET MAUI?
- Creating a new project
- Looking at the template
- Developing for Android
- Developing for iOS
- Developing for macOS
- Developing for Windows
- Developing for Tizen

The idea for this chapter is for you to use it as a reference, so that you will be able to implement a new project on your own.

Technical requirements

This chapter is a reference chapter and is not connected in any way with the book's other chapters.

You can find the source code for this chapter at https://github.com/PacktPublishing/Web-Development-with-Blazor-Second-Edition/tree/main/Chapter18.

What is .NET MAUI?

We'll start with a bit of history.

Xamarin is a software company founded in May 2011 by the engineers who created Mono, a free and open-source version of .NET Framework. Microsoft acquired the company in 2016 and it is now a vital part of the .NET development platform, providing tools and services for building native cross-platform mobile apps using C# and .NET. Xamarin's technology allows developers to write native iOS, Android, and Windows apps using a single shared code base, making it easier to develop and maintain apps for multiple platforms.

.NET **MAUI (Multi-Platform App UI)** is the new framework from Microsoft, which is an evolution of Xamarin.Forms.

This is a way to create one UI, deploy it to many different platforms, and get native controls on each platform. .NET MAUI can also host Blazor, which is called Blazor Hybrid. We will not get native controls when we use Blazor Hybrid. It will render web content.

Many years ago, I sat in a meeting with a bunch of consultants. The company I was working for wanted to invest in an app, and we turned to one of the big consultancy firms in Sweden to get some help on how we should proceed.

After a week, we had another meeting where they presented their findings. Their recommendation was to build natively and not use any of the cross-platform frameworks.

They had a bunch of arguments, but two that really stuck with me are as follows:

- Native apps look better and give the user a "real" device experience.
- Shared code (between platforms) means that if one platform has a bug, the same bug is now in all platforms.

Since .NET MAUI (formerly Xamarin.Forms) uses native controls, there is no way for the users to know the difference between developing a native app and developing using .NET MAUI. In the end it will look and feel like a native app. This is not true for Blazor Hybrid, which uses web controls. So there are some valid arguments for the first point. Now, we must ask ourselves, how important is that native look and feel? Looking at the apps on my iPhone, not many apps look the same, so I would argue it is not that important as long as you uphold a good UX. The second argument made me so angry. Were they trying to convince us that sharing code was terrible? Yes, they were. Sharing code between platforms is fantastic; you only need to write the code once, fix a bug once, and fix it on all platforms.

.NET MAUI gives us both options. We can use native UI with C# code or use Blazor Hybrid to get web controls.

Creating a new project

To develop cross-platform applications, we must install cross-platform tools in Visual Studio.

If you haven't done that, please open the Visual Studio installer and select the **.NET Multi-Platform App UI** development workflow.

.NET MAUI has a couple of templates: **.NET MAUI App**, **.NET MAUI Blazor App**, and **.NET MAUI Class Library**.

.NET MAUI App

The .NET MAUI template uses XAML to create applications.

XAML is also used for **WPF (Windows Presentation Foundation)** and **UWP (Universal Windows Platform)**. Every XAML version differs just a bit but if you have worked with WPF or UWP before, they should feel familiar.

The XAML is converted into native elements. This way, if our app runs on Windows, it will have the look and feel of a Windows application. If we run it on an iOS device, it will look and feel like a native iOS app.

This is probably our best option if we want to use our C# skills to create a cross-platform application. Using this approach, we will get the native feel without the need to write native code in Kotlin or Swift.

.NET MAUI Class Library

.NET MAUI Class Library is used to share content, classes, and functionality between applications.

.NET MAUI Blazor App

Since this is a book about Blazor, we will focus on the **.NET MAUI Blazor App** template. This is a template that embeds a Blazor application inside of a native shell.

For the .NET MAUI Blazor App project, we need at least:

- Android 7.0 (API 24) or higher
- iOS 14 or higher
- macOS 11 or higher, using Mac Catalyst

The .NET MAUI Blazor App project uses BlazorWebView to render the Blazor content. It is not the same as Blazor Server and does not run WebAssembly; it is simply the third option we have for hosting Blazor applications.

Let's start a new project and dig a bit deeper:

1. In Visual Studio, create a new .NET MAUI Blazor App project.
2. Name the project `BlazorHybridApp`, and make sure you select **.NET 7**.
3. At the top of Visual Studio, select **Windows Machine** and run the project.

That's it. We now have our first cross-platform Blazor Hybrid app!

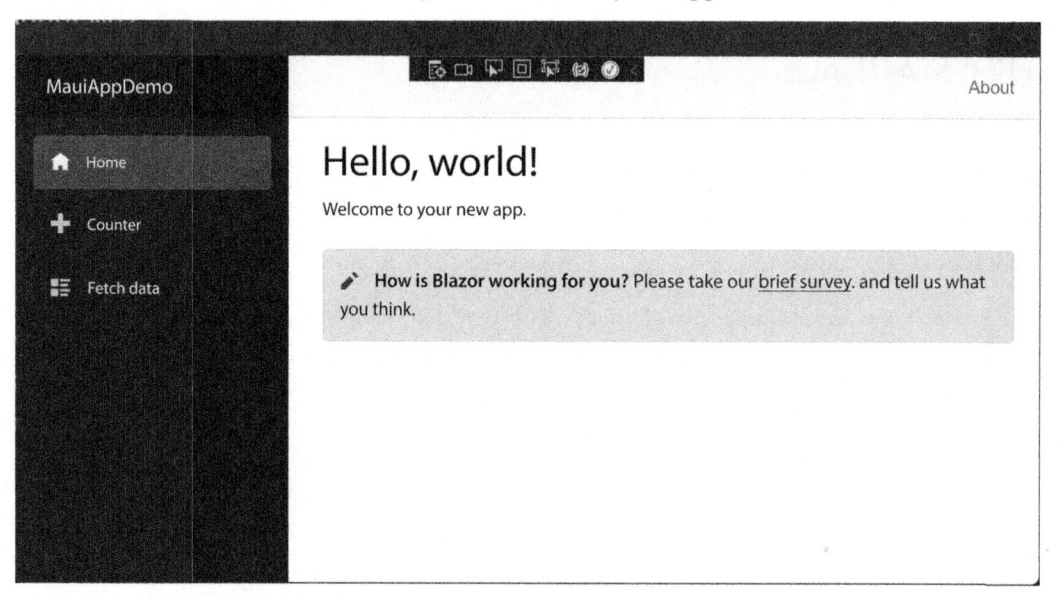

Figure 18.1: .NET MAUI app running on Windows

Great! We now have a project. In the next section, we will take a look at what the template looks like.

Looking at the template

When running the project, we should recognize the UI. It is the same *Hello, world!* page, the same counter, and the same weather forecast.

If we take a look in the `Pages` folder, we'll find the Razor components, and if we open the `Counter.razor` file, we will find a familiar component that looks like this:

```
@page "/counter"
<h1>Counter</h1>
```

```
<p role="status">Current count: @currentCount</p>
<button class="btn btn-primary" @onclick="IncrementCount">Click me</button>
@code {
    private int currentCount = 0;

    private void IncrementCount()
    {
        currentCount++;
    }
}
```

To create a Blazor Hybrid app, adding components like this is what you need to know to get started, but let's dig a bit deeper. The template is .NET MAUI App with some added Blazor startup code.

To understand what is happening, we will start in the Platforms folder. In the platforms folder, we will find different a folder for each platform we can develop for Android, iOS, Mac Catalyst, Tizen, and Windows.

This is the starting point for each platform, and they have a bit of a different implementation, but in the end, they all point to the file MauiProgram located at the project's root.

The MauiProgram class sets everything up, like fonts, dependency injection, etc.

```
namespace BlazorHybridApp;
public static class MauiProgram
{
    public static MauiApp CreateMauiApp()
    {
        var builder = MauiApp.CreateBuilder();
        builder
            .UseMauiApp<App>()
            .ConfigureFonts(fonts =>
            {
                fonts.AddFont("OpenSans-Regular.ttf", "OpenSansRegular");
            });

        builder.Services.AddMauiBlazorWebView();

#if DEBUG
```

```
        builder.Services.AddBlazorWebViewDeveloperTools();
        builder.Logging.AddDebug();
#endif

        builder.Services.AddSingleton<WeatherForecastService>();

        return builder.Build();
    }
}
```

The essential thing in the file is UseMauiApp<App>, which gives us a clue about what is happening next. The next step is to load the App.xaml.

The App.xaml file has a bunch of resources for styling. The Blazor magic starts to happen in App.xaml.cs:

```
namespace BlazorHybridApp;
public partial class App : Application
{
    public App()
    {
        InitializeComponent();
        MainPage = new MainPage();
    }
}
```

It sets the application MainPage to an instance of the class MainPage. In MainPage.xaml, we have reached the first Blazor reference in the app, the BlazorWebView:

```
<BlazorWebView x:Name="blazorWebView" HostPage="wwwroot/index.html">
    <BlazorWebView.RootComponents>
        <RootComponent Selector="#app" ComponentType="{x:Type local:Main}"
/>
    </BlazorWebView.RootComponents>
</BlazorWebView>
```

In this case, we are referring to index.html, located in the wwwroot folder, and also set up the root component (similar to what we do in Program.cs in Blazor Server and Blazor WebAssembly).

Here, we can also add XAML components, which makes it possible to mix XAML and Blazor components. Even though the implementation looks different, we should be familiar with the concepts.

The `index.html` is almost the same as in Blazor WebAssembly:

```html
<!DOCTYPE html>
<html lang="en">
<head>
    <meta charset="utf-8" />
    <meta name="viewport" content="width=device-width, initial-scale=1.0, maximum-scale=1.0, user-scalable=no, viewport-fit=cover" />
    <title>BlazorHybridApp</title>
    <base href="/" />
    <link rel="stylesheet" href="css/bootstrap/bootstrap.min.css" />
    <link href="css/app.css" rel="stylesheet" />
    <link href="BlazorHybridApp.styles.css" rel="stylesheet" />
</head>

<body>
    <div class="status-bar-safe-area"></div>
    <div id="app">Loading...</div>
    <div id="blazor-error-ui">
        An unhandled error has occurred.
        <a href="" class="reload">Reload</a>
        <a class="dismiss">🗙</a>
    </div>
    <script src="_framework/blazor.webview.js" autostart="false"></script>
</body>
</html>
```

The only difference worth mentioning is the JavaScript that differs from the others (Blazor Server and Blazor WebAssembly implementations). From this point, the application is now running pure Blazor.

As we can see in the `MainPage.xaml`, we are loading a Razor file called `Main`. The same file in Blazor Server and Blazor WebAssembly is called `App.razor`. The `Main.razor` file should also feel familiar:

```
<Router AppAssembly="@typeof(Main).Assembly">
```

```
        <Found Context="routeData">
            <RouteView RouteData="@routeData" DefaultLayout="@
    typeof(MainLayout)" />
            <FocusOnNavigate RouteData="@routeData" Selector="h1" />
        </Found>
        <NotFound>
            <LayoutView Layout="@typeof(MainLayout)">
                <p role="alert">Sorry, there's nothing at this address.</p>
            </LayoutView>
        </NotFound>
    </Router>
```

This is where we find the router, where we configure where to find the Razor components, and handle the requests that are not found.

We will not go deeper into the Blazor parts because everything past our router is the same as any other Blazor hosting model (Blazor Server and Blazor WebAssembly). There is a MainLayout, NavMenu, and component for each function (Hello, world!, Counter, and Weather).

With Blazor Server and Blazor WebAssembly, we need to make JavaScript calls to access local resources like Bluetooth, a battery, and a flashlight, to name a few. Blazor Hybrid adds the ability to write code that directly accesses local resources. We can access the flashlight (because we all love things that light up) by using this code:

```
try
{
    if (FlashlightSwitch.IsToggled)
        await Flashlight.Default.TurnOnAsync();
    else
        await Flashlight.Default.TurnOffAsync();
}
catch (FeatureNotSupportedException ex)
{
    // Handle not supported on device exception
}
catch (PermissionException ex)
{
    // Handle permission exception
}
```

```
catch (Exception ex)
{
    // Unable to turn on/off flashlight
}
```

This code will not work if we run a Blazor Server or Blazor WebAssembly app.

Next, we will get our amazing app to run on Android.

Developing for Android

There are two options when it comes to developing for Android. We can run our application in an *emulator* or on a *physical device*.

To publish our application we need to have a Google Developer license, but for development and testing we don't need one.

Running in an emulator

We first need to install an emulator to run our app on an Android emulator:

1. In Visual Studio, open the menu **Tools** | **Android** | **Android Device Manager**.
2. Press the **New** button, and configure a new device (the default settings should be OK):

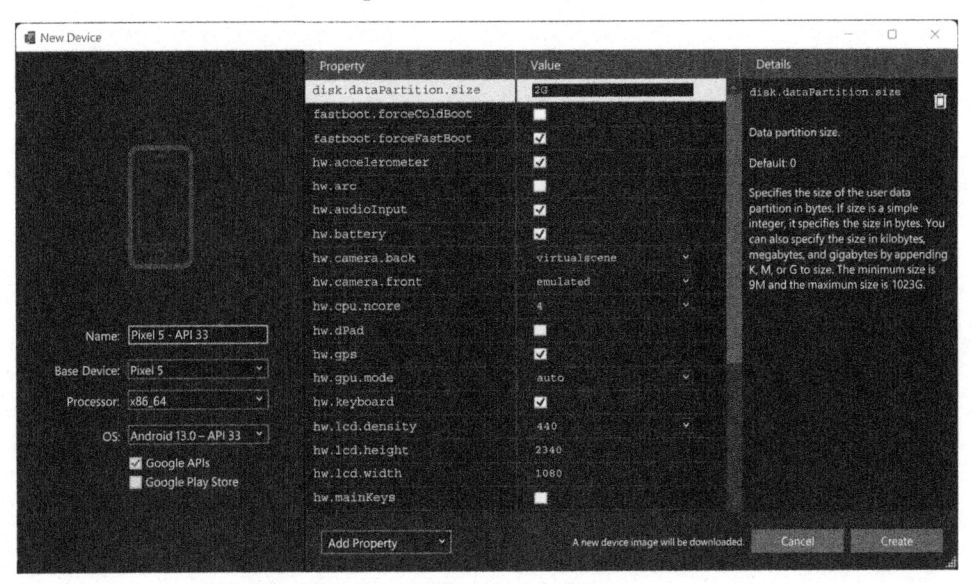

Figure 18.2: Android device configuration

3. Click **Create** to download a device image and configure it.

4. Select the newly created emulator at the top of Visual Studio and run the project. Starting the emulator will take a couple of minutes. When developing, make sure not to close the emulator for a faster deployment time.

To get the emulator to run fast, we can enable hardware acceleration, depending on the processor we use.

To enable hardware acceleration, please refer to the official documentation: `https:// learn.microsoft.com/en-us/xamarin/android/get-started/installation/android- emulator/hardware-acceleration?pivots=windows`

Great, we now have our app running inside an Android emulator:

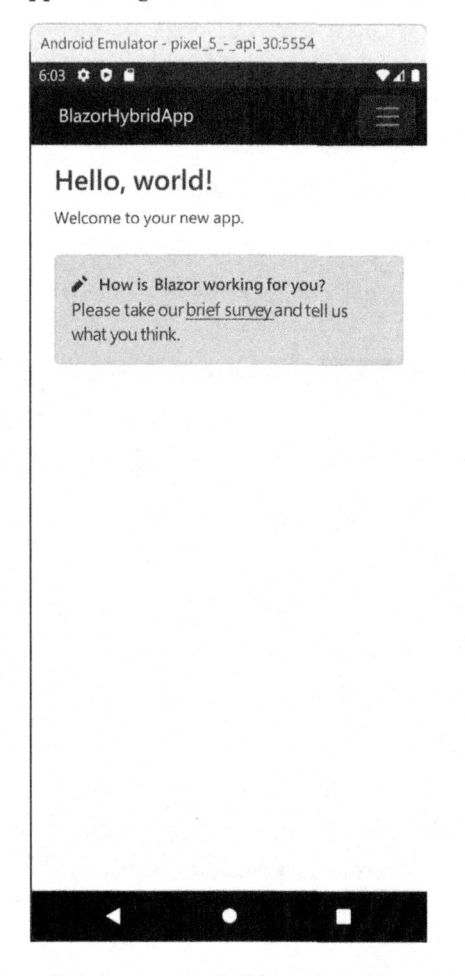

Figure 18.3: App running inside an Android emulator

Next, we will run the application on a physical device.

Running on a physical device

If we want to try our application on a physical device, we need to do a few things on our Android device. This may differ from device to device.

First, we need to make sure the phone is developer-unlocked:

1. Go to the **Settings** screen.
2. Select **About phone**.
3. Tap **Build Number** seven times until **You are now a developer!** is visible.

Second, we need to enable USB debugging:

1. Go to the **Settings** screen.
2. Select **Developer options**.
3. Turn on the **USB debugging** option.
4. Some devices also need to enable **Install via USB**.

We are now all set to try our app on a physical device.

1. In the menu at the top of Visual Studio, click the arrow under **Android local devices** and select your device.
2. Press **Run**, and Visual Studio will deploy the application to the device.

We should now have our application running on our device.

It is an extraordinary feeling to run code on another device. Over the years, I have developed over 100 applications for Windows 8 and Windows Phone. However, to this day, it still gives me the same feeling to see my application deploy to another physical device.

Next, we will look at what options we have for developing iOS.

Developing for iOS

Apple does not allow iOS code to be compiled on something that is not an Apple computer. There are also cloud options like MacinCloud and MacStadium, but we won't go into those options in this book.

This means we must own a Mac (to use the simulator) or have an Apple Developer license (to use **hot restart**).

Hot restart

To test our application on a physical device, we can use hot restart. The hot restart feature is only designed for us to test our application while we are developing it, and we will not be able to publish the application.

First, we need to have iTunes installed. If you don't have iTunes, you can install that from the Windows store.

In the top menu in Visual Studio, if we select **iOS Local Device**, we will get a nice wizard telling us precisely what we need to do. The first steps are informative and let us install iTunes.

Next, it's time to enter our App Store Connect API key information. To be able to supply that information, we need to have an Apple Developer account. At the time of writing, it costs $99.

There are excellent instructions on where to find that information.

You will be prompted with this screen:

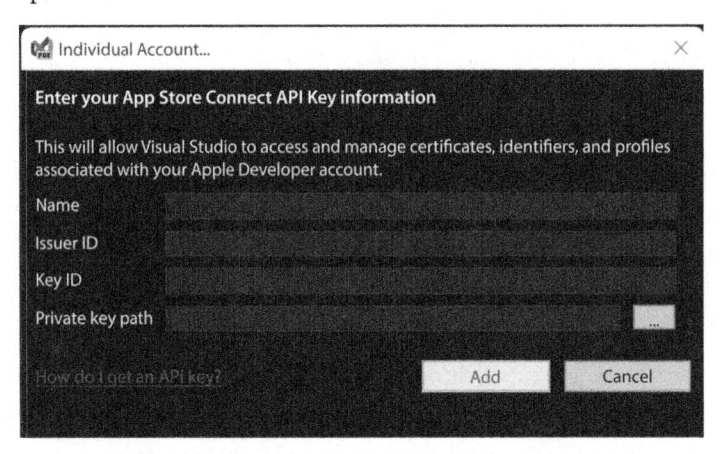

Figure 18.4: Apple Connect API Key information screen

1. You can create a new key by going to https://appstoreconnect.apple.com/access/api.
2. Click **Request API key** and then **Generate API Key**.
3. Enter the name Visual Studio and select **Access Developer**.
4. Copy the different values to Visual Studio, download the API key, and select the file as the **Private key path**.
5. Next, select a team, and we are all set.
6. Run the application and see it run on your iPhone:

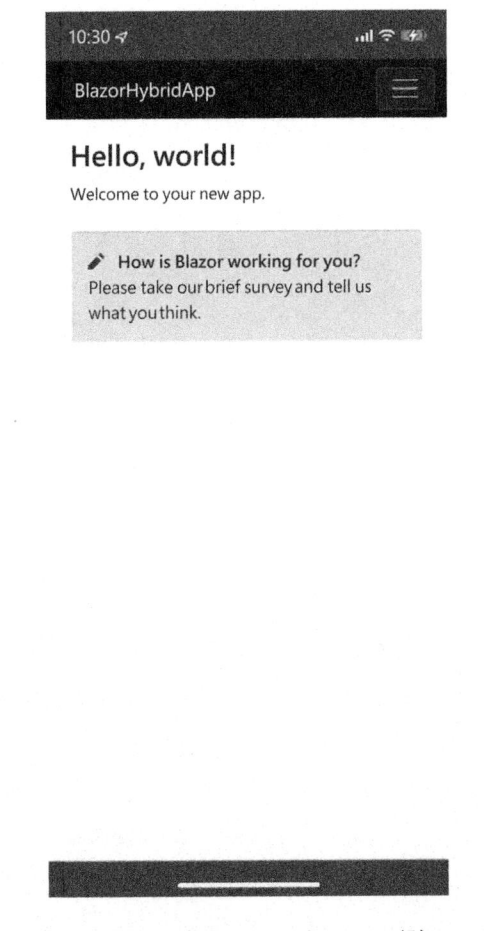

Figure 18.5: Application running on an iPhone

Next, we will look at how to set up a simulator.

Simulator

A simulator runs the app on a Mac but shows the result on a PC. A simulator differs from an emulator. An emulator runs the code on the machine (in our case, a PC). A simulator runs on top of the native OS (macOS), mimicking an iPad or an iPhone.

To get simulators to work, we need to have an Apple computer on the same network. Visual Studio will help us along the way to set everything up. We must install two things on the Apple computer, Xcode and Visual Studio for Mac or Mono. I went for Xcode and Visual Studio for Mac:

1. On your Mac, install Xcode from the App Store.
2. Install Visual Studio for Mac. You will find the installation files here: `https://visualstudio.microsoft.com/vs/mac/`.

We also need to open remote access to the Mac. We can do that by doing the following:

1. On the Mac, invoke Spotlight by pressing *cmd + space*, searching for `remote login`, and then opening the **Sharing System Preferences**.
2. Enable the **Remote Login** option to allow Visual Studio to connect to the Mac.
3. Set access for **Only these users** and ensure your machine user is included in the list or group.

We now have everything prepared on the Mac. In Visual Studio on the PC, we can now pair our Mac.

1. Select **Tools | iOS | Pair to Mac**.
2. Follow the instructions in the wizard (same as above).
3. Select the Mac from the list, and click **Connect**. Visual Studio can now help you install any versions of Mono you may need.
4. In the dropdown at the top of Visual Studio, we can select **iOS Simulators**, and then choose a device to run our app.

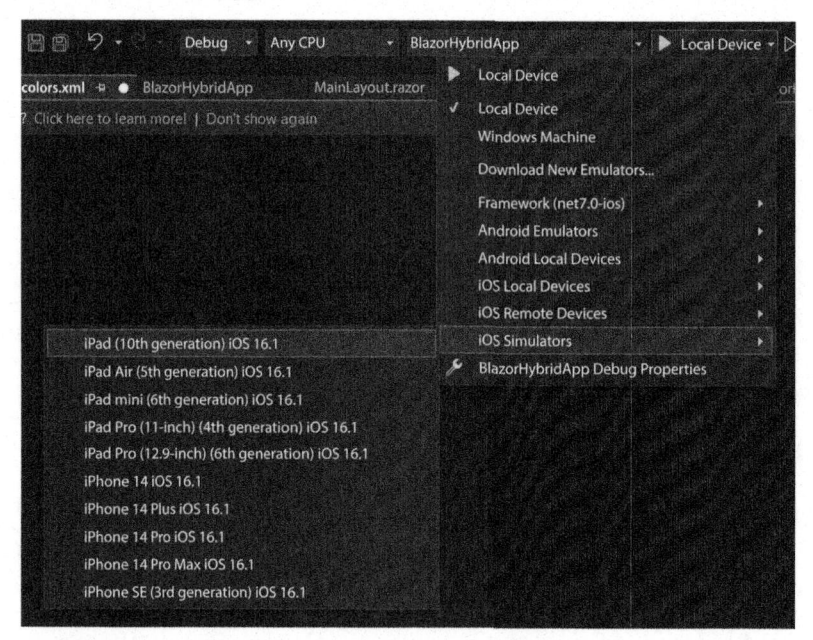

Figure 18.6: Device selection in Visual Studio

5. Run the app and the simulator will start. This is what the app would look like if we run it on an iPad Mini:

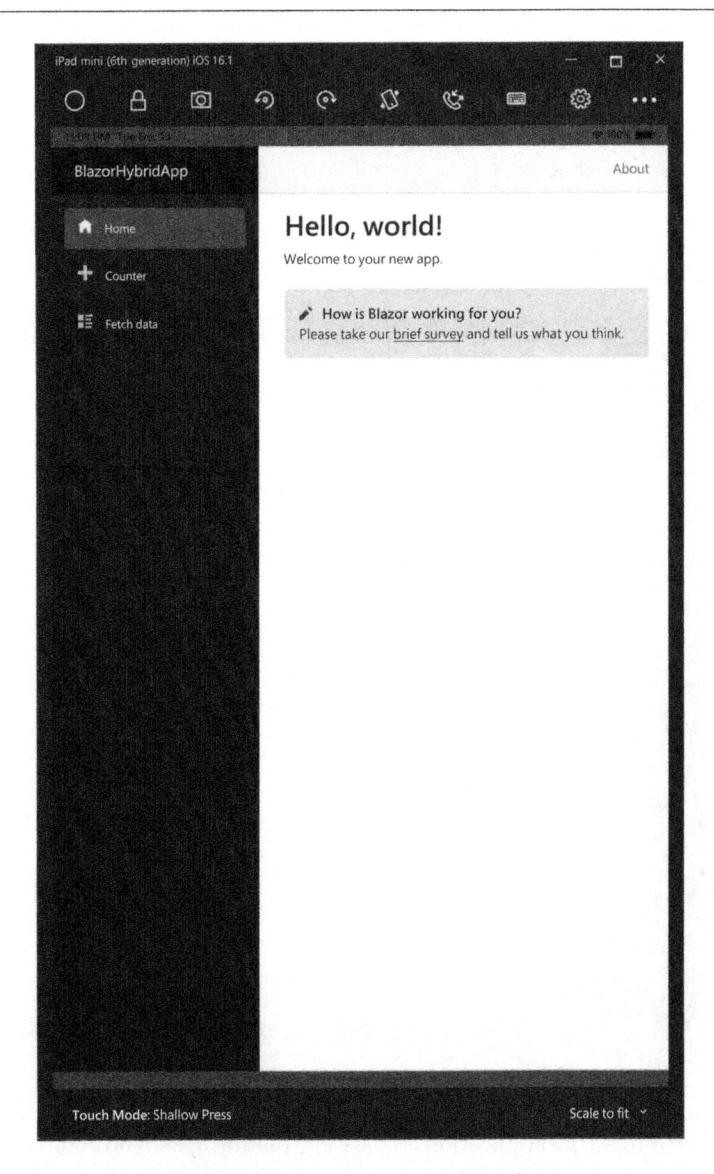

Figure 18.7: App running in iPad simulator

We now have two ways of running and testing on iOS devices. We can also connect an iPhone directly to the Mac and run the application over Wi-Fi. There is more information on debugging over Wi-Fi in the official docs: https://learn.microsoft.com/en-us/xamarin/ios/deploy-test/wireless-deployment.

Next, we will build an app for macOS.

Developing for macOS

We don't have an option for macOS to run or deploy from a Windows machine. To run our application on the Mac, follow these steps:

1. On the Mac, open our project in Visual Studio for Mac.
2. Run the project, and our app will show up:

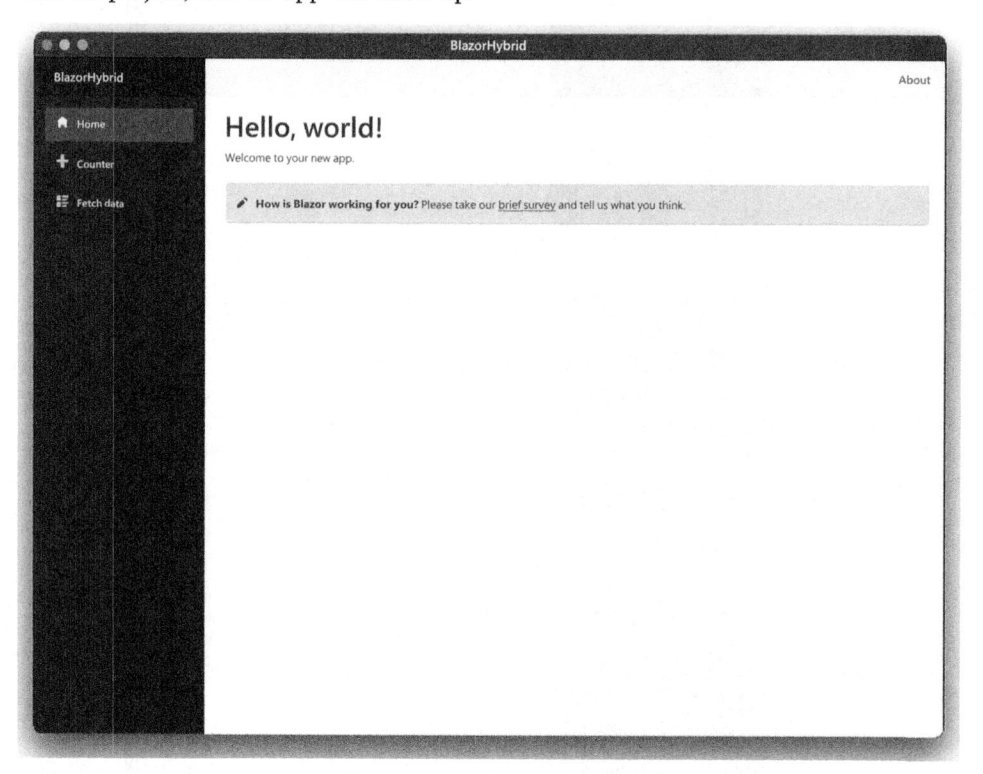

Figure 18.8: App running on macOS

In this case, we are running the application on the same platform, with no emulators or simulators, which is much less complicated than running it on a separate device.

Next, we will run our application on Windows.

Developing for Windows

Running the application on Windows is what we did in *step 3* of the *.NET MAUI Blazor App* section. To reiterate, perform the following step:

1. Change the dropdown to **Windows Machine** and run the project. We can see the result in *Figure 18.1* at the beginning of the chapter.

As with macOS, we run the application on the same platform, with no emulators or simulators, which is much less complicated than running it on a separate device.

Next, we will take a look at Tizen.

Developing for Tizen

Tizen is an operating system mainly for TVs and watches. My Samsung Gear S3 runs Tizen. Samsung manages Tizen and not Microsoft. This ability for other manufacturers to hook into the platform just shows how great the .NET MAUI platform is.

At the time of writing, the Tizen experience lags a bit. Since this is not an official platform and because of the state of the tooling, I have decided not to include a guide.

But Tizen is working on the tooling, so if you want to transfer your app to TVs running Tizen, you should look into it.

Summary

In this chapter, we looked at cross-platform development with Blazor Hybrid. I mentioned this before in this chapter, but it is worth mentioning again that running code on a phone or a device that is not a computer is such a fun thing to do. You can't beat that feeling. Even if you don't intend to develop for mobile devices, give it a try.

With .NET MAUI, we can leverage our existing C# knowledge and, perhaps more importantly, our Blazor knowledge to create mobile applications.

19
Where to Go from Here

The book is coming to an end, and I want to leave you with some of the things we have encountered while running Blazor in production ever since it was in preview. We will also talk about where to go from here.

In this chapter, we will cover the following topics:

- Learnings from running Blazor in production
- The next steps

Technical requirements

In this chapter, we are not using the code we have written throughout the book.

Learnings from running Blazor in production

Since Blazor was in preview, we have been running Blazor Server in production. In most cases, everything has run without issues. Occasionally, we encounter a few problems, and I will share those learnings with you in this section.

We will look at the following:

- Solving memory problems
- Solving concurrency problems
- Solving errors
- Old browsers

These are some of the things we ran into, and we have solved them all in a way that works for us.

Solving memory problems

Our latest upgrade did add many users and, with that, a bigger load on the server. The server manages memory quite well, but with this release, the backend system was a bit slow, so users pressed *F5* to reload a page. Then, the circuit disconnects, and a new circuit gets created. The old circuit waits for the user to connect to the server again for 3 minutes (by default).

The user now has a new circuit and will never connect to the old one again, but for 3 minutes, the user's state will still take up memory. This is probably not a problem for most applications, but we are loading a lot of data into memory – the data, the render tree, and everything surrounding that will be kept in memory.

So, what can we learn from that? Blazor is a single-page application. Reloading the page is like restarting an app, which means we should always make sure to add a possibility to update the data from within the page (if that makes sense for the application). We could also update the data as it changes, as we did in *Chapter 11, Managing State – Part 2*.

In our case, we added more memory to the server and then made sure there were reload buttons in the UI that refresh the data without reloading the whole page. The ultimate goal is to add real-time updates that continuously update the UI when the data changes.

If adding more memory to the server isn't an option, we can try to change the garbage collection from server to desktop. The .NET garbage collection has two modes:

- **Workstation** mode is optimized for running on a workstation that typically doesn't have a lot of memory. It runs the garbage collection multiple times per second.
- **Server** mode is optimized for servers where there is usually lots of memory and prioritizes speed, meaning it will only run the garbage collector every 2 seconds.

The mode of the garbage collector can be set in the project file or the `runtimeconfig.json` file by changing the `ServerGarbageCollection` node:

```
<PropertyGroup>
    <ServerGarbageCollection>true</ServerGarbageCollection>
</PropertyGroup>
```

Adding more memory is probably a better idea, though.

We have also noticed the importance of disposing of our database contexts. Make sure to use `IDbContextFactory` to create an instance of the data context and, when we are done, dispose of it, by using the `Using` keyword.

This method will only be available for a short time and then disposed of, freeing up memory fast.

Solving concurrency problems

We often ran into problems where the data context was already in use, and couldn't access the database from two different threads.

This is solved by using `IDbContextFactory` and disposing of the data context when we are finished using it.

In a non-Blazor site, having multiple components to load at the same time is never a problem (because the web is doing one thing at a time), so the fact that Blazor can do multiple things at the same time is something we need to think about when we design our architecture.

Solving errors

Blazor usually gives us an error that is easy to understand, but in some rare cases, we do run into problems that are hard to figure out. We can add detailed errors to our circuit (for Blazor Server) by adding the following option in `Startup.cs`:

```
services.AddServerSideBlazor().AddCircuitOptions(options => { options.DetailedErrors = true; });
```

By doing so, we will get more detailed errors. I don't recommend using detailed errors in a production scenario, however. With that said, we have the setting turned on for an internal app in production because the internal users are briefed on it and understand how to handle it. It makes it easier for us to help our users, and the error message is only visible in the developer tools of the web browser and not in the interface of the user.

Old browsers

Some of our customers were running old browsers on old systems, and even though Blazor supports all major browsers, that support doesn't include really old browsers. We ended up helping those customers upgrade to Edge or Chrome simply because we didn't think they should be browsing the web using browsers that no longer receive security patches.

Even our TV at home can run Blazor WebAssembly, so old browsers are probably not a big problem, but it can be worth thinking about when it comes to browser support. What browsers do we need/want to support?

The next steps

At this point, we know the difference between Blazor Server and Blazor WebAssembly. We know how to create reusable components, make APIs, manage state, and much more. But where do we go from here? What are the next steps?

The community

The Blazor community is not as big as other frameworks but is growing fast. Many people share content with the community through blogs or videos. YouTube and PluralSight have a lot of tutorials and courses. Twitch has a growing amount of Blazor content, but it is not always easy to find in the vast content catalog.

There are a number of resources worth mentioning:

- **My blog**: My blog has a lot of Blazor content and more to come: `https://engstromjimmy.com/`

    Twitter: `@EngstromJimmy`

- The **Blazm** component library that we have written can be found here: `http://blazm.net/`
- **Coding after Work** has many episodes of our podcast and our stream covering Blazor; please follow us on social media: `http://codingafterwork.com/FindUs`.
- **Daniel Roth** is the PM for Blazor. Amazing to listen to, he has been a guest on our podcast. Search for him on YouTube.

    Twitter: `@danroth27`

- **Steve Sanderson** is the guy who invented Blazor; he is definitely worth a follow. He continues to do groundbreaking things in his talks; search for him on YouTube. Make sure to see his NDC Oslo talk where he shows Blazor for the first time.

    Twitter: `@stevensanderson`

- **Awesome-Blazor** has a huge list of Blazor-related links and resources that can be found here: `https://github.com/AdrienTorris/awesome-blazor`
- **Jeff Fritz** shares Blazor knowledge (among other things) on Twitch. Twitch: `https://www.twitch.tv/csharpfritz`

    Twitter: `@csharpfritz`

- **Chris Sainty** has written a book on Blazor and has lots of content on his blog: https://chrissainty.com/

  Twitter: @chris_sainty

- **Junichi Sakamoto** has made loads of fantastic Blazor libraries, everything from connecting to gamepads to translation and pre-rendering.

  You can find his projects here:

  https://github.com/jsakamoto

  Twitter: @jsakamoto

- **Blazor University** has a lot of training material and is a great resource to learn more: https://blazor-university.com/

- **Gerald Versluis** has plenty of content on his YouTube channel related to all kinds of .NET things: https://youtube.com/GeraldVersluis

  Twitter: @jfversluis

- **Maddy Montaquilla** is amazing to watch; search for her on YouTube to watch her video.

  Twitter: @maddymontaquila

- **James Montemagno** has a great YouTube channel with loads of .NET MAUI content: https://www.youtube.com/JamesMontemagno

  Twitter: @JamesMontemagno

- **Daniel Hindrikes** has some great .NET MAUI content on this YouTube channel: https://www.youtube.com/@DanielHindrikes

  Twitter: @hindrikes

The components

Most third-party component vendors such as Progress Telerik, DevExpress, Syncfusion, Radzen, ComponentOne, and many more have invested in Blazor. Some cost money, and some are free. There are also a lot of open-source component libraries that we can use.

This question comes up a lot: *I am new to Blazor. What third-party vendor should I use?* My recommendation is to try to figure out what you need before investing in a library (either in terms of money or time).

Many vendors can do all the things we need but, in some cases, it will take a bit more effort to make an app work. We started to work on a grid component ourselves and after a while, we decided to make it open source.

This is how Blazm was born. We had a few special requirements (not anything fancy), but it required us to have to write a lot of code over and over again to make it work in a third-party vendor component.

We learned so much from writing our component, which is really easy to do. My recommendation is not to always write your own components. It is much better to focus on the actual business problem you are trying to solve.

For us, building a pretty advanced grid component taught us so much about the inner working of Blazor.

Think about what you need and try out the different vendors to see what works best for you, and perhaps it might be better to build the component yourself, at least in the beginning, to learn more about Blazor.

But always look at your code. If you repeat the same code, wrap it in a component. Always think: *Could this be a reusable component?*

We currently use a component vendor, but we are wrapping all the components in one of our components. This way, it is easy to set defaults and add logic that is right for us.

Summary

In this chapter, we looked at some of the things we have encountered while running Blazor in production. We also talked about where to go from here.

Throughout the book, we have learned how Blazor works and how to create basic and advanced components. We implemented security with both authentication and authorization. We created and consumed an API connected to a database.

We made JavaScript calls and real-time updates. We debugged our application and tested our code, and last but not least, we looked at deploying to production.

We are now ready to apply all this knowledge to the next adventure, another app. I hope you have had as much fun reading this book as I have had writing it. Being part of the Blazor community is so much fun and we learn new things every day.

Thank you for reading this book, and please stay in touch. I would love to learn more about the things you build!

Welcome to the Blazor community!

Join our community on Discord

Join our community's Discord space for discussions with the author and other readers:

`https://packt.link/WebDevBlazor2e`

‹packt›

packt.com

Subscribe to our online digital library for full access to over 7,000 books and videos, as well as industry leading tools to help you plan your personal development and advance your career. For more information, please visit our website.

Why subscribe?

- Spend less time learning and more time coding with practical eBooks and Videos from over 4,000 industry professionals
- Improve your learning with Skill Plans built especially for you
- Get a free eBook or video every month
- Fully searchable for easy access to vital information
- Copy and paste, print, and bookmark content

At www.packt.com, you can also read a collection of free technical articles, sign up for a range of free newsletters, and receive exclusive discounts and offers on Packt books and eBooks.

Other Books You May Enjoy

If you enjoyed this book, you may be interested in these other books by Packt:

Blazor WebAssembly by Example, Second Edition

Toi B. Wright

ISBN: 9781803241852

- Discover the power of the C# language for both server-side and client-side web development
- Build your first Blazor WebAssembly application with the Blazor WebAssembly App project template
- Learn how to debug a Blazor WebAssembly app, and use ahead-of-time compilation before deploying it on Microsoft's cloud platform

- Use templated components and the Razor class library to build and share a modal dialog box
- Learn how to use JavaScript with Blazor WebAssembly
- Build a progressive web app (PWA) to enable native app-like performance and speed
- Secure a Blazor WebAssembly app using Azure Active Directory
- Gain experience with ASP.NET Web APIs by building a task manager app

C# 11 and .NET 7 – Modern Cross-Platform Development Fundamentals, Seventh Edition

Mark J. Price

ISBN: 9781803237800

- Build rich web experiences using Blazor, Razor Pages, the Model-View-Controller (MVC) pattern, and other features of ASP.NET Core
- Write, test, and debug functions
- Query and manipulate data using LINQ
- Integrate and update databases in your apps using Entity Framework Core models
- Build and consume powerful services using the latest technologies, including Web API and Minimal API

Apps and Services with .NET 7

Mark J. Price

ISBN: 9781801813433

- Learn how to build more efficient, secure, and scalable apps and services
- Leverage specialized .NET libraries to improve your applications
- Implement popular third-party libraries like Serilog and FluentValidation
- Build cross-platform apps with .NET MAUI and integrate with native mobile features
- Get familiar with a variety of technologies for implementing services like gRPC and GraphQL
- Explore Blazor WebAssembly and use open-source Blazor component libraries
- Store and manage data locally and in the cloud with SQL Server and Cosmos DB

Packt is searching for authors like you

If you're interested in becoming an author for Packt, please visit authors.packtpub.com and apply today. We have worked with thousands of developers and tech professionals, just like you, to help them share their insight with the global tech community. You can make a general application, apply for a specific hot topic that we are recruiting an author for, or submit your own idea.

Share your thoughts

Now you've finished *Web Development with Blazor, Second Edition*, we'd love to hear your thoughts! Scan the QR code below to go straight to the Amazon review page for this book and share your feedback or leave a review on the site that you purchased it from.

https://packt.link/r/1803241497

Your review is important to us and the tech community and will help us make sure we're delivering excellent quality content.

Index

A

Actions 95, 96
admin interface
  usable making 184
admin interface, for blog
  blog posts, listing and editing 130-141
  building 121-123
  categories, listing and editing 123-126
  tags, listing and editing 126-129
alert component
  building 97-100
Angry Bots (Unity)
  reference link 6
Angular site
  Blazor, adding to 258-260
AOT (ahead-of-time) compilation 268, 269
API
  adding, to Blazor 60, 61
  adding, to handle blog posts 146-149
  adding, to handle categories 149, 150
  adding, to handle tags 150, 151
  configuring 173, 174
  mocking 239-243
  securing 173
API client
  creating 151-157

API controllers
  adding 146
API service
  creating 143, 144
  data access, adding 144, 145
application, for Android
  developing 297
  running, in emulator 297, 298
  running, on physical device 299
application, for iOS
  developing 299
  hot restart 300
application, for macOS
  developing 304
application, for Windows
  developing 305
Auth0 160
  adjusting 172, 173
  configuring 173
  roles, adding in 175, 176
authentication 159
  setting up 160, 161
authorization 159
Azure DevOps 252

B

binding 92, 119
  one-way binding 92-94
  to components 120
  to HTML elements 119
  two-way binding 94, 95

Blazm.Bluetooth 192

Blazm.Components 192

Blazor 7
  adding, to Angular site 258-260
  adding, to MVC/Razor Pages 261-263
  adding, to React site 260, 261
  API, adding to 60, 61
  characteristics 2
  components 9

Blazor application
  creating 20

Blazorators 286
  reference link 286

Blazor community 310
  resources 310, 311

Blazor Component 257, 258

Blazor Hybrid 14

Blazor Server 8
  advantages 9
  configuring 161-163
  CSS, adding to 184
  debugging 228, 229
  disadvantages 9
  hosting 252
  roles, adding to 176
  securing 164-167

Blazor Server App Empty template 21

Blazor Server application
  creating 22-27

Blazor Server App template 21

Blazor Server Program.cs 36-38

Blazor site
  Web components, adding to 263-265

Blazor WebAssembly 10, 11
  advantages 13
  debugging 230, 231
  debugging, in web browser 231-233
  disadvantages 12
  hosting 253
  roles, adding to 177-179
  securing 167-172
  versus Blazor Server 14

Blazor WebAssembly App Empty template 21

Blazor WebAssembly App template 21

BlazorWebAssembly.Client
  CSS, adding to 184

BlazorWebAssembly.Server project 144

blog
  making 186

BlogApiJsonDirectAccess 89

blog posts
  APIs, adding to handle 146-149

Bootstrap 44, 45
  URL 44

Bootswatch 183
  URL 182

browser storage
  Blazor Server, implementing 212-214
  implementing 211
  interface, creating 212
  shared code, implementing 215-218
  WebAssembly, implementing 214, 215

built-in components 100
  ErrorBoundary 107, 108

Index 325

focus, setting of UI 100, 101
HTML head, influencing 101-104
Virtualization component 104-107

bUnit 235, 236
authentication, testing 245, 246
authorization, testing 245, 246
reference link 248
test project, setting up 236-239

C

cascading parameters 83, 84
categories
APIs, adding to handle 149, 150
central processing unit (CPU) 269
ChildContent 97
code block 71
command line
used, for creating projects 34
community projects 286
Blazorators 286
C# source generators 286
InterfaceGenerator 286
Microsoft Learn 287
Roslyn SDK samples 287
components 64, 311
creating 84-89
components, creating ways 64, 78
class, inheriting 80
in partial class 79, 80
in Razor file 78
only code 80, 81
components library
creating 85, 86
using 86, 87

continuous delivery
options 251, 252
Continuous Integration and Continuous Delivery/Deployment (CI/CD) 252
Counter component 64-66
counter page 64
C# source generators 286
reference link 286
CSS 45, 183
adding, to BlazorServer 184
adding, to BlazorWebAssembly.Client 184
CSS isolation 187-190
Custom Elements 257
custom validation class attributes 115-118

D

data
storing, on server side 208
data project
creating 48
data classes, creating for blog post 49, 50
interface, creating 50, 51
interface, implementing 51-60
data, storing in URL 209
dependency injection 75, 76
reference link 76
scoped 77
service, injecting 77
singleton 76
transient 77
development environment
setting up 17
directives 73
attribute, adding 73

class, inheriting 74
generics 74
interface, adding 73
layout, modifying 74
namespace, setting 75
route, setting 75
using statement, adding 75
Distributed Application Runtime (Dapr) 145
Document Object Model (DOM) 4, 27
Doom
reference link 6
dotnet.exe 33
dotnet.wasm 11

E

emulator 301
reference link 13
ErrorBoundary 107, 108
EventCallback 95, 96
explicit Razor expressions 72
expression encoding 72, 73

F

FetchData component 66-70
form elements 109
EditForm 110, 111
InputBase<> 111
InputCheckbox 112
InputDate<TValue> 112
InputFile 113
InputNumber<TValue> 112
InputRadio 112
InputRadioGroup 113
InputSelect<TValue> 112

InputText 112
InputTextArea 112
forms
validation, adding 113, 114

G

generics 74
GitHub Actions 252

H

HeadOutlet 102
Highcharts 199, 200
hosting, options 252
application, hosting on IIS 253
Blazor Server, hosting 252
Blazor WebAssembly, hosting 253
Hot Reload 233
hot restart 300
HTTP Strict Transport Security (HSTS) 37

I

IBlogApi interface 89, 152
implicit Razor expressions 72
Index component 89
Index/_host 38
_Host (Blazor Server) 38-41
Index (WebAssembly) 41, 42
in-memory state container service
real-time updates, implementing on Blazor Server 219-222
real-time updates, implementing on Blazor WebAssembly 222-226
using 218, 219
InterfaceGenerator 283, 286
reference link 286

Index 327

Intermediate Language (IL) 268
Internet Information Server (IIS)
  application, hosting on 253
Inversion of Control (IoC) 75

J

JavaScript 3
  need for 192
  testing 247, 248
JavaScript, calling from .NET 192
  Global JavaScript 193
  JavaScript Isolation 193-195
JavaScript interop, in WebAssembly 202
  JavaScript, to .NET 204-206
  .NET, to JavaScript 203, 204
JavaScript library
  implementing 199-201

L

lazy loading 270-273
learnings, from running Blazor in production 307
  concurrency problems, solving 309
  errors, solving 309
  memory problems, solving 308
  old browsers 309
LESS 183
lifecycle events 82
  OnAfterRender 82
  OnAfterRenderAsync 82
  OnInitialized 82
  OnInitializedAsync 82
  OnParametersSet 82
  OnParametersSetAsync 82
  ShouldRender 82

LOB (Line of Business) 183
local storage 211

M

macOS
  Visual Studio 2022, installing on 19, 20
menu
  usable making 185, 186
Microsoft Learn 287
  reference link 287
Microsoft Visual Studio
  URL 18
Minimal APIs 145, 146
MVC/Razor Pages
  Blazor, adding to 261-263

N

native dependencies 273-275
.NET 5 6
.NET 6 7
.NET 7 6
.NET CLI
  reference link 35
.NET code, calling from JavaScript 195
  instance method call 196-198
  static .NET method call 195, 196
.NET Core 6
.NET garbage collection
  server mode 308
  workstation mode 308
.NET MAUI 14, 290, 291
.NET MAUI App 291
.NET MAUI Blazor App 291
.NET MAUI Class Library 291

.NET runtimes 6
.NET WebAssembly build tools 268

O

one-way binding 92-94

P

parameters 83
  cascading parameters 83, 84
prerendering
  on server 276
Program.cs 35
  Blazor Server Program.cs 36-38
  WebAssembly Program.cs 35, 36
progress indicators 275
Progressive Web Application
    (PWA) 13, 30, 273
projects
  creating, with command line 34
project structure
  App component 42, 43
  Index/_host 38
  MainLayout 43, 44
  Program.cs 35
Protected Browser Storage 212

Q

query string
  using 210

R

Razor component 38
Razor page 38

Razor syntax 70
  code blocks 71
  directives 73
  explicit Razor expressions 72
  expression encoding 72, 73
  implicit Razor expressions 72
React site
  Blazor, adding to 260, 261
RenderFragment
  alert component, building 97-100
  ChildContent 97
  default value 97
  using 96
REpresentational State Transfer (REST) 143
roles
  adding 175
  adding, in Auth0 175, 176
  adding, to Blazor Server 176
  adding, to Blazor WebAssembly 177-179
Roslyn SDK samples 287
  reference link 287
route constraints 209, 210

S

SASS 183
Search Engine Optimization (SEO) 104
server side
  data, storing on 208
session storage 212
SignalR 8
simulator 301
  working 301, 302
Single Instruction, Multiple Data (SIMD) 269
Single-Page Application (SPA) 12

Index

source generator 282, 283
  building 284-286
state 207
state persistence 277-279
state preloading 277-279
static files
  adding 182
stored procedures 282
style
  adding 183

T

tags
  APIs, adding to handle 150, 151
Tailwind 183
templates 20, 292-296
  Blazor Server App 21
  Blazor Server App Empty 21
  Blazor WebAssembly App 21
  Blazor WebAssembly App Empty 21
tests
  writing 243-245
Tizen 305
trimming 270
  reference link 270
two-way binding 94, 95
TypeScript 3

U

user state 207
UWP (Universal Windows Platform) 291

V

ValidationMessage component 114
ValidationSummary component 115
Virtualize component 96, 104-107
Visual Studio 2022 18
  editions 18
  installing, on macOS 19, 20
  installing, on Windows 18, 19
Visual Studio Code 20

W

wasm-tools 252
WebAssembly 4
  Angry Bots (Unity) example 6
  C, compiling 4, 5
  Doom example 6
  reference link, for projects 6
WebAssembly application
  creating 27-33
WebAssembly Program.cs 35, 36
web browser
  Blazor WebAssembly, debugging in 231-233
Web components 256
  adding, to Blazor site 263-265
Web Forms
  migrating from 265
WebSocket call 27
Windows
  Visual Studio 2022, installing on 18, 19
WPF (Windows Presentation Foundation) 291

X

Xamarin 290

Y

Yet Another Reverse Proxy (YARP) 265

Download a free PDF copy of this book

Thanks for purchasing this book!

Do you like to read on the go but are unable to carry your print books everywhere? Is your eBook purchase not compatible with the device of your choice?

Don't worry, now with every Packt book you get a DRM-free PDF version of that book at no cost.

Read anywhere, any place, on any device. Search, copy, and paste code from your favorite technical books directly into your application.

The perks don't stop there, you can get exclusive access to discounts, newsletters, and great free content in your inbox daily

Follow these simple steps to get the benefits:

1. Scan the QR code or visit the link below

https://packt.link/free-ebook/9781803241494

2. Submit your proof of purchase
3. That's it! We'll send your free PDF and other benefits to your email directly

Printed in Great Britain
by Amazon